OXFOR⸱⸱⸱ ⸱⸱⸱ D0675511

Series Editor: Steven Croft

More
Love Through the Ages

Edited by Julia Geddes and Anna Merrick

Oxford University Press

OXFORD

UNIVERSITY PRESS

Great Clarendon Street, Oxford OX2 6DP

Oxford University Press is a department of the University of Oxford.
It furthers the University's objective of excellence in research, scholarship,
and education by publishing worldwide in

Oxford   New York

Auckland   Cape Town   Dar es Salaam   Hong Kong   Karachi
Kuala Lumpur   Madrid   Melbourne   Mexico City   Nairobi
New Delhi   Shanghai   Taipei   Toronto

With offices in

Argentina   Austria   Brazil   Chile   Czech Republic   France   Greece
Guatemala   Hungary   Italy   Japan   South Korea   Poland   Portugal
Singapore   Switzerland   Thailand   Turkey   Ukraine   Vietnam

Oxford is a registered trade mark of Oxford University Press
in the UK and in certain other countries

British Library Cataloguing in Publication Data

Data available

ISBN: 978-0-19-912975-1

1 3 5 7 9 10 8 6 4 2

Typeset in India by TNQ Books and Journals Pvt. Ltd.

Printed in China by Printplus

Paper used in the production of this book is a natural, recyclable product made from wood
grown in sustainable forests. The manufacturing process conforms to the environmental
regulations of the country of origin.

The publishers would like to thank the following for permission to reproduce photographs:

Page 2: Mary Evans Picture Library; pages 8 and 176: Photostage; page 185: Mary Evans
Picture Library; pages 191, 200, and 204: Photostage; page 209: St Hilda's College, Oxford,
UK / The Bridgeman Art Library; page 218: National Portrait Gallery, London;
page 234: Carcanet Press

Contents

Acknowledgements

We gratefully acknowledge permission to reprint the following copyright material:

A.S. Byatt: extract from *Possession* (Chatto & Windus, 1990), reprinted by permission of The Random House Group Ltd and the author c/o Rogers, Coleridge & White Ltd, www.rcw.litagency.com.

E.M. Forster: extract from *A Room with a View* (Edward Arnold, 1908), reprinted by permission of The Provost and Scholars of King's College, Cambridge, and The Society of Authors as the Literary Representative of the Estate of E.M. Forster.

Ted Hughes: 'A Pink Wool Knitted Dress' from *Birthday Letters* (Faber, 1998), copyright © Ted Hughes 1998, reprinted by permission of the publishers.

Elizabeth Jennings: 'In a Garden' from *Collected Poems 1953-1985* (Carcanet, 1986), reprinted by permission of David Higham Associates Ltd.

Oscar Wilde: Letter to Lord Alfred Douglas, 20 May 1895 from *Complete Letters of Oscar Wilde* edited by Merlin Holland and Rupert Hart-Davis (Fourth Estate, 2000), collection copyright © Merlin Holland 2000, reprinted by permission of HarperCollins Publishers Ltd.

We have made every effort to trace and contact copyright holders before publication. If notified, the publisher will rectify any errors or omissions at the earliest opportunity.

Acknowledgements from Julia Geddes and Anna Merrick

We would like to thank Steven Croft for his helpful advice and guidance, and Jan Doorly for her insight, patience and encouragement. We would also like to thank our Upper Sixth Literature students for offering their perspective on the chosen extracts and their lively responses on the pairings produced.

Editors

Steven Croft, the series editor, holds degrees from Leeds and Sheffield universities. He has taught at secondary and tertiary level and headed the Department of English and Humanities in a tertiary college. He has 25 years' examining experience at A level and is currently a Principal Examiner for English. He has written several books on teaching English at A level, and his publications for Oxford University Press include *Exploring Literature*, *Success in AQA Language and Literature* and *Exploring Language and Literature*.

Julia Geddes has a degree in English and Philosophy, and an MA in English Literature from the University of Leeds. She is currently Head of English in a large sixth form college in the north of England. She is also a Senior Examiner and Moderator and has been the author of several study guides for A level students. She presents conferences for students and provides support for teachers working with A level specifications.

Anna Merrick has a degree in English and an MA from the University of Cambridge. She is currently second in department at a large sixth form college. She also works as a Senior Examiner and has presented advice and guidance to teachers on the delivery of English Literature specifications. She has written several student workbooks and guides for teachers of A level English Literature.

Foreword

Oxford Student Texts have, over a number of years, established a reputation for presenting literary texts to students in both a scholarly and an accessible way. In response to developments in the structure and approach of A level study, several new editions have been published to help students prepare for the changing emphasis and demands of these courses. These editions have been written with a key focus on a specific area of study and contain a range of texts by a wide variety of writers intended to give a flavour of that area and provide contextual linking material that will help students develop their wider reading on a particular period or topic. Each volume in the series consists of four main sections which link together to provide an integrated approach.

The first part provides important background information about the period or thematic area and the factors that played an important part in shaping literary works. This discussion sets the various texts in context and explores some key contextual factors.

This section is followed by the texts themselves. The texts are presented without accompanying notes so that students can engage with them on their own terms without the influence of secondary ideas. To encourage this approach, the Notes are placed in the third section, immediately following the texts. The Notes provide a brief explanation of individual texts to help set them in context and also give explanations of particular words, phrases, images, allusions and so forth, to help students gain a full understanding of the particular text. They also raise questions or highlight particular issues or ideas which are important to consider when arriving at interpretations.

The fourth section, Interpretations, goes on to discuss a range of issues in more detail. This involves an examination of the influence of contextual factors as well as looking at such aspects as language and style, and various critical views or interpretations. A range of activities for students to carry out, together with discussions as to how these might be approached, are integrated into this section.

At the end of each volume there is a selection of Essay Questions, a Chronology and where appropriate a Further Reading list.

We hope you enjoy reading these texts and working with these supporting materials, and wish you every success in your studies.

Steven Croft   *Series Editor*

The Literature of Love in Context

Early writing about love

Throughout the ages, love has been represented in a variety of literary forms and has acted as a powerful focus for writers. The fifteenth-century Paston letters (see page 20) are among the earliest surviving love letters in English, part of an archive of letters spanning four generations. These letters offer the reader insights into customs and practices connected with love and marriage in the late medieval period, and suggest that they were not always what we would call 'romantic'.

In the Middle Ages, the English word 'romance' alluded to the origin of certain stories in French: 'romance' narratives were concerned with chivalry, and usually told of knights fighting for honour as well as love. They often depicted historical adventures in a courtly setting, with tests of virtue and the idea of a quest; tales of the recovery of lost fortunes were also a feature of the genre. A popular narrative of the time, which is known to have influenced the writing of Geoffrey Chaucer, was *Le Roman de la Rose*, a tale of courtly love outside marriage (see page 86).

Chaucer is perhaps the most celebrated writer of this early period of English literature, and love is an important theme in his work. His poems *The Parliament of Fowls* (about 1382) and *Troilus and Criseyde* (about 1385), for example, are tales of thwarted love. Chaucer's most famous work is *The Canterbury Tales*, in which a group of pilgrims set off on their journey to Canterbury Cathedral and each one is charged with telling a tale on the way. Many of these tales are concerned with love, and they reflect a variety of views about and attitudes towards love relationships. From the courtly, chivalric love of *The Knight's Tale* (see page 17) to the bawdy, comic portrayal of the Wife of Bath (see page 19), Chaucer explores the many different forms love can take. Sometimes the tales satirize the foolish expectations of humanity; at other times they celebrate the beauty of romance and romantic ideals.

WIFE OF BATH.

The Wife of Bath as depicted in the Ellesmere manuscript of
The Canterbury Tales

When considering the literature of the Tudor period (the
sixteenth century), we can also see the many ways in which love was
important in the writing of the time. It was during this era that Henry
Howard, Earl of Surrey (1517–1547) introduced the unrhymed
pentameters that we now call blank verse, a form that was taken up
by dramatists such as William Shakespeare, Christopher Marlowe
and John Webster in presenting their ideas about, among other
things, love. Surrey was the first to use this form in a published
work: his translation of Virgil's *Aeneid*. He was also among the first
to use the sonnet form in English. Like many of his contemporaries,
Surrey wrote of love as a battleground where men pursued the
object of their affection but often suffered when their advances
were spurned. For example, in his poem *'The lover comforteth
himself with the worthiness of his love'*, he compares the pains of his
love with the suffering of the Greeks in the Trojan war, suggesting
that 'after raging storms of care/ Joyful at length may be my fare'.

The imagery used reflects the idea of love as a war of the passions, and this is an image we see repeated throughout the period.

Many other types of love and issues connected with this theme were explored in the Tudor era. Sir Thomas More (1478–1535), for example, considers the love of God in his *Twelve Properties or Conditions of a Lover*. Here he lists what he believes to be the demands of love on the individual, stating, for example, that the lover is 'To serve his love, nothing thinking of any reward or profit'. He goes on to detail how each property should be viewed in terms of an individual's relationship with God. Clearly these properties are to be applied to both religious and worldly love.

Poets such as Sir Thomas Wyatt (1503–1542) and Samuel Daniel (1562–1619) were also influential in the development of love poetry during this era. Wyatt was greatly influenced by the Italian writer Francesco Petrarca, known in English as Petrarch, and he is credited with introducing the Petrarchan sonnet form to English writing. In Wyatt's collection of sonnets we are offered a variety of views and complaints about love and its effects on the suffering individual. In one sonnet Wyatt uses a phrase taken directly from Petrarch, *Of Love, Fortune, and the Lover's Mind*, as the title and develops this into a complaint against the dire effects of love: 'Love slayeth mine heart'. This sense that love is painful and challenging yet infinitely rewarding is perhaps what best characterizes the era.

Interestingly, although Sir Walter Ralegh (1554–1618) is perhaps best remembered for his exploratory sea voyages, he was also a celebrated writer and poet who challenged the Petrarchan style by writing in quatrains, in such poems as *The Nymph's Reply to the Shepherd*, and in other varied styles.

The sonnets of Shakespeare stand out among the many love poems written during the Elizabethan and Jacobean period, and are perhaps some of the most famous love poetry of all time. Influenced by the work of writers such as Wyatt and Sir Philip Sidney (1554–1586), Shakespeare's collection of sonnets reflects a range of different views on love. Adapting the rather formal

3

Petrarchan structure into something a little less rigid, he explores conventional love in works such as Sonnet 128, '*How oft, when thou, my music, music play'st*', as well as taking more diverse approaches, including ideas such as the ravaging effects of time upon love, a thought explored in '*That time of year thou mayst in me behold*' (Sonnet 73).

Social and political influences on the presentation of love can be seen during the Elizabethan period. Edmund Spenser's seminal 1590 work *The Faerie Queene*, for example, is an allegorical tale of the Faerie Queene or Gloriana, who represents Elizabeth I. Book 1 of the poem is centred on the struggles of the Red Cross Knight (representing England) and his true love Una (representing the Anglican Church) against the wiles of many hostile characters (symbolizing the Catholic Church and Mary Queen of Scots). The poem is deeply rooted in politics but it portrays chivalric acts of valour and the rewards of the love of a beautiful woman, illustrating the way in which the theme of love is used to present other, sometimes radical, ideas.

Renaissance drama

An important development within writing of this time was the rising popularity of tragic drama in the 1590s. The development of this form brought with it a new presentation of the theme of love. Among the earliest writers of this kind of drama was Thomas Kyd, with *The Spanish Tragedy*. Unrequited love is a common theme of writing of this period.

It was Marlowe and Shakespeare who launched the English theatre into its greatest glory. Marlowe, who was renowned for his fiery disposition, wrote several striking and successful plays before he was killed in a brawl at the age of 29. In his most famous plays, love is often presented as self-seeking, as in *Dr Faustus*, where Faustus lusts after Helen of Troy, 'the face that launched a thousand ships', and in *Edward II*, where the king's homosexual relationship with Piers Gaveston proves to be his downfall.

Shakespeare's plays also challenged the expected presentation of love. Although many of his characters reflect traditional views of courtship and marriage, he created resourceful women who, if necessary, woo reluctant males, an image that challenges the stereotypical presentation of gender roles. The dark complexities of love are fully explored in plays such as *Othello* (see page 25) and *King Lear* (see page 27), as Shakespeare invites the audience to engage with the problems of jealousy, greed, lust and self-love. Even in those texts that could be considered traditional romances, Shakespeare constantly challenges ideas about love; comedies such *As You Like It* (see page 23), *Twelfth Night* and *A Midsummer Night's Dream* set a different tone by humorously exploring the varying roles men and women play within relationships.

Shakespeare addresses another type of love in his history plays: love of one's country. This can be seen for example in the dying John of Gaunt's speech in *Richard II*. In his later plays, such as *The Tempest* (see page 30), *The Winter's Tale* and *Pericles*, Shakespeare concerns himself with filial love, especially that between a father and daughter, and with the idea of reconciliation and healing where people who love each other have been parted or relationships have gone wrong.

In the Jacobean period dramatists such as John Webster wrote tragedies concerned with revenge, intrigue, and lust. Webster's two most famous plays, *The White Devil* (1612) and *The Duchess of Malfi* (1613, see page 33), concern themselves with passionate relationships and violent revenge. Horrors are perpetrated on the Duchess of Malfi as punishment for defying the customs of arranged marriage and the authority of her brothers by secretly marrying the man she loves. Thomas Middleton's *The Revenger's Tragedy* (1606) also depicts revenge, taken this time for the murder of a bride-to-be.

Writers of the seventeenth and eighteenth centuries

One of the greatest poets of this era is John Donne (1572–1631), whose love poems are characterized by sharp wit and irony as he attempts to draw meaning from his experience (see *The Sun Rising* on page 35). The preoccupation with questions of love, death and religious faith marks out Donne and his successors, who are often referred to as the Metaphysical poets. It is interesting to note that, although Donne's earlier work concentrates on romantic love, his later poems present the love of God, as in his Holy Sonnets. An important later Metaphysical poet is Andrew Marvell (see page 37), whose most famous poem, *To His Coy Mistress*, is regularly listed as one of the nation's favourite love poems.

At this time we see an increase in satirical writing about love. The idea that love could be corrupted and corrupting haunted literature, but the portrayal of men idealizing women and the great love between parent and child, for example, also dominated the writing of the time. The work of the dramatist and poet Ben Jonson (1572–1637), for example, reflects these ideas, while also considering the nature of love itself (see *Death and Love*, page 36). In his tender poem *On My First Daughter*, we read not only of his pain and sorrow on losing his daughter but of his overarching belief in a benevolent God who had taken her to his care.

Another important figure in seventeenth-century English literature who founded his writing on the teachings of the Bible was John Milton. He married Mary Powell, a young woman of 17, when he was 34, and she returned to her parents a few weeks after their marriage. However, the couple were eventually reconciled and they had four children; sadly, on the birth of their daughter Deborah, Mary died. Six weeks later their 15-month-old son John also died. Milton was left bereft not just of wife and child but was also losing his sight, and in a few years he was totally blind. Milton created some of the greatest works in the English language in his head and then dictated them to his aides from memory.

The most famous of his works is *Paradise Lost*, published in 1667 (see pages 38 and 115). It depicts Satan's temptation of Eve in the Garden of Eden, and it is interesting to consider the ways Milton presents a love relationship through the images of Adam and Eve before and after their fall from God's favour. In Book 4 he describes the pair as Satan first encounters them, and we see the biblical image of the humility of the ideal woman translated into poetry, as Milton insists on the authority and superiority of Adam in contrast to the subordinate role of his partner.

Through weakness and vanity, Milton's Eve succumbs to the temptation of Satan and in turn tempts Adam, ultimately leading to the loss of Paradise, but Milton maintains his presentation of the woman as one who is simply misguided; at the close of Book 12 the couple are reconciled to each other and their loss, as they 'hand in hand with wandering steps and slow,/ Through Eden took their solitary way'. However, the image of woman as a temptress likely to lure a man away from his pure and spiritual self can be found in literature throughout the ages; Thomas Hardy is among those who expose the injustice of this image, in for example *Far From the Madding Crowd* (1874, see page 65) and *Tess of the d'Urbervilles* (1891).

During the Restoration period at the end of the seventeenth century, writers revelled in a new freedom to challenge society's attitudes and values through humorous representations of male and female exploits in love. In *The Country Wife* (see page 40), for example, William Wycherley exposes the foolishness of male jealousy and insistence upon defining women as possessions. In *The Rover* (see page 44), Aphra Behn uses comic drama to explore a serious issue, that of the predatory male and the problems brought about by unequal relations between the sexes.

The comic drama developed into what has now become known as the comedy of sentiment and manners, as exemplified by George Etherege in *The Man of Mode* (1676), William Congreve in *The Way of the World* (1700), and George Farquhar (see page 48) in *The Recruiting Officer*. The genre was developed further, towards the end of eighteenth century, by Richard Brinsley Sheridan in *The Rivals* (see page 54) and *The School for Scandal*.

A 2010 production of *The Rivals* with Harry Hadden-Paton as Jack
Absolute and Robin Soans as Sir Anthony

The eighteenth century also saw the rise of the novel, with
writers such as Samuel Richardson and Henry Fielding. One
popular early form consisted of a series of letters by a fictional
character telling his or her story, as in Richardson's *Pamela* (see
page 49), which explores the transcendence of female virtue and
the weakness of male desire.

Romantic literature and the Victorian era

The eighteenth and early nineteenth centuries are characterized
as the Age of Enlightenment, a time when philosophical thinking
and new ideas on politics and religion dominated. Though
writers of the time often aimed to reflect and challenge these
new philosophies, the theme of love still prevailed in literature.

Authors such as Mary Shelley and Nathaniel Hawthorne explored ideas about the changing moral structure of the modern world, but often portrayed their ideas through relationships. Shelley's striking novel *Frankenstein* (1818), for example, considers the progress of science and challenges ideas about the human soul, but at its heart is the traumatic, destructive search for love by Frankenstein's monstrous creation.

The Romantic poets, writers such as William Blake, S.T. Coleridge and William Wordsworth, were interested in love of the landscape and often tried to capture in their writing a feeling of the sublime and an overwhelming passion for nature and for God. Works such as Coleridge's *The Rime of the Ancient Mariner*, for example, explore the power of nature and supernatural phenomena with the intensity that typifies the Romantic movement. Though other poems of the age can be seen to reflect ideas about love relationships (see Lord Byron's poem on page 60), many writers of the time emphasized spiritual aspects of the natural world. Byron was part of the second generation of Romantic poets, along with John Keats (see page 60) and P.B. Shelley. As well as poems about love (see page 62), Shelley wrote works with a political message, and long visionary poems.

Queen Victoria came to the throne in 1837, and in the Victorian era the Industrial Revolution brought widespread social change and great expansion in the British economy. With this increased wealth and mobility, alliances through marriage became an important means of maintaining a family's inheritance and status. As a result, courtship and marriage conventions became rather regimented and instead of focusing on love, the writing of the time tended to deal with the way relationships adapted to these conventions. Strict social codes made falling in love with an 'unsuitable' person problematic, and even where the partnership was considered socially acceptable, complex conventions of courtship had to be adhered to, among the more prosperous classes at least. In particular, there was a strict set of rules that governed the way in which a single woman must behave. She would not, for example, be able to travel in a closed carriage with a man unless he was a relative, and she would always be chaperoned when in male company. The presentation of love in the literature of the time is therefore interesting for what it tells us about the social climate, the role of women and the division of the classes.

The development of the novel in this era added a new dimension to the ways in which love was presented. The publication of extended stories in magazines as well as the rise in popularity of libraries, which lent copies of the latest novels, brought this form of writing to a wider audience. The genre developed into one that gave writers the chance to explore a wide range of situations and views, with complex plots developed on a broad canvas. The Brontë sisters created determined and passionate heroines such as Jane Eyre in the novel of that name and Cathy in *Wuthering Heights*. While these novels describe the kind of romantic love the Victorians enjoyed reading about, they do not necessarily reflect the realities of the time for the majority of people, when love often had to be worked towards within marriages that were entered into for more material reasons.

Other female writers of the time were also beginning to challenge the way in which women and love were presented. Poets such as Elizabeth Barrett Browning and Christina Rossetti, for example, were exploring the issue of love and marriage by considering the sacrifice of individualism that had to be made by women if they were to become wives. In her poem *Aurora Leigh* (1856), Barrett Browning's heroine struggles for an independent life and the poet seems to be suggesting that to be married is to give up all freedom. Her main concern was that a loss of freedom would lead to a loss of creativity and individuality. It is important to note, however, that although many poems seem to reflect a preoccupation with the fear of love as something that will defeat the individual, Barrett Browning also created some of the most eloquent love poems in her *Sonnets from the Portuguese* (1850) where she expresses her love for the poet Robert Browning and reflects on elements of their courtship. Similarly, Rossetti's poetry reflects her fear that marriage would be a restriction. Robert Browning, however, explores the complexities of love from a male perspective (see page 65). Although his poetry is best remembered for its use of the dramatic monologue, he nevertheless adopted many different structural patterns to prevent varying ideas on love.

Other important Victorian poets were Alfred, Lord Tennyson, and Matthew Arnold (see page 64). Many late Victorian writers questioned well-established social and economic customs, and the presentation of love in literature from the latter half of the century often challenged traditional views of marriage in a more drastic way. Oscar Wilde's 1893 play *A Woman of No Importance*, for example, champions the 'fallen woman' and questions society's views about sex outside marriage. Whereas previous literature had focused on courtship and often celebrated the idea of a happy, monogamous and heterosexual marriage, Wilde's writings often explored atypical love. In his *Ballad of Reading Gaol* and his love letters to Lord Alfred Douglas (see page 70), Wilde explores the pain of complex yet unconditional love for another man in a society that criminalized homosexual love. Wilde was considered one of the new radicals and his literature reflects a changing perception of love that included quite direct criticism of the institution of marriage, and an interest in those who challenged social norms.

Modern and post-modern writing

As the economic and cultural expansion of the Victorian age came to a close, and particularly after the end of the First World War in 1918, the modern era promoted radical thinking and a change in political and social consciousness from the stoicism of the earlier years. The rise of Marxist ideologies, feminism and the growing interest in the work of psycho-analysts such as Sigmund Freud meant that the social climate was fast-changing. Increased social mobility and technological developments were reflected in more liberal, often controversial, literary works. A more diverse range of topics were taken up in literature, but love remained a fascinating subject that appealed to readers and was still important to all the literary genres.

The First World War had an enormous impact on the literature of the time. A wide range of writings depict the horror and grief caused by the war, but there are many examples of writing from a variety of genres (poetry, prose and non-fiction in particular) that focus on the theme of love. Many of these pieces illustrate the changing relationship between men and women during these years as the deployment of so many men to the battlefields meant women were forced to become more independent; this undoubtedly impacted on the relationships between the genders.

The creation of the 'modern novel' is often attributed to writers such as Virginia Woolf and James Joyce, and with the development of techniques such as the stream of consciousness in prose and free verse in poetry, writers reflected their thoughts and feelings in a more versatile way. In Woolf's *Mrs Dalloway* (1925) for example, we enter the mind of the protagonist Clarissa through a stream of consciousness. She reflects on her 'sensible' choice of husband – she selected the rather dull but financially stable and socially reliable Richard, rather than following her heart. Like previous presentations of love through the ages, Woolf reflects the way in which social issues impact on our experience of relationships. By presenting Clarissa's plight through a fragmented narrative that directly illustrates the way in which she is thinking, Woolf draws readers in and allows them to experience Clarissa's inner turmoil.

W.B. Yeats (see pages 76 and 162) was an important figure in early twentieth-century poetry, and also wrote plays. In his poetry he used traditional forms, but increasingly experimented with plain and striking diction. Famously, his love for the elusive Maud Gonne had a lasting effect on his poetry.

In post-modern literature (in general terms, that written since the Second World War) a more liberal social climate and freedom from censorship have influenced writing on love, leading to a range of tones and styles. Certainly there is no longer seen to be a need for a happy ending to a love story. In *Possession*, for example, A.S. Byatt interweaves a Victorian love story with a modern exploration of less formalized relationships (see pages 77 and 166).

Poets such as Elizabeth Jennings (see *In a Garden*, page 77) also offer contemporary, critical views of relationships, fusing these with a consideration of the effect of the secularization of modern society upon love. Collections such as Sylvia Plath's *Ariel* and Simon Armitage's *The Dead Sea Poems* both explore ideas from an autobiographical viewpoint, but do so very differently. Plath, struggling to deal with her psychological instability and depression, explores the pain of being unable to love and be loved. In her poem *Elm*, Plath comments that 'Love is a shadow' and goes on to describe her fear of 'this dark thing / That sleeps in me', almost as if her inability to love haunts her. Plath was married to fellow poet Ted Hughes, but they became estranged; many years after her suicide, he became Poet Laureate and later wrote about their relationship in his collection *Birthday Letters* (see pages 81 and 170). One of Plath's striking presentations of the pain of loss is given in her poem *Daddy*, where she explores the devastating impact her father's death had upon her. Armitage, on the other hand, focuses more on the strength that familial love can provide, as well as exploring the importance of finding your own identity and being comfortable with who you are as an individual before you can build meaningful relationships with others.

In the literature of today, love is still a central topic of creative writing. The work of Poet Laureate Carol Ann Duffy often reflects on different types of love. Her collection *Standing Female Nude* looks at, among other things, issues to do with social perceptions of beauty and sexuality, and *The World's Wife* and *Mean Time* present some challenging views of relationships and female identity.

In contemporary novels, from the terrifying images of parental love in *We Need to Talk About Kevin* by Lionel Shriver, to the exploration of the roles of women in love in Khaled Hosseini's *A Thousand Splendid Suns*, to the various humorous relationships in the works of Hanif Kureishi, love is still a core theme. Although it can be seen as we look through the ages that the purpose of presenting love and the types of love in literature across different literary eras may change, the sense that it is a fundamental part of the human condition remains a constant. The fact that it can challenge, liberate, damage and rejuvenate all of us makes love perhaps the most enthralling aspect of writing in literature old and new.

More
Love Through the Ages

Late Middle Ages

The Knight's Tale: Geoffrey Chaucer

      This Palamon answerde and seyde agayn,
'Cosyn, for sothe, of this opinioun
Thow hast a veyn ymaginacioun.
This prison caused me nat for to crye,
But I was hurt right now thurghout myn ye   5
Into myn herte, that wol my bane be.
The fairnesse of that lady that I see
Yond in the gardyn romen to and fro
Is cause of al my criyng and my wo.
I noot wher she be womman or goddesse,   10
But Venus is it soothly, as I gesse.'
And therwithal, on knees doun he fil,
And seyde, 'Venus, if it be thy wil
Yow in this gardyn thus to transfigure
Bifore me, sorweful, wrecched creature,   15
Out of this prisoun help that we may scapen.
And if so be my destynee be shapen
By eterne word to dyen in prisoun,
Of oure lynage have som compassioun,
That is so lowe ybroght by tirannye.'   20
And with that word Arcite gan espye
Wher as this lady romed to and fro,
And with that sighte hir beautee hurte hym so,
That, if that Palamon was wounded sore,
Arcite is hurt as muche as he, or moore.   25
And with a sigh he seyde pitously,
'The fresshe beautee sleeth me sodeynly
Of hire that rometh in the yonder place;

And but I have hir mercy and hir grace,
That I may seen hire atte leeste weye, 30
I nam but deed; ther nis namoore to seye.'
    This Palamon, whan he tho wordes herde,
Dispitously he looked and answerde,
'Wheither seistow this in ernest or in pley?'
    'Nay,' quod Arcite, 'in ernest, by my fey! 35
God helpe me so, me list ful yvele pleye.'
    This Palamon gan knytte his browes tweye.
'It nere,' quod he, 'to thee no greet honour
For to be fals, ne for to be traitour
To me, that am thy cosyn and thy brother 40
Ysworn ful depe, and ech of us til oother,
That nevere, for to dyen in the peyne,
Til that the deeth departe shal us tweyne,
Neither of us in love to hyndre oother,
Ne in noon oother cas, my leeve brother, 45
But that thou sholdest trewely forthren me
In every cas, as I shal forthren thee –
This was thyn ooth, and myn also, certeyn;
I woot right wel, thou darst it nat withseyn.
Thus artow of my conseil, out of doute, 50
And now thou woldest falsly been aboute
To love my lady, whom I love and serve,
And evere shal til that myn herte sterve.
Nay, certes, false Arcite, thow shalt nat so.
I loved hire first, and tolde thee my wo 55
As to my conseil and my brother sworn
To forthre me, as I have toold biforn.
For which thou art ybounden as a knyght
To helpen me, if it lay in thy myght,
Or elles artow fals, I dar wel seyn.' 60

The Wife of Bath's Tale: Geoffrey Chaucer

'Now ther ye seye that I am foul and old,
Than drede you noght to been a cokewold;
For filthe and eelde, also moot I thee,
Been grete wardeyns upon chastitee.
But nathelees, syn I knowe youre delit,   5
I shal fulfille youre worldly appetit.
    'Chese now,' quod she, 'oon of thise thynges tweye:
To han me foul and old til that I deye,
And be to yow a trewe, humble wyf,
And nevere yow displese in al my lyf,   10
Or elles ye wol han me yong and fair,
And take youre aventure of the repair
That shal be to youre hous by cause of me,
Or in som oother place, may wel be.
Now chese yourselven, wheither that yow liketh.'   15
    This knyght avyseth hym and sore siketh,
But atte laste, he seyde in this manere:
'My lady and my love, and wyf so deere,
I put me in youre wise governance;
Cheseth youreself which may be moost plesance   20
And moost honour to yow and me also.
I do no fors the wheither of the two,
For as yow liketh, it suffiseth me.'
    'Thanne have I gete of yow maistrie,' quod she,
'Syn I may chese and governe as me lest?'   25
    'Ye, certes, wyf,' quod he, 'I holde it best.'
    'Kys me,' quod she, 'we be no lenger wrothe,
For, by my trouthe, I wol be to yow bothe –
This is to seyn, ye, bothe fair and good.
I prey to God that I moote sterven wood,   30
But I to yow be also good and trewe

As evere was wyf, syn that the world was newe.
And but I be to-morn as fair to seene
As any lady, emperice, or queene,
That is bitwixe the est and eke the west,   35
Dooth with my lyf and deth right as yow lest.
Cast up the curtyn, looke how that it is.'
    And whan the knyght saugh verraily al this,
That she so fair was, and so yong therto,
For joye he hente hire in hise armes two.   40
His herte bathed in a bath of blisse.
A thousand tyme a-rewe he gan hire kisse,
And she obeyed hym in every thyng
That myghte doon hym plesance or likyng.
    And thus they lyve unto hir lyves ende   45
In parfit joye; and Jhesu Crist us sende
Housbondes meeke, yonge, and fressh abedde,
And grace t'overbyde hem that we wedde;
And eek I praye Jhesu shorte hir lyves
That noght wol be governed by hir wyves;   50
And olde and angry nygardes of dispence,
God sende hem soone verray pestilence!

The Paston Letters: From Margery Brews to John Paston

Sent from Topcroft, February 1476 or 1477

Unto my right well-beloved Valentine, John Paston,
Esq., be this Bill delivered, &c.
    Right reverend and worshipful, and my right well-beloved
Valentine, I recommend me unto you, full heartily desiring
to hear of your welfare, which I beseech Almighty God long   5
for to preserve unto his pleasure and your heart's desire.

And if it please you to hear of my welfare, I am not in good heele of body nor of heart, nor shall I be till I hear from you.

> For there wottys no creature what pain that I endure, 10
> And for to be dead, I dare it not dyscur

And my lady my mother hath laboured the matter to my father full diligently, but she can no more get than ye already know of, for the which God knoweth I am full sorry. But if that ye love me, as I trust verily 15 that ye do, ye will not leave me therefore; for if that ye had not half the livelihood that ye have, for to do the greatest labour that any woman alive might, I would not forsake you.

> And if ye command me to keep me true wherever
>   I go, 20
> I wis I will de all my might you to love, and never
>   no mo.
> And if my friends say that I do amiss,
> They shall not me let so for to do,
> Mine heart me bids evermore to love you
> Truly over all earthly thing, 25
> And if they be never so wrath,
> I trust it shall be better in time coming.

No more to you at this time, but the Holy Trinity have you in keeping; and I beseech you that this bill be not seen of none earthly creature save only yourself, &c. 30

And this letter was endited at Topcroft, with full heavy heart, &c.

By your own
Margery Brews

***

Unto my right well-beloved cousin, John Paston, Esq., be this letter delivered, &c.

Most worshipful and well-beloved Valentine, in my most humble wise I recommend myself unto you, &c. I thank you with all my heart for the letter you sent me by John Beckerton, from which I know for certain that you intend to come to Topcroft shortly, with no other errand or business except to bring to a conclusion the business between my father and you. I would be the happiest one alive if only the business might come to fruition. And you say that, if you come and find the business no further advanced than you did before, you would no more put my father and my lady my mother to any expense or trouble in that matter for a good while after, which makes my heart full heavy. And if you come and the business comes to nothing, then I will be even sorrier and full of sadness.

As for myself, I have done and endured in the business as much as I know how to or am able to, as God knows. And I want you to understand that my father refuses to part with any more money than one hundred pounds and fifty marks in this business, which is far from fulfilling your wishes.

For which reason, if you could be content with that amount and my poor person, I would be the happiest maid on earth. And if you do not consider yourself satisfied with that, or believe that you could get more money, as I have understood from you before, good, faithful and loving Valentine, do not take the trouble to visit any more on this business. Rather, let it be finished and never spoken of again, on condition that I may be your faithful friend and petitioner for the duration of my life.

No more to you now, but may Almighty Jesus preserve you, in both body and soul, &c.

By your Valentine
Margery Brews

William Shakespeare

As You Like It

ROSALIND [*disguised*]   There is a man haunts the forest
that abuses our young plants with carving 'Rosalind'
on their barks; hangs odes upon hawthorns and elegies
on brambles; all, forsooth, deifying the name of
Rosalind. If I could meet that fancy-monger, I would   5
give him some good counsel, for he seems to have the
quotidian of love upon him.

ORLANDO   I am he that is so love-shaked. I pray you tell
me your remedy.

ROSALIND   There is none of my uncle's marks upon you.   10
He taught me how to know a man in love; in which
cage of rushes I am sure you are not prisoner.

ORLANDO   What were his marks?

ROSALIND   A lean cheek, which you have not; a blue eye
and sunken, which you have not; an unquestionable   15
spirit, which you have not; a beard neglected, which
you have not – but I pardon you for that, for simply
your having in beard is a younger brother's revenue.
Then your hose should be ungartered, your bonnet
unbanded, your sleeve unbuttoned, your shoe untied,   20
and everything about you demonstrating a careless
desolation. But you are no such man: you are rather
point-device in your accoutrements, as loving yourself
than seeming the lover of any other.

ORLANDO   Fair youth, I would I could make thee believe   25
I love.

ROSALIND   Me believe it! You may as soon make her that
you love believe it, which I warrant she is apter to do

than to confess she does. That is one of the points in
the which women still give the lie to their consciences.   30
But in good sooth, are you he that hangs the verses on
the trees, wherein Rosalind is so admired?

ORLANDO   I swear to thee youth, by the white hand of
Rosalind, I am that he, that unfortunate he.

ROSALIND   But are you so much in love as your rhymes   35
speak?

ORLANDO   Neither rhyme nor reason can express how
much.

ROSALIND   Love is merely a madness, and I tell you,
deserves as well a dark house and a whip as madmen   40
do; and the reason why they are not so punished and
cured is that the lunacy is so ordinary that the whippers
are in love too. Yet I profess curing it by counsel.

ORLANDO   Did you ever cure any so?

ROSALIND   Yes, one, and in this manner. He was to   45
imagine me his love, his mistress; and I set him every
day to woo me. At which time would I, being but a
moonish youth, grieve, be effeminate, changeable,
longing and liking, proud, fantastical, apish, shallow,
inconstant, full of tears, full of smiles, for every   50
passion something and for no passion truly anything,
as boys and women are for the most part cattle of this
colour; would now like him, now loathe him; then
entertain him, then forswear him; now weep for him,
then spit at him; that I drave my suitor from his mad   55
humour of love to a living humour of madness, which
was, to forswear the full stream of the world and to
live in a nook merely monastic. And thus I cured him,
and this way will I take upon me to wash your liver as
clean as a sound sheep's heart, that there shall not be   60
one spot of love in't.

ORLANDO   I would not be cured, youth.

ROSALIND   I would cure you, if you would but call me
Rosalind and come every day to my cote and woo me.

ORLANDO   Now by the faith of my love, I will. Tell me   65
where it is.

ROSALIND   Go with me to it, and I'll show it you; and by
the way, you shall tell me where in the forest you live.
Will you go?

ORLANDO   With all my heart, good youth.   70

ROSALIND   Nay, you must call me Rosalind.

Othello

OTHELLO   Her father lov'd me, oft invited me,
Still question'd me the story of my life,
From year to year; the battles, sieges, fortunes,
That I have pass'd:
I ran it through, even from my boyish days,   5
To the very moment that he bade me tell it.
Wherein I spake of most disastrous chances,
Of moving accidents by flood and field;
Of hair-breadth scapes i' th' imminent deadly breach;
Of being taken by the insolent foe;   10
And sold to slavery, of my redemption thence,
And with it all my travel's history;
Wherein of antres vast, and deserts idle,
Rough quarries, rocks and hills, whose heads touch
    heaven,
It was my hint to speak, such was the process: 15
And of the Cannibals, that each other eat;
The Anthropophagi, and men whose heads
Do grow beneath their shoulders: this to hear
Would Desdemona seriously incline;

But still the house-affairs would draw her thence,   20
And ever as she could with haste dispatch,
She'ld come again, and with a greedy ear
Devour up my discourse; which I observing,
Took once a pliant hour, and found good means
To draw from her a prayer of earnest heart,   25
That I would all my pilgrimage dilate,
Whereof by parcel she had something heard,
But not intentively: I did consent,
And often did beguile her of her tears,
When I did speak of some distressed stroke   30
That my youth suffer'd: my story being done,
She gave me for my pains a world of sighs;
She swore i' faith 'twas strange, 'twas passing strange;
'Twas pitiful, 'twas wondrous pitiful;
She wish'd she had not heard it, yet she wish'd   35
That heaven had made her such a man: she thank'd me,
And bade me, if I had a friend that lov'd her,
I should but teach him how to tell my story,
And that would woo her. Upon this hint I spake:
She lov'd me for the dangers I had pass'd,   40
And I lov'd her that she did pity them.
This only is the witchcraft I have us'd:
Here comes the lady, let her witness it.
   Enter Desdemona, Iago, Attendants
DUKE   I think this tale would win my daughter too.
  Good Brabantio,   45
  Take up this mangled matter at the best;
  Men do their broken weapons rather use,
  Than their bare hands.
BRABANTIO   I pray you, hear her speak.
  If she confess that she was half the wooer,
  Destruction light on me, if my bad blame   50

Light on the man! Come hither, gentle mistress:
Do you perceive in all this noble company,
Where most you owe obedience?
DESDEMONA   My noble father,
    I do perceive here a divided duty:
    To you I am bound for life and education,   55
    My life and education both do learn me
    How to respect you, you are lord of all my duty,
    I am hitherto your daughter: but here's my husband:
    And so much duty as my mother show'd
    To you, preferring you before her father,   60
    So much I challenge, that I may profess,
    Due to the Moor my lord.
BRABANTIO   God bu'y, I ha' done:
    Please it your grace, on to the state-affairs;
    I had rather to adopt a child than get it;
    Come hither, Moor: 65
    I here do give thee that, with all my heart,
    Which, but thou hast already, with all my heart
    I would keep from thee. For your sake (jewel)
    I am glad at soul I have no other child,
    For thy escape would teach me tyranny,   70
    To hang clogs on 'em; I have done, my lord.

King Lear

Re-enter Lear, with Cordelia dead in his arms; Officer
KING LEAR   Howl, howl, howl! O! you are men of stones:
    Had I your tongues and eyes, I'd use them so
    That heaven's vault should crack. She's gone for ever.
    I know when one is dead, and when one lives;
    She's dead as earth. Lend me a looking-glass;   5

If that her breath will mist or stain the stone,
Why, then she lives.
KENT   Is this the promis'd end?
EDGAR   Or image of that horror?
ALBANY   Fall and cease.
KING LEAR   This feather stirs; she lives! if it be so,
It is a chance which does redeem all sorrows   10
That ever I have felt.
KENT [*Kneeling*]   O my good master!
KING LEAR   Prithee, away.
EDGAR   'Tis noble Kent, your friend.
KING LEAR   A plague upon you, murderers, traitors all!
I might have sav'd her; now she's gone for ever!
Cordelia, Cordelia! stay a little. Ha!   15
What is't thou say'st? Her voice was ever soft,
Gentle and low, an excellent thing in woman.
I kill'd the slave that was a-hanging thee.
CAPTAIN   'Tis true, my lords, he did.
KING LEAR   Did I not, fellow?
I have seen the day, with my good biting falchion   20
I would have made them skip: I am old now,
And these same crosses spoil me. Who are you?
Mine eyes are not o'th'best: I'll tell you straight.
KENT   If Fortune brag of two she lov'd and hated,
One of them we behold.   25
KING LEAR   This is a dull sight. Are you not Kent?
KENT   The same;
Your servant Kent. Where is your servant Caius?
KING LEAR   He's a good fellow, I can tell you that;
He'll strike, and quickly too. He's dead and rotten.
KENT   No, my good Lord; I am the very man, –   30
KING LEAR   I'll see that straight.
KENT   That, from your first of difference and decay,
Have follow'd your sad steps, –

KING LEAR   You are welcome hither.
KENT   Nor no man else. All's cheerless, dark, and deadly:
   Your eldest daughters have fordone themselves,   35
   And desperately are dead.
KING LEAR   Ay, so I think.
ALBANY   He knows not what he says, and vain is it
   That we present us to him.
EDGAR   Very bootless.
   Enter an Officer
OFFICER   Edmund is dead, my Lord.
ALBANY   That's but a trifle here.
   You lords and noble friends, know our intent;   40
   What comfort to this great decay may come
   Shall be appli'd: for us, we will resign,
   During the life of this old Majesty,
   To him our absolute power: [*To Edgar and Kent*]
                     You, to your rights,
   With boot and such addition as your honours   45
   Have more than merited. All friends shall taste
   The wages of their virtue, and all foes
   The cup of their deservings. O! see, see!
KING LEAR   And my poor fool is hang'd! No, no, no life!
   Why should a dog, a horse, a rat, have life,   50
   And thou no breath at all? Thou'lt come no more,
   Never, never, never, never, never!
   Pray you, undo this button: thank you, Sir.
   Do you see this? Look on her, look, her lips,
   Look there, look there! [*Dies*]
EDGAR   He faints! My Lord, my Lord!   55
KENT   Break, heart; I prithee, break!
EDGAR   Look up, my Lord.
KENT   Vex not his ghost: O! let him pass; he hates him
   That would upon the rack of this tough world
   Stretch him out longer.

EDGAR   He is gone, indeed.
KENT   The wonder is he hath endur'd so long: 60
    He but usurp'd his life.
ALBANY   Bear them from hence. Our present business
    Is general woe. [*To Kent and Edgar*] Friends of my soul,
        you twain
    Rule in this realm, and the gor'd state sustain.
KENT   I have a journey, sir, shortly to go;   65
    My master calls me, I must not say no.
EDGAR   The weight of this sad time we must obey;
    Speak what we feel, not what we ought to say.
    The oldest hath borne most: we that are young
    Shall never see so much, nor live so long.   70
        [*Exeunt, with a dead march*]

The Tempest

FERDINAND   Where should this music be? i' th' air or
        the earth?
    It sounds no more: and, sure, it waits upon
    Some god o' th' island. Sitting on a bank,
    Weeping again the King my father's wrack,
    This music crept by me upon the waters,   5
    Allaying both their fury and my passion
    With its sweet air: thence I have follow'd it,
    Or it hath drawn me rather. But 'tis gone.
    No, it begins again.

                    Ariel's song

        Full fathom five thy father lies;   10
        Of his bones are coral made;
        Those are pearls that were his eyes:

Nothing of him that doth fade,
But doth suffer a sea-change
Into something rich and strange. 15
Sea-nymphs hourly ring his knell:

Burthen: Ding-dong.

ARIEL Hark! now I hear them, – Ding-dong, bell.
FERDINAND The ditty does remember my drown'd
   father.
   This is no mortal business, nor no sound 20
   That the earth owes: – I hear it now above me.
PROSPERO The fringed curtains of thine eye advance,
   And say what thou seest yond.
MIRANDA   What is 't? a spirit?
   Lord, how it looks about! Believe me, sir,
   It carries a brave form. But 'tis a spirit. 25
PROSPERO No, wench; it eats and sleeps and hath such
   senses
   As we have, such. This gallant which thou seest
   Was in the wrack; and, but he's something stain'd
   With grief (that's beauty's canker) thou mightst call him
   A goodly person: he hath lost his fellows, 30
   And strays about to find 'em.
MIRANDA   I might call him
   A thing divine; for nothing natural
   I ever saw so noble.
PROSPERO [*Aside*]   It goes on, I see,
   As my soul prompts it. Spirit, fine spirit! I'll free thee
   Within two days for this.
FERDINAND   Most sure the goddess 35
   On whom these airs attend! Vouchsafe my prayer
   May know if you remain upon this island;
   And that you will some good instruction give

How I may bear me here: my prime request,
Which I do last pronounce, is, O you wonder!   40
If you be maid or no?
MIRANDA   No wonder, sir;
But certainly a maid.
FERDINAND   My language! heavens!
I am the best of them that speak this speech,
Were I but where 'tis spoken.
PROSPERO   How? the best?
What wert thou, if the King of Naples heard thee?   45
FERDINAND A single thing, as I am now, that wonders
To hear thee speak of Naples. He does hear me;
And that he does I weep: myself am Naples,
Who with mine eyes, never since at ebb, beheld
The King my father wrack'd.
MIRANDA   Alack, for mercy!   50
FERDINAND Yes, faith, and all his lords; the Duke of
Milan
And his brave son being twain.
PROSPERO [*Aside*]   The Duke of Milan
And his more braver daughter could control thee,
If now 'twere fit to do 't. At the first sight
They have chang'd eyes. Delicate Ariel,   55
I'll set thee free for this. [*To Ferdinand*] A word, good
sir;
I fear you have done yourself some wrong: a word.
MIRANDA Why speaks my father so ungently? This
Is the third man that e'er I saw; the first
That e'er I sigh'd for: pity move my father   60
To be inclin'd my way!
FERDINAND   O, if a virgin,
And your affection not gone forth, I'll make you
The Queen of Naples.

Early seventeenth century

The Duchess of Malfi: John Webster

DUCHESS   The misery of us that are born great:
   We are forced to woo, because none dare woo us;
   And as a tyrant doubles with his words,
   And fearfully equivocates, so we
   Are forced to express our violent passions   5
   In riddles, and in dreams, and leave the path
   Of simple virtue, which was never made
   To seem the thing it is not. Go, go brag
   You have left me heartless: mine is in your bosom,
   I hope 'twill multiply love there. You do tremble: 10
   Make not your heart so dead a piece of flesh
   To fear more than to love me. Sir, be confident;
   What is't distracts you? This is flesh, and blood, sir;
   'Tis not the figure cut in alabaster
   Kneels at my husband's tomb. Awake, awake, man.   15
   I do here put off all vain ceremony,
   And only do appear to you a young widow
   That claims you for her husband, and like a widow
   I use but half a blush in't.
ANTONIO   Truth speak for me:
   I will remain the constant sanctuary   20
   Of your good name.
DUCHESS   I thank you, gentle love,
   And 'cause you shall not come to me in debt,
   Being now my steward, here upon your lips
   I sign your *Quietus est*.
     [*Kisses him*]
   This you should have begged now.   25

I have seen children oft eat sweetmeats thus,
As fearful to devour them too soon.
ANTONIO　But for your brothers?
DUCHESS　　　　　　　　Do not think of them.
All discord, without this circumference,
Is only to be pitied, and not feared;　　　　　　　30
Yet, should they know it, time will easily
Scatter the tempest.
ANTONIO　　　　These words should be mine,
And all the parts you have spoke, if some part of it
Would not have savoured flattery.
DUCHESS　Kneel.　　　　　　　　　　　　35
　　　[*They kneel. Cariola comes from behind the arras*]
ANTONIO　Hah?
DUCHESS　Be not amazed, this woman's of my counsel.
I have heard lawyers say, a contract in a chamber
Per verba de presenti is absolute marriage.
Bless, heaven, this sacred Gordian, which let violence　40
Never untwine.
ANTONIO　And may our sweet affections, like the spheres,
Be still in motion.
DUCHESS　　　　　Quickening, and make
The like soft music.
ANTONIO　That we may imitate the loving palms,　　45
Best emblem of a peaceful marriage,
That ne'er bore fruit divided.
DUCHESS　What can the church force more?
ANTONIO　That Fortune may not know an accident,
Either of joy or sorrow, to divide　　　　　　50
Our fixèd wishes.
DUCHESS　　　　　How can the church build faster?
We now are man and wife, and 'tis the church
That must but echo this. – Maid, stand apart –
I now am blind.

ANTONIO   What's your conceit in this?
DUCHESS   I would have you lead your fortune by the hand,   55
   Unto your marriage bed
   (You speak in me this, for we now are one):
   We'll only lie, and talk together, and plot
   T'appease my humorous kindred; and if you please,
   Like the old tale, in 'Alexander and Lodovic',   60
   Lay a naked sword between us, keep us chaste.
   O, let me shroud my blushes in your bosom,
   Since 'tis the treasury of all my secrets.
    [*Exeunt Duchess and Antonio*]

The Sun Rising: John Donne

    Busy old fool, unruly sun,
     Why dost thou thus,
Through windows, and through curtains call on us?
Must to thy motions lovers' seasons run?
     Saucy pedantic wretch, go chide   5
     Late school-boys, and sour prentices,
  Go tell court-huntsmen, that the King will ride,
  Call country ants to harvest offices;
Love, all alike, no season knows, nor clime,
Nor hours, days, months, which are the rags of time.   10

    Thy beams, so reverend, and strong
     Why shouldst thou think?
I could eclipse and cloud them with a wink,
But that I would not lose her sight so long:
     If her eyes have not blinded thine,   15
     Look, and tomorrow late, tell me,
  Whether both th'Indias of spice and mine
  Be where thou left'st them, or lie here with me.

35

Ask for those kings whom thou saw'st yesterday,
And thou shalt hear, All here in one bed lay.   20

       She'is all states, and all princes, I,
         Nothing else is.
Princes do but play us; compared to this,
All honour's mimic; all wealth alchemy.
         Thou sun art half as happy as we,   25
           In that the world's contracted thus;
       Thine age asks ease, and since thy duties be
        To warm the world, that's done in warming us.
Shine here to us, and thou art everywhere;
This bed thy centre is, these walls, thy sphere.   30

Death and Love: Ben Jonson

Though I am young, and cannot tell
      Either what Death or Love is well,
Yet I have heard they both bear darts,
      And both do aim at human hearts.
And then again, I have been told   5
      Love wounds with heat, as Death with cold;
So that I fear they do but bring
      Extremes to touch, and mean one thing.

As in a ruin we it call
      One thing to be blown up, or fall;   10
Or to our end like way may have
      By a flash of lightning, or a wave;
So Love's inflamèd shaft or brand
      May kill as soon as Death's cold hand;
Except Love's fires the virtue have   15
      To fight the frost out of the grave.

The Fair Singer: Andrew Marvell

I

To make a final conquest of all me,
Love did compose so sweet an enemy,
In whom both beauties to my death agree,
Joining themselves in fatal harmony;
That while she with her eyes my heart does bind,   5
She with her voice might captivate my mind.

II

I could have fled from one but singly fair:
My disentangled soul itself might save,
Breaking the curlèd trammels of her hair.
But how should I avoid to be her slave,   10
Whose subtle art invisibly can wreathe
My fetters of the very air I breathe?

III

It had been easy fighting in some plain,
Where victory might hang in equal choice.
But all resistance against her is vain,   15
Who has th'advantage both of eyes and voice,
And all my forces needs must be undone,
She having gainèd both the wind and sun.

Restoration

Paradise Lost: John Milton

                          'O thou for whom
And from whom I was formed flesh of thy flesh,
And without whom am to no end, my guide
And head, what thou hast said is just and right.
For we to him indeed all praises owe,   5
And daily thanks, I chiefly who enjoy
So far the happier lot, enjoying thee
Pre-eminent by so much odds, while thou
Like consort to thyself canst nowhere find.
That day I oft remember, when from sleep   10
I first awaked, and found myself reposed
Under a shade of flowers, much wondering where
And what I was, whence thither brought, and how.
Not distant far from thence a murmuring sound
Of waters issued from a cave and spread   15
Into a liquid plain, then stood unmoved
Pure as the expanse of heaven; I thither went
With unexperienced thought, and laid me down
On the green bank, to look into the clear
Smooth lake, that to me seemed another sky.   20
As I bent down to look, just opposite,
A shape within the watery gleam appeared
Bending to look on me, I started back,
It started back, but pleased I soon returned,
Pleased it returned as soon with answering looks   25
Of sympathy and love; there I had fixed
Mine eyes till now, and pined with vain desire,
Had not a voice thus warned me, "What thou seest,
What there thou seest fair creature is thyself,

With thee it came and goes: but follow me,   30
And I will bring thee where no shadow stays
Thy coming, and thy soft embraces, he
Whose image thou art, him thou shall enjoy
Inseparably thine, to him shalt bear
Multitudes like thyself, and thence be called   35
Mother of human race": what could I do,
But follow straight, invisibly thus led?
Till I espied thee, fair indeed and tall,
Under a platan, yet methought less fair,
Less winning soft, less amiably mild,   40
Than that smooth watery image; back I turned,
Thou following cried'st aloud, "Return fair Eve,
Whom fly'st thou? Whom thou fly'st, of him thou art,
His flesh, his bone; to give thee being I lent
Out of my side to thee, nearest my heart   45
Substantial life, to have thee by my side
Henceforth an individual solace dear;
Part of my soul I seek thee, and thee claim
My other half": with that thy gentle hand
Seized mine, I yielded, and from that time see   50
How beauty is excelled by manly grace
And wisdom, which alone is truly fair.'
        So spake our general mother, and with eyes
Of conjugal attraction unreproved,
And meek surrender, half embracing leaned   55
On our first father, half her swelling breast
Naked met his under the flowing gold
Of her loose tresses hid: he in delight
Both of her beauty and submissive charms
Smiled with superior love, as Jupiter   60
On Juno smiles, when he impregns the clouds
That shed May flowers; and pressed her matron lip
With kisses pure[…]

The Country Wife: William Wycherley

[*Pinchwife's lodging*]
[*Enter*] *Alethea and Mrs Pinchwife* [*at opposite doors*]

ALETHEA   Sister, what ails you? You are grown melancholy.

MRS PINCHWIFE   Would it not make anyone melancholy,
to see you go every day fluttering about abroad, whilst
I must stay at home like a poor, lonely, sullen bird in
a cage?   5

ALETHEA   Ay, sister, but you came young, and just from
the nest, to your cage, so that I thought you liked it,
and could be as cheerful in't as others that took their
flight themselves early, and are hopping abroad in the
open air.   10

MRS PINCHWIFE   Nay, I confess I was quiet enough, till my
husband told me what pure lives the London ladies live
abroad, with their dancing, meetings, and junketings,
and dressed every day in their best gowns – and, I
warrant you, play at ninepins every day of the week,   15
so they do.

Enter Pinchwife

PINCHWIFE   Come, what's here to do? You are putting the
town pleasures in her head, and setting her a-longing.

ALETHEA   Yes, after ninepins. You suffer none to give
her those longings you mean, but yourself.   20

PINCHWIFE   I tell her of the vanities of the town like a
confessor.

ALETHEA   A confessor! Just such a confessor as he that
by forbidding a silly ostler to grease the horses' teeth,
taught him to do't.   25

PINCHWIFE   Come, Mistress Flippant, good precepts are
lost when bad examples are still before us. The liberty
you take abroad makes her hanker after it, and out

of humour at home, poor wretch! She desired not to
come to London; I would bring her.   30

ALETHEA   Very well.

PINCHWIFE   She has been this week in town, and never
desired, till this afternoon, to go abroad.

ALETHEA   Was she not at a play yesterday?

PINCHWIFE   Yes, but she ne'er asked me; I was myself   35
the cause of her going.

ALETHEA   Then if she ask you again, you are the cause
of her asking, and not my example.

PINCHWIFE   Well, tomorrow night I shall be rid of you;
and the next day, before 'tis light, she and I'll be rid   40
of the town, and my dreadful apprehensions. [*To Mrs
Pinchwife*] Come, be not melancholy, for thou sha't go
into the country after tomorrow, dearest.

ALETHEA   Great comfort.

MRS PINCHWIFE   Pish, what d'ye tell me of the country   45
for?

PINCHWIFE   How's this! What, pish at the country?

MRS PINCHWIFE   Let me alone, I am not well.

PINCHWIFE   Oh, if that be all – what ails my dearest?

MRS PINCHWIFE   Truly, I don't know – but I have not   50
been well since you told me there was a gallant at the
play in love with me.

PINCHWIFE   Ha!

ALETHEA   That's by my example too.

PINCHWIFE   Nay, if you are not well, but are so concerned   55
because a lewd fellow chanced to lie, and say he liked
you, you'll make me sick too.

MRS PINCHWIFE   Of what sickness?

PINCHWIFE   Oh, of that which is worse than the plague –
jealousy.   60

MRS PINCHWIFE   Pish, you jeer; I'm sure there's no such
disease in our receipt-book at home.

PINCHWIFE   No, thou never met'st with it, poor innocent. (*Aside*) Well, if thou cuckold me, 'twill be my own fault – for cuckolds and bastards are generally makers 65 of their own fortune.

MRS PINCHWIFE   Well, but pray, bud, let's go to a play tonight.

PINCHWIFE   'Tis just done – she comes from it. But why are you so eager to see a play? 70

MRS PINCHWIFE   Faith, dear, not that I care one pin for their talk there; but I like to look upon the player-men, and would see, if I could, the gallant you say loves me – that's all, dear bud.

PINCHWIFE   Is that all, dear bud? 75

ALETHEA   This proceeds from my example.

MRS PINCHWIFE   But if the play be done, let's go abroad however, dear bud.

PINCHWIFE   Come, have a little patience, and thou shalt go into the country on Friday. 80

MRS PINCHWIFE   Therefore I would see first some sights, to tell my neighbours of. Nay, I *will* go abroad, that's once.

ALETHEA   I'm the cause of this desire, too.

PINCHWIFE   But now I think on't, who was the cause 85 of Horner's coming to my lodging today? That was you.

ALETHEA   No, you – because you would not let him see your handsome wife out of your lodging.

MRS PINCHWIFE   Why! Oh Lord! Did the gentleman 90 come hither to see me indeed?

PINCHWIFE   No, no. – You are not cause of that damned question too, Mistress Alethea? (*Aside*) Well, she's in the right of it; he is in love with my wife, and comes after her – 'tis so. But I'll nip his love in the 95 bud, lest he should follow us into the country, and

break his chariot-wheel near our house, on purpose
for an excuse to come to't. But I think I know the
town.

MRS PINCHWIFE   Come, pray, bud, let's go abroad before   100
'tis late – for I *will* go, that's flat and plain.

PINCHWIFE (*aside*)   So! The obstinacy already of a town
wife, and I must, whilst she's here, humour her like
one. – Sister, how shall we do, that she may not be
seen, or known?   105

ALETHEA   Let her put on her mask.

PINCHWIFE   Pshaw, a mask makes people but the more
inquisitive, and is as ridiculous a disguise as a stage
beard. Her shape, stature, habit will be known. And
if we should meet with Horner, he would be sure to   110
take acquaintance with us, must wish her joy, kiss her,
talk to her, leer upon her, and the devil and all. No I'll
not use her to a mask, 'tis dangerous; for masks have
made more cuckolds than the best faces that ever were
known.   115

ALETHEA   How will you do, then?

MRS PINCHWIFE   Nay, shall we go? The Exchange will be
shut, and I have a mind to see that.

PINCHWIFE   So – I have it; I'll dress her up in the suit we
are to carry down to her brother, little Sir James. Nay,   120
I understand the town tricks. Come let's go dress her.
A mask! No; a woman masked, like a covered dish,
gives a man curiosity and appetite, when (it may be)
uncovered 'twould turn his stomach. No, no.

ALETHEA   Indeed, your comparison is something a   125
greasy one. But I had a gentle gallant used to say, a
beauty masked, like the sun in eclipse, gathers together
more gazers than if it shined out.

Exeunt

Song: Aphra Behn

Love in fantastic triumph sate
    Whilst bleeding hearts around him flowed,
For whom fresh pains he did create
    And strange tyrannic power he showed:
From thy bright eyes he took his fires,   5
    Which round about in sport he hurled;
But 'twas from mine he took desires
    Enough to undo the amorous world.

From me he took his sighs and tears,
    From thee his pride and cruelty;   10
From me his languishments and fears,
    And every killing dart from thee.
Thus thou and I the god have armed
    And set him up a deity;
But my poor heart alone is harmed,   15
    Whilst thine the victor is, and free!

The Rover: Aphra Behn

The garden in the night
Enter Florinda in an undress, with a key and a little box
FLORINDA   Well, thus far I'm in my way to happiness: I
have got myself free from Callis; my brother too, I find
by yonder light, is got into his cabinet, and thinks not
of me; I have by good fortune got the key of the garden
back-door. I'll open it to prevent Belvile's knocking; a   5
little noise will now alarm my brother. Now am I as
fearful as a young thief. (*Unlocks the door*) Hark, what
noise is that? Oh, 'twas the wind that played amongst

the boughs. Belvile stays long, methinks; it's time. Stay, for fear of a surprise I'll hide these jewels in yonder 10 jessamine.

[*Florinda*] *goes to lay down the box. Enter Willmore, drunk*

WILLMORE What the devil is become of these fellows, Belvile and Frederick? They promised to stay at the next corner for me, but who the devil knows the corner of a full moon? Now, whereabouts am I? Ha, what have 15 we here, a garden! A very convenient place to sleep in. Ha, what has God sent us here? A female! By this light, a woman! I'm a dog if it be not a very wench!

FLORINDA [*aside*] He's come! – Ha, who's there?

WILLMORE Sweet soul! let me salute thy shoe-string. 20

FLORINDA [*aside*] 'Tis not my Belvile. Good heavens! I know him not. – Who are you, and from whence come you?

WILLMORE Prithee, prithee, child, not so many hard questions. Let it suffice I am here, child. Come, come 25 kiss me.

FLORINDA Good gods! what luck is mine?

WILLMORE Only good luck child, parlous good luck. Come hither. [*Aside*] 'Tis a delicate shining wench; by this hand, she's perfumed, and smells like any 30 nosegay. – Prithee, dear soul, let's not play the fool, and lose time, precious time; for as Gad shall save me, I'm as honest a fellow as breathes, though I'm a little disguised at present. Come, I say; why, thou mayst be free with me, I'll be very secret. I'll not boast who 'twas 35 obliged me, not I: for hang me if I know thy name.

FLORINDA Heavens! what a filthy beast is this!

WILLMORE I am so, and thou ought'st the sooner to lie with me for that reason: for look you, child, there will be no sin in't, because 'twas neither designed nor 40 premeditated; 'tis pure accident on both sides, that's a

45

certain thing now. Indeed, should I make love to you, and vow you fidelity, and swear and lie till you believed and yielded, that were to make it wilful fornication, the crying sin of the nation. Thou art therefore, as   45
thou art a good Christian, obliged in conscience to deny me nothing. Now, come, be kind without any more idle prating.

FLORINDA   Oh, I am ruined! – Wicked man, unhand me.

WILLMORE   Wicked! Egad, child, a judge, were he young   50
and vigorous, and saw those eyes of thine, would know 'twas they gave the first blow, the first provocation. Come, prithee let's lose no time, I say; this is a fine convenient place.

FLORINDA   Sir, let me go, I conjure you, or I'll call out.   55

WILLMORE   Aye, aye, you were best to call witness to see how finely you treat me, do.

FLORINDA   I'll cry murder, rape, or anything, if you do not instantly let me go.

WILLMORE   A rape! Come, come, you lie, you baggage,   60
you lie: what, I'll warrant you would fain have the world believe now that you are not so forward as I. No, not you! Why, at this time of night, was your cobweb door set open, dear spider, but to catch flies? Ha, come, or I shall be damnably angry. Why what a coil is here!   65

FLORINDA   Sir, can you think –

WILLMORE   – That you would do't for nothing? Oh, oh, I find what you would be at. Look here, here's a pistole for you. Here's a work indeed! Here, take it I say.

FLORINDA   For heaven's sake, sir, as you're a gentleman –   70

WILLMORE   So – now, now – she would be wheedling me for more. – What, you will not take it then, you are resolved you will not? Come, come, take it, or I'll put it up again, for look ye, I never give more. Why how now mistress, are you so high i'th' mouth a pistole   75

won't down with you? Ha, why, what a work's here!
In good time! Come, no struggling to be gone; but an
y'are good at a dumb wrestle, I'm for ye, look ye, I'm
for ye.

> [*Florinda*] *struggles with* [*Willmore*]. *Enter Belvile and
> Frederick*

BELVILE   The door is open. A pox of this mad fellow,   80
I'm angry that we've lost him; I durst have sworn he
had followed us.

FREDERICK   But you were so hasty, colonel, to be gone.

FLORINDA   Help, help! Murder! Help! Oh, I am ruined.

BELVILE   Ha, sure that's Florinda's voice! [*Belvile*] *comes*   85
up to [*Florinda and Willmore*] A man! – Villain, let go
that lady.

Eighteenth century

Letter: From George Farquhar to Anne Oldfield

Sunday, after Sermon

I came, I saw, and was conquered; never had man more
to say, yet can I say nothing; where others go to save their
souls, there have I lost mine; but I hope that Divinity
which has the justest title to its service has received it;
but I will endeavour to suspend these raptures for a   5
moment, and talk calmly.– Nothing on earth, madam
can charm, beyond your wit but your beauty: after this
not to love you would proclaim me a fool; and to say
I did when I thought otherwise would pronounce me a
knave; if anybody called me either I should resent it; and   10
if you but think me either I shall break my heart.

You have already, madam, seen enough of me to create
a liking or an aversion; your sense is above your sex, then
let your proceeding be so likewise, and tell me plainly
what I have to hope for. Were I to consult my merits my   15
humility would chide any shadow of hope; but after a
sight of such a face whose whole composition is a smile
of good nature, why should I be so unjust as to suspect
you of cruelty.

Let me either live in London and be happy or retire   20
again to my desert to check my vanity that drew me
thence; but let me beg you to receive my sentence from
your own mouth, that I may hear you speak and see you
look at the same time; then let me be unfortunate if I
can.   25

If you are not the lady in mourning that sat upon my
right hand at church, you may go to the devil, for I'm
sure you're a witch.

Pamela: Samuel Richardson

'Well, Pamela,' he was pleased to say, 'I am glad you
wanted not intreaty, or a new command, to come to me.
I love to be obliged. Give me your hand.' I did so; and
he looked at me very steadily, and pressing my hand all
the time, at last said, 'I will now talk to you in a serious   5
manner.

'You have a good deal of prudence, and a penetration
beyond your *years*, and, as I thought, beyond your
opportunities. You seem to me to have an open, frank, and
generous mind; and in person you are so lovely, that in my   10
eyes, you excel all your sex. All these accomplishments
have engaged my affections so deeply, that, as I have often
said, I cannot live without you; and I would divide, with
all my soul, my estate with you, to make you mine upon
my own terms.' Here he paused. 'Ah, sir', said I, offering   15
gently to withdraw my hand; but he held it the faster.
'Hear me out,' said he. 'These terms you have absolutely
rejected; yet in such a manner as makes me admire you the
more. Your pretty chit-chat to Mrs Jewkes the last Sunday
night, so full of beautiful simplicity, half disarmed my   20
resolution, before I approached your bed. And I see you
on all occasions so watchful for your virtue, that though
I hoped to find it otherwise, I cannot but confess, my
passion for you is increased by it. But now what shall I
say further, Pamela? I will make you my adviser in this   25
matter; though not, perhaps, my definitive judge.

'You cannot believe,' proceeded he, 'that I am a *very* abandoned man. I have hitherto been guilty of no *very* enormous actions. The causing you to be carried off to this house, and confining you here, may, perhaps, be one of the most violent actions of my life. Had I been utterly given up to my passions, I should before now have gratified them, and not have shewn that remorse and compassion for you, which have reprieved you more than once when absolutely in my power.

'But, what can I do? Consider the pride of my condition. I cannot endure the thought of marriage, even with a person of equal or superior degree to myself; and have declined several proposals of that kind: how, then, with the distance between us, in the world's judgment, can I think of making *you* my wife? Yet I must have you; I cannot bear the thoughts of any other man's supplanting me in your affections. And the very apprehension of that has made me hate the name of Williams, and use him in a manner unworthy of my nature.

'Now, Pamela, judge for me; and, since I have told you thus candidly my mind, and I see yours is big with some important meaning, by your eyes, your blushes, and that sweet confusion which I behold struggling in your bosom, tell me with like openness and candour, what you think I ought to do, and what you would have me do.'

It is impossible for me to express the agitations of my mind on this unexpected declaration, and made in so condescending a manner; for, alas for me! I found I had need of all my poor discretion, to ward off the blow which this treatment gave to my most guarded thoughts. I threw myself at his feet; for I trembled, and could hardly stand. 'O sir,' said I, 'spare your poor servant's confusion! O spare the poor Pamela!' 'Speak out,' said he, 'and tell me, what you think I ought to do?' 'I cannot say what you *ought* to do,' answered I: 'but I only beg you will not seek to ruin me; and if you think me virtuous, if you think me sincerely honest, let me go to my poor parents. I will vow to you, that I will never suffer myself to be engaged without your approbation.' 65

Still he insisted upon a more explicit answer to his question, of what I thought he *ought* to do. And I said, 'As to *my* poor thoughts, of what you ought to do, I must needs say, that, indeed, I think you ought to regard the world's opinion, and avoid doing any thing disgraceful to your birth and fortune; and therefore, if you really honour the poor Pamela with your favour, a little time, absence, and the conversation of worthier persons of my sex, will effectually enable you to overcome a regard so unworthy of your condition: and this, sir, is the best advice I can offer.' 70 75

'Charming creature! lovely Pamela!' said he, (with an ardour that was never before so agreeable to me) 'this generous manner is of a piece with all the rest of your conduct. But tell me still more explicitly, what you would advise me to in the case.' 80

'O sir!' said I, 'take not advantage of my credulity, and of my free and open heart: but were I the first lady in the land, instead of the poor abject Pamela Andrews, I would, I *could* tell you. But I can say no more.' And I held down my face, all covered over with confusion. 85

O my dear father and mother! now I know you will indeed be concerned for me, since now I am concerned for myself: for now I begin to be afraid, I know too well the reason why all his hard trials of me, and my black apprehensions, would not let me hate him. 90

But be assured still, by the Divine Aid, that I shall do nothing unworthy of your Pamela; and if I find that this

appearance of true love is only assumed to delude me, I   95
shall think nothing in this world so vile and so odious;
and nothing, if he be not the worst of his kind, (as he
says, and I hope, he is not) so desperately guileful as the
heart of man.

The Art of Coquetry: Charlotte Lennox

First form your artful looks with studious care,
From mild to grave, from tender to severe.
Oft on the careless youth your glances dart,
A tender meaning let each glance impart.
Whene'er he meets your looks, with modest price   5
And soft confusion turn your eyes aside,
Let a soft sigh steal out, as if by chance,
Then cautious turn, and steal another glance.
Caught by these arts, with pride and hope elate,
The destined victim rushes on his fate: 10
Pleased, his imagined victory pursues,
And the kind maid with soft attention views,
Contemplates now her shape, her air, her face,
And thinks each feature wears an added grace;
Till gratitude, which first his bosom proves,   15
By slow degrees sublimed, at length he loves.
'Tis harder still to fix than gain a heart;
What's won by beauty must be kept by art.
Too kind a treatment the best lover cloys,
And oft despair the growing flame destroys: 20
Sometimes with smiles receive him, sometimes tears,
Perhaps he mourns his ill-requited pains
Condemns your sway, and strives to break his chains;
Behaves as if he now your scorn defied,

And thinks at least he shall alarm your pride: 25
But with indifference view the seeming chance,
And let your eyes to seek new conquests range;
While his torn breast with jealous fury burns,
He hopes, despairs, adores and hates by turns;
With anguish now repents the weak deceit,   30
And powerful passion bears him to your feet.
Strive not the jealous love to perplex,
Ill suits suspicion with that haughty sex;
Rashly they judge, and always think the worst,
And love is often banish'd by distrust.   35
To these an open free behaviour wear,
Avoid disguise, and seem at least sincere;
Whene'er you meet affect a glad surprise,
And give a melting softness to your eyes;
By some unguarded work your love reveal,   40
And anxiously the rising blush conceal.
By arts like these the jealous you deceive,
Then most deluded when they most believe.
But while in all you seek to raise desire,
Beware the fatal passion you inspire: 45
Each soft intruding wish in time reprove,
And guard against the sweet invader love.
Not for the tender were these rules design'd,
Who in their faces show their yielding mind:
Whose eyes a native languishment can wear,   50
Whose smiles are artless, and whose blush sincere;
But for the nymph who liberty can prize,
And vindicate the triumph of her eyes:
Who o'er mankind a haughty rule maintains,
Whose wit can manage what her beauty gains;   55
Such by these arts their empire may improve,
And unsubdu'd controul the world by love.

The Rivals: Richard Brinsley Sheridan

SIR ANTHONY   Now, Jack, I am sensible that the income
of your commission, and what I have hitherto allowed
you, is but a small pittance for a lad of your spirit.

ABSOLUTE   Sir, you are very good.

SIR ANTHONY   And it is my wish, while yet I live, to have   5
my boy make some figure in the world. I have resolved,
therefore, to fix you at once in a noble independence.

ABSOLUTE   Sir, your kindness overpowers me. Such
generosity makes the gratitude of reason more lively
than the sensations even of filial affection.   10

SIR ANTHONY   I am glad you are so sensible of my
attention – and you shall be master of a large estate in
a few weeks.

ABSOLUTE   Let my future life, sir, speak my gratitude; I
cannot express the sense I have of your munificence.   15
Yet, sir, I presume you would not wish me to quit the
army?

SIR ANTHONY   O, that shall be as your wife chooses.

ABSOLUTE   My wife, sir!

SIR ANTHONY   Ay, ay, settle that between you; settle that   20
between you.

ABSOLUTE   A *wife*, sir, did you say?

SIR ANTHONY   Ay, a wife. Why, did not I mention her
before?

ABSOLUTE   Not a word of her, sir.   25

SIR ANTHONY   Odso, I mustn't forget *her*, though. Yes,
Jack, the independence I was talking of is by a marriage.
The fortune is saddled with a wife. But I suppose that
makes no difference.

ABSOLUTE   Sir! Sir! You amaze me!   30

SIR ANTHONY   Why, what the devil's the matter with the
fool? Just now you were all gratitude and duty.

ABSOLUTE   I was, sir. You talked to me of independence and a fortune, but not a word of a wife.

SIR ANTHONY   Why, what difference does that make? Od's life, sir, if you have the estate, you must take it with the livestock on it, as it stands!

ABSOLUTE   If my happiness is to be the price, I must beg leave to decline the purchase. Pray, sir, who is the lady?

SIR ANTHONY   What's that to you, sir? Come, give me your promise to love and to marry her directly.

ABSOLUTE   Sure, sir, this is not very reasonable – to summon my affections for a lady I know nothing of!

SIR ANTHONY   I am sure, sir, 'tis more unreasonable in you to *object* to a lady you know nothing of.

ABSOLUTE   Then, sir, I must tell you plainly that my inclinations are fixed on another. My heart is engaged to an angel.

SIR ANTHONY   Then pray let it send an excuse. It is very sorry, but *business* prevents its waiting on her.

ABSOLUTE   But my vows are pledged to her.

SIR ANTHONY   Let her foreclose, Jack; let her foreclose. They are not worth redeeming. Besides, you have the angel's vows in exchange, I suppose; so there can be no loss there.

ABSOLUTE   You must excuse me, sir, if I tell you, once for all, that in this point I cannot obey you.

SIR ANTHONY   Harkee, Jack. I have heard you for some time with patience. I have been cool, quite cool; but take care. You know I am compliance itself, when I am not thwarted – no one more easily led, when I have my own way; but don't put me in a frenzy!

ABSOLUTE   Sir, I must repeat it. In this I cannot obey you.

SIR ANTHONY   Now damn me, if ever I call you Jack again while I live!

ABSOLUTE   Nay, sir, but hear me.

SIR ANTHONY   Sir, I won't hear a word; not a word! Not
one word! So give me your promise by a nod, and I'll
tell you what, Jack – I mean, you dog – if you don't, by –   70

ABSOLUTE   What, sir, promise to link myself to some
mass of ugliness! To –

SIR ANTHONY   Zounds, sirrah, the lady shall be as ugly as
I choose. She shall have a hump on each shoulder. She
shall be as crooked as the Crescent. Her one eye shall   75
roll like the bull's in Cox's Museum. She shall have a
skin like a mummy and the beard of a Jew. She shall be
all this, sirrah! Yet I'll make you ogle her all day, and sit
up all night to write sonnets on her beauty.

ABSOLUTE   This is reason and moderation indeed!   80

SIR ANTHONY   None of your sneering, puppy! No grinning,
jackanapes!

ABSOLUTE   Indeed, sir, I never was in a worse humour
for mirth in my life.

SIR ANTHONY   'Tis false, sir! I know you are laughing in   85
your sleeve. I know you'll grin when I am gone, sirrah!

ABSOLUTE   Sir, I hope I know my duty better.

SIR ANTHONY   None of your passion, sir! None of your
violence, if you please! It won't do with me, I promise
you.   90

ABSOLUTE   Indeed, sir, I never was cooler in my life.

SIR ANTHONY   'Tis a confounded lie! I know you are in a
passion in your heart; I know you are, you hypocritical
young dog! But it won't do.

ABSOLUTE   Nay, sir, upon my word.   95

SIR ANTHONY   So you will fly out! Can't you be cool,
like me? What the devil good can *passion* do! *Passion*
is of no service, you impudent, insolent, overbearing
reprobate! There you sneer again! Don't provoke me!
But you rely upon the mildness of my temper. You   100

56

do, you dog! You play upon the meekness of my disposition! Yet take care. The patience of a saint may be overcome at last! But mark! I give you six hours and a half to consider of this. If you then agree, without any condition, to do everything on earth that I choose, 105 why, confound you, I may in time forgive you. If not, zounds, don't enter the same hemisphere with me! Don't dare to breathe the same air, or use the same light with me; but get an atmosphere and a sun of your own! I'll strip you of your commission; I'll lodge a 110 five-and-threepence in the hands of trustees, and you shall live on the interest. I'll disown you, I'll disinherit you, I'll unget you! And damn me, if ever I call you Jack again!

Exit Sir Anthony Absolute

ABSOLUTE (*alone*) Mild, gentle, considerate father, I 115 kiss your hands. What a tender method of giving his opinion in these matters Sir Anthony has! I dare not trust him with the truth. I wonder what old, wealthy hag it is that he wants to bestow on me! Yet he married himself for love, and was in his youth a bold intriguer 120 and a gay companion!

The Romantics

Journal: Dorothy Wordsworth

On Monday, 4th October 1802, my brother William was married to Mary Hutchinson. I slept a good deal of the night, and rose fresh and well in the morning. At a little after 8 o'clock I saw them go down the avenue towards the church. William had parted from me upstairs. 5
When they were absent my dear little Sara prepared the breakfast. I kept myself as quiet as I could, but when I saw the two men running up the walk, coming to tell us it was over, I could stand it no longer, and threw myself on the bed, where I lay in stillness, neither hearing or seeing 10
anything till Sara came upstairs to me, and said, 'They are coming'. This forced me from the bed where I lay, and I moved, I knew not how, straight forward, faster than my strength could carry me, till I met my beloved William, and fell upon his bosom. He and John Hutchinson led 15
me to the house, and there I stayed to welcome my dear Mary. As soon as we had breakfasted, we departed. It rained when we set off. Poor Mary was much agitated, when she parted from her brothers and sisters, and her home. Nothing particular occurred till we reached Kirby. 20
We had sunshine and showers, pleasant talk, love and chearfulness. We were obliged to stay two hours at K. while the horses were feeding. We wrote a few lines to Sara, and then walked out; the sun shone, and we went to the churchyard after we had put a letter into the post- 25
office for the *York Herald*. We sauntered about, and read the gravestones. There was one to the memory of five children, who had all died within five years, and the

longest lived had only lived four years. There was another stone erected to the memory of an unfortunate woman (as we supposed, by a stranger). The verses engraved upon it expressed that she had been neglected by her relations, and counselled the readers of those words to look within, and recollect their own frailties. We left Kirby at about half-past two. There is not much variety of prospect from K. to Helmsley, but the country is very pleasant, being rich and woody, and Helmsley itself stands very sweetly at the foot of the rising grounds of Duncombe Park, which is scattered over with tall woods; and, lifting itself above the common buildings of the town, stands Helmsley Castle, now a ruin, formerly inhabited by the gay Duke of Buckingham. Every foot of the road was, of itself, interesting to us, for we had travelled along it on foot, Wm and I, when we went to fetch our dear Mary, and had sate upon the turf by the roadside more than once. Before we reached Helmsley, our driver told us that he could not take us any further, so we stopped at the same inn where we had slept before. My heart danced at the sight of its cleanly outside, bright yellow walls, casements overshadowed with jasmine, and its low, double gavel-ended front. We were not shown into the same parlour where Wm and I were; it was a small room with a drawing over the chimney piece which the woman told us had been bought at a sale. Mary and I warmed ourselves at the kitchen fire. We then walked into the garden, and looked over a gate, up to the old ruin which stands at the top of a mount, and round about it the moats are grown up into soft green cradles, hollows surrounded with green grassy hillocks, and these are overshadowed by old trees, chiefly ashes. I prevailed upon William to go up with me to the ruins. We left Mary sitting by the kitchen fire.

So, We'll Go No More A-Roving: Lord Byron

So, we'll go no more a-roving
    So late into the night,
Though the heart be still as loving,
    And the moon be still as bright.

For the sword outwears its sheath,   5
    And the soul wears out the breast,
And the heart must pause to breathe,
    And love itself have rest.

Though the night was made for loving,
    And the day returns too soon,   10
Yet we'll go no more a-roving
    By the light of the moon.

La Belle Dame sans Merci: John Keats

I
O what can ail thee, knight-at-arms,
    Alone and palely loitering?
The sedge has withered from the lake,
    And no birds sing.

II
O what can ail thee, knight-at-arms,   5
    So haggard and so woe-begone?
The squirrel's granary is full,
    And the harvest's done.

III

I see a lily on thy brow,
    With anguish moist and fever-dew,   10
And on thy cheeks a fading rose
    Fast withereth too.

IV

I met a lady in the meads,
    Full beautiful – a faery's child,
Her hair was long, her foot was light,   15
    And her eyes were wild.

V

I made a garland for her head,
    And bracelets too, and fragrant zone;
She looked at me as she did love,
    And made sweet moan.   20

VI

I set her on my pacing steed,
    And nothing else saw all day long,
For sidelong would she bend, and sing
    A faery's song.

VII

She found me roots of relish sweet,   25
    And honey wild, and manna-dew,
And sure in language strange she said –
    'I love thee true'.

VIII

She took me to her elfin grot,
    And there she wept and sighed full sore,   30
And there I shut her wild wild eyes
    With kisses four.

IX

And there she lullèd me asleep,
    And there I dreamed – Ah! woe betide! –
The latest dream I ever dreamt 35
    On the cold hill side.

X

I saw pale kings and princes too,
    Pale warriors, death-pale were they all;
They cried – 'La Belle Dame sans Merci
    Thee hath in thrall!' 40

XI

I saw their starved lips in the gloam,
    With horrid warning gapèd wide,
And I awoke and found me here,
    On the cold hill's side.

XII

And this is why I sojourn here, 45
    Alone and palely loitering,
Though the sedge is withered from the lake,
    And no birds sing.

To... : Percy Bysshe Shelley

One word is too often profaned
    For me to profane it;
One feeling too falsely disdained
    For thee to disdain it;
One hope is too like despair 5
    For prudence to smother;

And pity from thee more dear
    Than that from another.

I can give not what men call love:
    But wilt thou accept not   10
The worship the heart lifts above
    And the heavens reject not,
The desire of the moth for the star,
    Of the night for the morrow,
The devotion to something afar   15
    From the sphere of our sorrow?

The Victorians

To Marguerite: Matthew Arnold

Yes! in the sea of life enisled,
With echoing straits between us thrown,
Dotting the shoreless watery wild,
We mortal millions live *alone*.
The islands feel the enclasping flow,   5
And then their endless bounds they know.

But when the moon their hollows lights,
And they are swept by balms of spring,
And in their glens, on starry nights,
The nightingales divinely sing;   10
And lovely notes, from shore to shore,
Across the sounds and channels pour –

Oh! then a longing like despair
Is to their farthest caverns sent;
For surely once, they feel, we were   15
Parts of a single continent!
Now round us spreads the watery plain –
Oh might our marges meet again!

Who order'd that their longing's fire
Should be, as soon as kindled, cool'd?   20
Who renders vain their deep desire? –
A God, a God their severance ruled!
And bade betwixt their shores to be
The unplumb'd, salt, estranging sea.

The Lost Mistress: Robert Browning

All's over, then: does truth sound bitter
    As one at first believes?
Hark, 'tis the sparrows' good-night twitter
    About your cottage eaves!

And the leaf-buds on the vine are woolly,   5
    I noticed that, today;
One day more bursts them open fully
    – You know the red turns grey.

Tomorrow we meet the same then, dearest?
    May I take your hand in mine?   10
Mere friends are we, – well, friends the merest
    Keep much that I resign:

For each glance of the eye so bright and black,
    Though I keep with heart's endeavour, –
Your voice, when you wish the snowdrops back,   15
    Though it stay in my soul for ever! –

Yet I will but say what mere friends say,
    Or only a thought stronger;
I will hold your hand but as long as all may,
    Or so very little longer!   20

Far From the Madding Crowd: Thomas Hardy

He pointed to about a yard in front of him.
    Bathsheba's adventurous spirit was beginning to find
some grains of relish in these highly novel proceedings.
She took up her position as directed, facing Troy.

'Now just to learn whether you have pluck enough to   5
let me do what I wish, I'll give you a preliminary test.'

He flourished the sword by way of introduction number
two, and the next thing of which she was conscious was
that the point and blade of the sword were darting with
a gleam towards her left side, just above her hip; then of   10
their reappearance on her right side, emerging as it were
from between her ribs, having apparently passed through
her body. The third item of consciousness was that of
seeing the same sword, perfectly clean and free from
blood held vertically in Troy's hand (in the position   15
technically called 'recover swords'). All was as quick as
electricity.

'Oh!' she cried out in affright, pressing her hand to
her side. 'Have you run me through? – no, you have not!
Whatever have you done!'   20

'I have not touched you,' said Troy, quietly. 'It was
mere sleight of hand. The sword passed behind you.
Now you are not afraid, are you? Because if you are I
can't perform. I give my word that I will not only not
hurt you, but not once touch you.'   25

'I don't think I am afraid. You are quite sure you will
not hurt me?'

'Quite sure.'

'Is the sword very sharp?'

'O no – only stand as still as a statue. Now!'   30

In an instant the atmosphere was transformed to
Bathsheba's eyes. Beams of light caught from the low
sun's rays, above, around, in front of her, well-nigh shut
out earth and heaven – all emitted in the marvellous
evolutions of Troy's reflecting blade, which seemed   35
everywhere at once, and yet nowhere specially. These
circling gleams were accompanied by a keen rush that
was almost a whistling – also springing from all sides of

her at once. In short, she was enclosed in a firmament of light, and of sharp hisses, resembling a sky-full of meteors close at hand.

Never since the broadsword became the national weapon had there been more dexterity shown in its management than by the hands of Sergeant Troy, and never had he been in such splendid temper for the performance as now in the evening sunshine among the ferns with Bathsheba. It may safely be asserted with respect to the closeness of his cuts, that had it been possible for the edge of the sword to leave in the air a permanent substance wherever it flew past, the space left untouched would have been almost a mould of Bathsheba's figure.

Behind the luminous streams of this *aurora militaris*, she could see the hue of Troy's sword arm, spread in a scarlet haze over the space covered by its motions, like a twanged harpstring, and behind all Troy himself, mostly facing her; sometimes, to show the rear cuts, half turned away, his eye nevertheless always keenly measuring her breadth and outline, and his lips tightly closed in sustained effort. Next, his movements lapsed slower, and she could see them individually. The hissing of the sword ceased, and he stopped entirely.

'That outer loose lock of hair wants tidying,' he said, before she had moved or spoken. 'Wait: I'll do it for you.'

An arc of silver shone on her right side: the sword had descended. The lock dropped to the ground.

'Bravely borne!' said Troy. 'You didn't flinch a shade's thickness. Wonderful in a woman!'

'It was because I didn't expect it. O, you have spoilt my hair!'

'Only once more.'

'No – no! I am afraid of you – indeed I am!' she cried.

'I won't touch you at all – not even your hair. I am only going to kill that caterpillar settling on you. Now: still!'

It appeared that a caterpillar had come from the fern and chosen the front of her bodice as his resting place. She saw the point glisten towards her bosom, and seemingly enter it. Bathsheba closed her eyes in the full persuasion that she was killed at last. However, feeling just as usual, she opened them again.

'There it is, look,' said the sergeant, holding his sword before her eyes.

The caterpillar was spitted upon its point.

'Why, it is magic!' said Bathsheba, amazed.

'O no – dexterity. I merely gave point to your bosom where the caterpillar was, and instead of running you through checked the extension a thousandth of an inch short of your surface.'

'But how could you chop off a curl of my hair with a sword that has no edge?'

'No edge! This sword will shave like a razor. Look here.'

He touched the palm of his hand with the blade, and then lifting it, showed her a thin shaving of scarf-skin dangling therefrom.

'But you said before beginning that it was blunt and couldn't cut me!'

'That was to get you to stand still, and so make sure of your safety. The risk of injuring you through your moving was too great not to force me to tell you a fib to escape it.'

She shuddered. 'I have been within an inch of my life, and didn't know it!'

'More precisely speaking, you have been within half

68

an inch of being pared alive two hundred and ninety-five times.'

'Cruel, cruel, 'tis of you!'

'You have been perfectly safe, nevertheless. My sword never errs.' And Troy returned the weapon to the scabbard.

Bathsheba, overcome by a hundred tumultuous feelings resulting from the scene, abstractedly sat down on a tuft of heather.

'I must leave you now,' said Troy softly. 'And I'll venture to take and keep this in remembrance of you.'

She saw him stoop to the grass, pick up the winding lock which he had severed from her manifold tresses, twist it round his fingers, unfasten a button in the breast of his coat, and carefully put it inside. She felt powerless to withstand or deny him. He was altogether too much for her, and Bathsheba seemed as one who, facing a reviving wind, finds it blow so strongly that it stops the breath.

He drew near and said, 'I must be leaving you.' He drew nearer still. A minute later and she saw his scarlet form disappear amid the ferny thicket, almost in a flash, like a brand swiftly waved.

That minute's interval had brought the blood beating into her face, set her stinging as if aflame to the very hollows of her feet, and enlarged emotion to a compass which quite swamped thought. It had brought upon her a stroke resulting, as did that of Moses in Horeb, in a liquid stream – here a stream of tears. She felt like one who has sinned a great sin.

The circumstance had been the gentle dip of Troy's mouth downwards upon her own. He had kissed her.

Letter: From Oscar Wilde to Lord Alfred Douglas

20 May 1895

My child,

Today it was asked to have the verdicts rendered separately. Taylor is probably being judged at this moment, so that I have been able to come back here. My sweet rose, my delicate flower, my lily of lilies, it is perhaps in prison that I am going to test the power of love. I am going 5 to see if I cannot make the bitter waters sweet by the intensity of the love I bear you. I have had moments when I thought it would be wiser to separate. Ah! moments of weakness and madness! Now I see that that would have mutilated my life, ruined my art, broken the 10 musical chords which make a perfect soul. Even covered with mud I shall praise you, from the deepest abysses I shall cry to you. In my solitude you will be with me. I am determined not to revolt but to accept every outrage through devotion to love, to let my body be dishonoured 15 so long as my soul may always keep the image of you. From your silken hair to your delicate feet you are perfection to me. Pleasure hides love from us but pain reveals it in its essence. O dearest of created things, if someone wounded by silence and solitude comes to you, 20 dishonoured, a laughing-stock to men, oh! you can close his wounds by touching them and restore his soul which unhappiness had for a moment smothered. Nothing will be difficult for you then, and remember, it is that hope which makes me live, and that hope alone. What wisdom 25 is to the philosopher, what God is to his saint, you are to me. To keep you in my soul, such is the goal of this pain which men call life. O my love, you whom I cherish above all things, white narcissus in an unmown field, think of the burden which falls to you, a burden which 30 love alone can make light. But be not saddened by that, rather be happy to have filled with an immortal love the soul of a man who now weeps in hell, and yet carries heaven in his heart. I love you, I love you, my heart is a rose which your love has brought to bloom, my life is a 35 desert fanned by the delicious breeze of your breath, and whose cool springs are your eyes; the imprint of your little feet makes valleys of shade for me, the odour of your hair is like myrrh, and wherever you go you exhale the perfumes of the cassia tree. 40

Love me always, love me always. You have been the supreme, the perfect love of my life; there can be no other.

I decided that it was nobler and more beautiful to stay. We could not have been together. I did not want to be 45 called a coward or a deserter. A false name, a disguise, a hunted life, all that is not for me, to whom you have been revealed on that high hill where beautiful things are transfigured.

O sweetest of all boys, most loved of all loves, my 50 soul clings to your soul, my life is your life, and in all the worlds of pain and pleasure you are my ideal of admiration and joy.

Oscar

Early twentieth century

A Room with a View: E.M. Forster

At the end of five minutes Lucy departed in search of
Mr Beebe and Mr Eager[...]

She addressed herself to the drivers, who were
sprawling in the carriages, perfuming the cushions with
cigars. The miscreant, a bony young man scorched black   5
by the sun, rose to greet her with the courtesy of a host
and the assurance of a relative.

'*Dove?*' said Lucy, after much anxious thought.

His face lit up. Of course he knew where. Not so far
either. His arm swept three-fourths of the horizon. He   10
should just think he did know where. He pressed his
finger-tips to his forehead and then pushed them towards
her, as if oozing with visible extract of knowledge.

More seemed necessary. What was the Italian for
'clergymen'?   15

'*Dove buoni uomini?*' said she at last.

Good? Scarcely the adjective for those noble beings!
He showed her his cigar.

'*Uno – piu – piccolo,*' was her next remark, implying
'Has the cigar been given to you by Mr Beebe, the smaller   20
of the two good men?'

She was correct as usual. He tied the horse to a tree,
kicked it to make it stay quiet, dusted the carriage, arranged
his hair, remoulded his hat, encouraged his moustache,
and in rather less than a quarter of a minute was ready to   25
conduct her. Italians are born knowing the way. It would
seem that the whole earth lay before them, not as a map,
but as a chess-board, whereon they continually behold

the changing pieces as well as the squares. Anyone can find places, but the finding of people is a gift from God. 30

He only stopped once, to pick her some great blue violets. She thanked him with real pleasure. In the company of this common man the world was beautiful and direct. For the first time she felt the influence of spring. His arm swept the horizon gracefully; violets, like 35 other things, existed in great profusion there; would she like to see them?

'*Ma buoni uomini.*' He bowed. Certainly. Good men first, violets afterwards. They proceeded briskly through the undergrowth, which became thicker and 40 thicker. They were nearing the edge of the promontory, and the view was stealing round them, but the brown network of the bushes shattered it into countless pieces. He was occupied in his cigar, and in holding back the pliant boughs. She was rejoicing in her escape 45 from dullness. Not a step, not a twig, was unimportant to her.

'What is that?'

There was a voice in the wood, in the distance behind them. The voice of Mr Eager? He shrugged his shoulders. 50 An Italian's ignorance is sometimes more remarkable than his knowledge. She could not make him understand that perhaps they had missed the clergymen. The view was forming at last; she could discern the river, the golden plain, other hills. 55

'*Eccolo!*' he exclaimed.

At the same moment the ground gave way, and with a cry she fell out of the wood. Light and beauty enveloped her. She had fallen onto a little open terrace, which was covered with violets from end to end. 60

'Courage!' cried her companion, now standing some six feet above. 'Courage and love.'

She did not answer. From her feet the ground sloped sharply into the view, and violets ran down in rivulets and streams and cataracts, irrigating the hillside with blue, 65 eddying round the tree stems, collecting into pools in the hollows, covering the grass with spots of azure foam. But never again were they in such profusion; this terrace was the well-head, the primal source whence beauty gushed out to water the earth. 70

Standing at its brink, like a swimmer who prepares, was the good man. But he was not the good man that she had expected, and he was alone.

George had turned at the sound of her arrival. For a moment he contemplated her, as one who had fallen 75 out of heaven. He saw radiant joy in her face, he saw the flowers beat against her dress in blue waves. The bushes above them closed. He stepped quickly forward and kissed her.

Before she could speak, almost before she could feel, 80 a voice called, 'Lucy! Lucy! Lucy!' The silence of life had been broken by Miss Bartlett, who stood brown against the view.

The Going: Thomas Hardy

Why did you give no hint that night
That quickly after the morrow's dawn,
And calmly, as if indifferent quite,
You would close your term here, up and be gone
    Where I could not follow 5
    With wing of swallow
To gain one glimpse of you ever anon!

Never to bid good-bye,
    Or lip me the softest call,
Or utter a wish for a word, while I   10
Saw morning harden upon the wall,
        Unmoved, unknowing
        That your great going
Had place that moment, and altered all.

Why do you make me leave the house   15
And think for a breath it is you I see
At the end of the alley of bending boughs
Where so often at dusk you used to be;
        Till in darkening dankness
        The yawning blankness   20
Of the perspective sickens me!

    You were she who abode
    By those red-veined rocks far West,
You were the swan-necked one who rode
 Along the beetling Beeny Crest,   25
        And, reining nigh me,
        Would muse and eye me,
While Life unrolled us its very best.

Why, then, latterly did we not speak,
Did we not think of those days long dead,   30
And ere your vanishing strive to seek
That time's renewal? We might have said,
        'In this bright spring weather
        We'll visit together
Those places that once we visited.'   35

        Well, well! All's past amend,
        Unchangeable. It must go.

I seem but a dead man held on end
To sink down soon... O you could not know
    That such swift fleeing   40
    No soul foreseeing –
Not even I – would undo me so!

Leda and the Swan: W.B. Yeats

A sudden blow: the great wings beating still
Above the staggering girl, her thighs caressed
By the dark webs, her nape caught in his bill,
He holds her helpless breast upon his breast.

How can those terrified vague fingers push   5
The feathered glory from her loosening thighs?
And how can body, laid in that white rush,
But feel the strange heart beating where it lies?

A shudder in the loins engenders there
The broken wall, the burning roof and tower   10
And Agamemnon dead.
                  Being so caught up,
So mastered by the brute blood of the air,
Did she put on his knowledge with his power
Before the indifferent beak could let her drop?

Post Second World War

In a Garden: Elizabeth Jennings

When the gardener has gone this garden
Looks wistful and seems waiting an event.
It is so spruce, a metaphor of Eden
And even more so since the gardener went,

Quietly godlike, but, of course, he had   5
Not made me promise anything, and I
Had no one tempting me to make the bad
Choice. Yet I still felt lost and wonder why.

Even the beech tree from next door which shares
Its shadow with me, seemed a kind of threat.   10
Everything was too neat, and someone cares

In the wrong way. I need not have stood long
Mocked by the smell of a mown lawn, and yet
I did. Sickness for Eden was so strong.

Possession: A.S. Byatt

The lady was dressed elegantly if not in the first flight
of fashion; she wore a grey-striped muslin dress over
which she had cast an Indian shawl with marine-blue
and peacock paisleys on a dove-grey ground; she had
a small grey silk bonnet, under the brim of which   5
appeared a few white silk rosebuds. She was very fair,
pale-skinned, with eyes, not unduly large, of a strange

green colour which transmuted itself as the light varied. She was not exactly beautiful – her face was too long for perfection, and not in the first flush of youth, though the bones were well-cut and the mouth an elegant curve, no pouting rosebud. Her teeth were a little large for an exacting taste, but they were strong and white. It was hard to tell whether she was a married lady or a spinster, and hard too, to decide what her circumstances might be. Everything about her was both neat and tastefully chosen, breathing no hint of extravagance, but betraying no signs of poverty or skimping to the curious eye. Her white kid gloves were supple and showed no signs of wear. Her little feet, which appeared from time to time as the carriage movement displaced the large bell of her skirt, were encased in a gleaming pair of laced boots in emerald green leather. If she was aware of her travelling companion's interest, she showed no sign of it, unless it were that her eyes were studiously averted from his person, and that circumstance might have indicated only a proper modesty.

It was indeed only when they were well beyond York that the question of their relationship might have been resolved, for the gentleman leaned forward and asked, very earnestly, if she was quite comfortable and not tired. And by then there were no other passengers, for the most part had changed trains, or reached their destination at York, and none was proceeding beyond Malton and Pickering, so that the two were alone in the carriage. She looked directly at him then, and said no, she was not in the least tired; she considered for a moment and added precisely that she was not in a state of mind that allowed of tiredness, she believed. Whereupon they did smile at each other, and he leaned forward and possessed himself of one of the little gloved hands, which lay still and then clasped his. There were matters, he said, that they had an urgent need to discuss before they arrived, things which they had had no time or peace to make clear in the haste and turmoil of setting off, things to which there was a degree of awkwardness attached, which he hoped, with resolution, they could overcome.

He had been planning this speech since they left King's Cross. He had been quite unable to imagine how he would say it, or how she would respond.

She said she was listening attentively. The little hand in his curled and crisped. He gripped it.

'We are travelling together,' he said. 'We decided – you decided – to come. What I do not know is whether you would wish – whether you would choose – to lodge and manage yourself separately from me after this point – or whether – or whether – you would wish to travel as my wife. It is a large step – It is attended with all sorts of inconvenience, hazard and – embarrassment. I have rooms reserved in Scarborough where a wife could well – find space. Or I could reserve other rooms – under some false name. Or you may not wish to take this step at all – you may wish to be lodged separately and respectably elsewhere. Forgive this baldnesss. I am truly trying to discover your wishes. We left in so exalted a state – I wish decisions could arise naturally – but you see how it is.'

'I want to be with you,' she said. 'I took a vast step. If it is taken, it is taken. I am quite happy to be called your wife, wherever you choose, for this time. That is what I had understood I – we – had decided.'

She spoke quickly and clearly; but the gloved hands, in their warm kid, turned and turned in his. He said, still in the quiet, dispassionate tone they had so far employed:

'You take my breath away. This is generosity –'

'This is necessity.'

'But you are not sad, you are not in doubt, you are not –'

'That doesn't come into it. This is necessity. You know that.' She turned her face away and looked out, through a stream of fine cinders, at the slow fields. 'I am afraid, of course. But that seems to be of no real importance. None of the old considerations – none of the old cares – seem to be of any importance. They are not tissue paper, but seem so.'

'You must not regret this, my dear.'

'And you must not speak nonsense. Of course I shall regret. So will you, will you not? But that, too, is of no importance at this time.'

They were silent, for a time. Then he said, choosing his words carefully, 'If you are to come with me as my wife – I hope you will accept this ring. It is a family ring – it belonged to my mother. It is a plain gold band, engraved with daisies.'

'I too have brought a ring. It belonged to a great-aunt, Sophie de Kercoz. It has a green stone – look – jade – a simple stone, with an engraved S.'

'You would prefer not to accept my ring?'

'I did not say that. I was giving proof of foresight and resolution. I shall be happy to wear your ring.'

He peeled off the little white glove, and pushed his ring over her fine one with its green stone, so that the two lay together. It fitted, though loosely. He would have liked to say something – with this ring I thee wed, with my body I thee worship – but these good and true words were doubly treacherous to two women. Their unspoken presence hung in the air. He seized the little hand and carried it to his lips. Then he sat back and turned the glove reflectively in his hands, pushing its soft leather

pockets back into shape, one by one, smoothing their   110
fine creases.

All the way from London, he had been violently confused
by her real presence in the opposite inaccessible corner.
For months he had been possessed by the imagination
of her. She had been distant and closed away, a princess   115
in a tower, and his imagination's work had been all to
make her present, all of her, to his mind and senses,
the quickness of her and the mystery, the whiteness
of her, which was part of her extreme magnetism, and
the green look of those piercing or occluded eyes. Her   120
presence had been unimaginable, or more strictly, *only*
to be imagined. Yet here she was, and he was engaged in
observing the ways in which she resembled, or differed
from, the woman he dreamed, or reached for in sleep, or
would fight for.   125

A Pink Wool Knitted Dress: Ted Hughes

In your pink wool knitted dress
Before anything had smudged anything
You stood at the altar. Bloomsday.

Rain – so that a just-bought umbrella
Was the only furnishing about me   5
Newer than three years inured.
My tie – sole, drab, veteran RAF black –
Was the used-up symbol of a tie.
My cord jacket – thrice-dyed black, exhausted,
Just hanging on to itself.   10

I was a post-war, utility son-in-law!
Not quite the Frog-Prince. Maybe the Swineherd
Stealing this daughter's pedigree dreams
From under her watchtowered searchlit future.

No ceremony could conscript me   15
Out of my uniform. I wore my whole wardrobe –
Except for the odd, spare, identical item.
My wedding, like Nature, wanted to hide.
However – if we were going to be married
It had better be Westminster Abbey. Why not?   20
The Dean told us why not. That is how
I learned that I had a Parish Church.
St George of the Chimney Sweeps.
So we squeezed into marriage finally.
Your mother, brave even in this   25
US Foreign Affairs gamble,
Acted all bridesmaids and all guests,
Even – magnanimity – represented
My family
Who had heard nothing about it.   30
I had invited only their ancestors.
I had not even confided my theft of you
To a closest friend. For Best Man – my squire
To hold the meanwhile rings –
We requisitioned the sexton. Twist of the outrage: 35
He was packing children into a bus,
Taking them to the Zoo – in that downpour!
All the prison animals had to be patient
While we married.
                                    You were transfigured.
So slender and new and naked,   40
A nodding spray of wet lilac.
You shook, you sobbed with joy, you were ocean depth

Brimming with God.
You said you saw the heavens open
And show riches, ready to drop upon us.   45
Levitated beside you, I stood subjected
To a strange tense: the spellbound future.

In that echo-gaunt, weekday chancel
I see you
Wrestling to contain your flames   50
In your pink wool knitted dress
And in your eye-pupils – great cut jewels
Jostling their tear-flames, truly like big jewels
Shaken in a dice-cup and held up to me.

Notes

sd = stage direction

Late Middle Ages

The Knight's Tale: Geoffrey Chaucer (c. 1390)

Geoffrey Chaucer, who died in 1400, wrote *The Canterbury Tales* in the last dozen or so years of his life. It was a huge undertaking, and was unfinished at his death. In the *General Prologue* the reader is presented with a group of pilgrims, one of whom is the narrator himself, who are about to set out from the Tabard Inn in Southwark to travel to the shrine of St Thomas à Becket at Canterbury. It is agreed that they will all tell stories to pass the time on the journey. Lots are drawn, and by chance – or perhaps by design – it falls to the Knight to tell the first tale; this is fitting as he is of the highest social rank among the pilgrims.

The tales give the reader a very clear picture of medieval society, including its attitudes towards love and romance across the different social classes, as the pilgrims are from a wide variety of backgrounds and have vividly contrasting personalities.

In this extract from the Knight's story, Arcite and Palamon – two noblemen from Thebes who are close friends – are in prison after being captured during Theseus's campaign against the Thebans. It is from their prison window overlooking a palace garden that both young men fall in love with the unattainable Emelye, which results in divisions between them. Throughout the passage Chaucer exploits the conventions of 'courtly love', an elaborate set of conventions where love is an experience somewhere between erotic desire and spiritual devotion. Courtly love involved a nobleman dedicating himself to worshipping a woman from afar, and was not generally linked to marriage. In medieval society, marriage was often seen as a business transaction quite separate from love.

Chaucer uses the conventions of courtly love in adopting language originally used to describe religious love as a way of exploring secular love, and the perspective is almost entirely male (the woman is at times seen as a tormentor of the men's emotions). The art of love had a particular code of behaviour, most famously set out for aristocratic readers in the French romance *Le Roman de la Rose*. This French poem uses the allegory of a Dreamer who finds his way into a rose garden (the garden of love, from which all unpleasant aspects of human life have been removed). Once in the garden, the Dreamer sees the beautiful Rose and is wounded through the eye with an arrow from the bow of the God of Love. In the extract, we see Chaucer depicting a very similar pattern of events. The passage begins after Arcite has expressed the opinion that the reason Palamon is pale and distressed is because they have been imprisoned.

 1 **agayn** in reply.
 2 **Cosyn** kinsman.
  for sothe truly.
 3 Palamon insists Arcite's assertions are merely an empty fantasy (*veyn ymaginacioun*).
 5 **ye** eye.
 5–6 The description of the wounding through his eye into his heart echoes the conventions of courtly love, as does Palamon's insistence that it will be his *bane* (cause of death).
 7–10 The image of the young woman roaming in the garden mirrors the *Roman de la Rose* (see headnote above). Palamon also questions whether he sees a *womman or goddesse*; in keeping with courtly traditions he elevates his beloved and worships her from afar.
 10 **noot wher** do not know whether.
 11 **Venus** the goddess of love.
 13–20 Palamon prays to *Venus* to beg help in escaping from prison, and *compassioun* on his *lynage* (noble birth).
 16 **scapen** escape.
 21 **gan espye** saw.
 23–5 The description of Arcite being similarly *wounded* by the sight of the *lady* is a further development of the courtly love imagery. What is the effect of this doubling?
 27–31 The suddenness of the wound and its fatal nature are foregrounded. In keeping with courtly convention, Arcite uses both hyperbole (exaggeration) and religious language as he calls for *hir mercy and hir grace*.

27 **sleeth**   kills.

29 **but**   unless.

30 **atte leeste weye**   at the very least.

31 **nam but deed**   am as good as dead.

33 **Dispitously**   angrily.

34 **Wheither seistow**   do you say.

35 **fey**   faith. As ever with knights, honour is a key issue and it is to this quality that Arcite turns as he swears on his faith that he is *in ernest*.

36 **me list ful yvele pleye**   I have no desire to play around (or joke).

37 **tweye**   two.

38–40 Palamon appeals to ideas of *honour* and *brother*hood.

38 **nere... no**   would not be... any.

40–41 **thy brother/ Ysworn ful depe**   Palamon reminds Arcite of their deeply sworn oath to be as brothers to one another.

41 **til**   to.

42 **in the peyne**   in pain, under torture.

44 They have sworn never to betray one another in love.

45 **leeve**   dear.

46, 47 **forthren**   support, help.

49 **woot**   know.
   withseyn   deny.

50 **artow**   you are.
   of my conseil   in my confidence (i.e. knowing my secrets).

53 **sterve**   die.

55–60 By an interesting exercise in logic, Palamon claims the lady as his own since he saw her first, and told Arcite about his devotion to her. Ironically neither he nor Arcite has spoken a single word to this young woman.

The Wife of Bath's Tale: Geoffrey Chaucer (c. 1390)

See the headnote on page 85 for *The Canterbury Tales*. The Wife of Bath is one of the most striking characters among Chaucer's pilgrims. She is introduced in the *General Prologue* as bold and outspoken; the reader quickly learns that she has been married several times and has inherited considerable wealth from her husbands. Her appearance is rather ostentatious, and her clothes demonstrate not just her comfortable financial position but also her confidence (see the illustration on page 2). She is an experienced woman of the world and feels she knows all there is to know about courtship and love, which the narrator calls 'the olde daunce', suggesting that there is a set of expected moves a couple will make. This is a typical representation of love and courtship at this time.

The story the Wife narrates suggests that all women desire to be in control, to have *maistrie* in their relationships. As a woman who has gained independence for herself through mastering her numerous husbands, her story seems to reflect her own views.

The tale describes what happens after a knight rapes a young woman. He is saved from capital punishment by the queen, who banishes him from court for a year with the task of riding through the kingdom to discover what it is that women most desire. His life will be forfeited at the end of the year if he doesn't return with a convincing answer. The knight searches high and low but is unsuccessful in his quest until, about to despair and return to the queen to meet his fate, he meets an ugly old woman who tells him that she knows the answer and will tell him, if he agrees to grant her a wish. He returns with the old woman to court, where he reports to the queen and the assembled court the secret that has been revealed to him: that all women desire *maistrie* over their lovers and husbands. Neither the queen nor any other woman at court is able to deny the truth of this, and the knight is granted his reprieve, whereupon the old woman – to his horror – demands his hand in marriage.

The extract begins as the knight and the old woman discuss their future on their wedding night. It is interesting to note that it is the old woman who is speaking as the extract begins and hers is the main voice that we hear throughout the extract. In terms of the power structure of the relationship, this illustrates an unusual arrangement for the time in which the tale is set, when one might expect a woman to be silent and powerless.

1–2　The woman tells the knight that because she is *foul and old* he does not have to live in the perennial fear of the married man, especially one married to a beautiful young woman: that he will be cuckolded by his wife (that is, she will sleep with another man). This fear was especially strong when the first son produced in a marriage would inherit the husband's wealth and estate; men were understandably keen to be assured of the faithfulness of their wives so as to be confident that the son was their own child.

3　**filthe and eelde**　ugliness and old age.
also moot I thee　as I hope to thrive.

4　**wardeyns**　guardians.

5　**youre delit**　what pleases you.

6　**worldly appetit**　The woman refers to her understanding of men's sexual requirements and promises that she can fulfil these. The fact that these desires are referred to as *worldly* reminds the reader of the perceived division between sacred and secular love at this time, where sacred love is offered to God, and *worldly* love involves sexual desire. This viewpoint can be seen in literature about love throughout the ages: some modern writers still play on ideas of sacred and profane types of love (for example, see Elizabeth Jennings's poem *In a Garden* on page 77).

7　**Chese now**　Notice how the woman addresses her husband using imperatives. By instructing him to choose whether he wishes her to be old and ugly (therefore chaste) or young and beautiful (therefore always a source of concern to him) she seems to be giving him power, but does the imperative show that it is she who remains in control of the transaction?

12–13　The woman suggests that a young, beautiful wife can be a danger *to youre hous*, suggesting the threat to the knight's estate as well as his reputation if she were to be unfaithful to him.

12　**aventure**　chance.
repair　many visits.

15　**wheither**　whichever.

16　**avyseth hym and sore siketh**　considers carefully and sighs deeply.

18 The respectful tone with which the knight addresses the old woman here is entirely different from the contemptuous way he addressed her when they first met, and illustrates how much the old woman (and indeed the queen) has taught him already.

19 By putting himself in his wife's control, the knight shows his respect for her and also shows that he may already have learned the lesson she offered him: that all women desire the upper hand in marriage.

20 **plesance** pleasurable.

23 **suffiseth** is enough for.

24–5 The woman seeks to confirm that this means he has given her control of their dealings – which she has told him is what women prefer. There is a neat symmetry in the structure of the tale, which demonstrates the knight's conversion: the man who began by unlawfully taking a woman's chastity is now granting *maistrie* to his wife. As a result, she agrees to be *bothe fair and good* to him (line 29).

25 **me lest** I please.

27 **wrothe** angry.

30 **moote sterven wood** might die insane.

31 **But** unless.

33 **but I be** if I am not.

35 **eke** also.

36 Having been granted control, the woman now says to her husband that he may do to her as he wishes, even kill her, if she fails to keep her promises. The woman demonstrates trust in him, in return for his showing her the same courtesy.

40 **hente hire in hise armes two** took her in his arms.

41 The metaphor suggests how completely engulfed in his *blisse* the knight is at his new situation.

42 **a-rewe** in succession.

43 A modern reader might see this line as rather a sting in the tail of the story, but the following lines do suggest the playful tones of the Wife of Bath and remind us that, even if the repentant rapist has been rewarded with a beautiful, young and true wife, he has been granted this only because he put himself under her command.

46–8 **Jhesu Crist... we wedde** This is clearly the voice of the Wife of Bath, boldly asking Christ to send all women such

husbands. The adjective *meeke* reminds the reader of the
original message of the tale: the husband must grant the wife
the control she desires.

48 **overbyde**   outlive.

49 **shorte hir lyves**   shorten their lives.

51 **olde and angry nygardes of dispence**   old, bad-tempered
misers who scant their wives' requests for money.
Thus the strident tone of the Wife ends the tale in an
uncompromising fashion. This voice clearly illustrates that
it is dangerous to make assumptions about gender roles and
views in literature about love: as early as the 1390s, Chaucer
created a female character who voices strong desires and
aspirations.

The Paston Letters: From Margery Brews to John Paston (1476 or 1477)

The Pastons were a wealthy family who lived in Norfolk. Their
surviving letters, which span four generations, have been preserved
and offer a vivid picture of life at the time. These letters are
from Margery Brews to her prospective fiancé John Paston, and
together with others the family wrote they have been called the
oldest surviving love letters in the English language. However,
their content often seems more like the negotiation of a business
deal. They serve to highlight the way marriage was seen at this
time as a matter of property rights, and also the powerlessness
of women, who were subject to first their father's and then their
husband's will.

These letters concern themselves with negotiations about the
size of Brews's dowry (the money offered by her father upon her
marriage), which the Paston family considered too small. The
couple did eventually marry in 1477.

The lines displayed as verse in the first letter may make up
Brews's own Valentine poem; it is not certain that she intended
them to be read in this way, but her use of language does seem
to differ in these lines, and the first two pairs form rhyming
couplets.

2 **Bill**   letter.

3 **Right reverend and worshipful**   The terms used to address
Paston indicate the subordinate status that the writer is
adopting, one that women were usually accorded at this
time. The man is addressed in quasi-religious terms that
simultaneously assure him of the vehemence of her love.

5–6 **your welfare… heart's desire**   Her pleas that God keep
Paston in good health can be seen as a typical greeting of the
time, indicating her society's deeply religious character.

8 **heele**   health. The writer informs her loved one that she
will not be in full health or in good spirits until he responds
to her letter. The suggestion of love-sickness is in keeping
with the conventions of the period, with its traditions of
courtly love, but it is quite unusual to see the woman as the
sufferer.

10 **wottys**   knows.

11 **for to be dead**   even if I must die. The threat of death from
love-sickness was not an uncommon idea.
dyscur   discover, reveal.

12 **the matter**   Presumably this refers to the issue of her dowry.

16–19 **for if that… not forsake you**   The writer asserts that she
would not abandon her loved one if he had only half as
much money, implying that she therefore hopes he will not
forsake her on financial grounds.

21 **I wis I will de all my might**   certainly I will do all in my
power.
no mo   anything else.

22 **friends**   those close to her: friends and relations. She vows
to value him alone above or despite the advice of her friends
and family.

23 **let**   prevent.

26 **if they be never so wrath**   no matter how angry they are.

27 The writer acknowledges that there are impediments to their
love at this time, but finds comfort in the reassurance that
things can get better.

28–9 **the Holy Trinity have you in keeping**   Once more she
wishes for the blessings of heaven upon her loved one.

29–30 **that this bill be not seen**   Notice that the writer asks for the
secrecy of her Valentine letter to be respected.

The second letter seems more concerned with the financial negotiations for the prospective marriage, but also shows the writer subtly assuming some control and suggesting that she has value in terms other than monetary ones.

8 **business** The repeated use of this word offers a clear indication that marriage is a transaction in which love can have little or no influence.

9–10 **I would be the happiest one alive** The simplicity of this declaration suggests the innocence of the writer and also her acceptance of her situation.

17–18 **as much as I know how to or am able to** Is there a hint here of the pain she has so far *endured* for love?

20 **one hundred pounds and fifty marks** Mention of the monetary sum reinforces the representation of women as property to be bought and sold. The tone is conciliatory but realistic, as the writer acknowledges her limited influence in the affair.

22–4 **if you could be content... happiest maid on earth** These lines create a sense of pathos as the writer shows humility in accepting that the money on offer may not be enough to secure her lover. The representation of women as having a monetary value in the marriage market, but little power of choice, remained prominent in writing on love until the middle of the nineteenth century.

27–8 **do not take the trouble to visit any more** The tone at this point can be read in two ways. On the one hand the writer appears to accept her lot and acknowledge her lowly position in the light of the fact that her lover could *get more money* if he chose a wife from a richer family. Alternatively, the tone may be seen as more challenging, as the young man is reminded of his desire for money, something she has *understood from* him *before*. The adjectives *good, faithful and loving* can be read as rather ironic under the circumstances.

28–30 **let it be finished... duration of my life** A feminist reading suggests that the writer attempts here to assert some authority as she takes it upon herself to redefine the relationship in terms of friendship. Clearly she wishes to maintain the link with her lover, but if he chooses a wife who can offer a better financial settlement, the writer insists the subject of their possible liaison should *be finished and never spoken of again*. She concludes in a modest and simple tone, asking that from this point she should be seen as a *faithful friend and petitioner*. The word *petitioner* implies someone who will be supportive and prepared to make appeals or requests on behalf of the young man. This hints at a sense of empowerment despite her inferior status.

31–2 **may Almighty Jesus… body and soul** The final lines change the mood of the letter as the writer moves the focus from the secular world of financial bargaining to a spiritual blessing. This leaves the reader in no doubt about the writer's commitment both to her faith and to the spiritual welfare of her potential husband.

William Shakespeare

As You Like It (c. 1599)

In this pastoral comedy a young noblewoman, Rosalind, is forced to flee the treacherous court and take refuge in the Forest of Arden because her uncle, who has already usurped her father's dukedom and banished him, subsequently turns against her too. Before being driven from court she had watched a wrestling competition where she had fallen in love with the young challenger, Orlando.

Once safely in the forest, Rosalind disguises herself as a boy in order to protect her identity and her chastity. A series of coincidences brings her into the company of Orlando again, as he also has sought refuge in the forest. She finds that he is in love with her and has been carving her name on trees and writing love poems about her. Unable to admit to Orlando that she is the woman he loves, she plots to spend as much time with him as she can by pretending to teach him about love and, comically, how to go about wooing his loved one.

In this extract, with Rosalind in her disguise as a sceptical young boy, they discuss the nature of love. Rosalind invokes the ancient idea that love is a sickness and imagines herself as the doctor who can cure it.

7 **quotidian** attack of fever.

12 **cage of rushes** flimsy, easily penetrated prison.

14 **A lean cheek** Rosalind proceeds to outline the traditional symptoms of love-sickness and claims Orlando lacks these signs of love.

blue eye eye with dark shadows caused by sleeplessness.

15 **unquestionable** i.e. irritable or sullen.

23 **point-device** neat and precise.

30 **women still give the lie to their consciences** Rosalind alludes to the female practice of refusing to admit their love even to themselves.

35 **are you so much in love** Rosalind implies that Orlando's declarations of love may be exaggerated, hinting at the conventional practice in love poetry of expressing love in hyperbolic terms. What lies behind her question?

39–41 **Love is merely a madness... as madmen do** Rosalind expresses the common view of love as an aberration or mental sickness. The following lines refer to unsympathetic contemporary reactions to mental illnesses, with her allusions to use of the *whip* and confinement to *a dark house*. She pretends to think that lovers ought to be treated like this, but are not because love is so common an ailment.

43 **counsel** advice.

45–6 **He was to imagine me his love** Rosalind begins to outline her plan to 'cure' Orlando of his love-sickness. Note that this plan will require them to spend much time together.

48 **moonish** changeable.

54 **entertain** receive kindly.

forswear him give him up.

55–6 **from his mad humour... humour of madness** *Humour* can simply mean mood, but it also refers to the Renaissance belief in the theory of the four humours: it was thought that a person's temperament was controlled by the balance of the body's four fluids – blood, yellow bile, black bile and phlegm. While these were in perfect balance in the body, the person would be even-tempered. An excess of a particular humour would cause a person to be too 'sanguine', 'choleric', 'melancholic', or 'phlegmatic'. As a person in love was likely to display an uneven temperament, Rosalind is hinting at an imbalance of humours leading to *madness*.

59–60 **wash your liver as clean as a sound sheep's heart** The liver was believed to be the seat of the passions. In this metaphor, love is envisaged as unclean, an unwanted impurity to be washed away.

62 **I would not** I do not want to.

64 **come every day** In a comedic piece of dramatic irony, the audience is here invited to recognize Rosalind's invitation to Orlando as revealing her true feelings towards him.
cote humble cottage.

65 **Now by the faith of my love, I will** Having initially refused Rosalind's offer of a *cure*, Orlando here appears to change his mind, apparently seeing the attempt to cure him as a test of the strength of his love. As a typical lover, he will also relish the opportunity to talk about his love as often as possible.

Othello (c. 1603)

In *Othello* Shakespeare presents a hero who is from the beginning of the play defined by his colour. As a black foreigner he is an outsider in Venice, but as a man who has achieved military distinction he is revered by the Venetian state for the service he has done. In this extract he has been accused of luring the daughter of a state senator, Brabantio, into marriage through witchcraft or unlawful arts. While the gathered company await the arrival of Desdemona, the young woman in question, Othello relates how the couple fell in love. The detail offered here presents Othello as a man of action and quite different from his audience, the noblemen of Venice.

3 **battles, sieges, fortunes** This triplet illustrates the nature of Othello's life up to this point; his major experiences have been on the battlefield, and this implies that his understanding of the role of lover and husband is limited.

8 **by flood and field** at sea and on the battlefield.

13 **antres** caves. The breadth of Othello's *travels* suggests he
is extremely knowledgeable about the world beyond the
confines of Venice, adding to his aura of mystery.
idle empty or sterile.

14 **hills, whose heads touch heaven** This hyperbolic
description, and the following mention of strange peoples,
reveal an imaginative, poetic side to Othello.

17 **The Anthropophagi** a mythical race of cannibals described
in ancient legends.

17–18 **men whose heads/ Do grow beneath their shoulders** Legends
told of a race of men who had no heads, whose facial features
were in their chests.

19 Desdemona's reaction, as described by Othello, is
important here, as she is clearly affected by the wonder of
Othello's descriptions. Othello presents himself as a man
of vast experience, in contrast to the naive young woman
who has spent her life within the confines of her father's
home.

22–3 **with a greedy ear/ Devour up** The use of synaesthesia
(mixing of the senses) to describe Desdemona's reaction
suggests her appetite for Othello's stories, and the way in
which they make him desirable to her.

24 **a pliant hour** This phrase suggests that Othello chose a time
when Desdemona appeared most malleable and receptive.

25–6 **prayer of earnest heart... my pilgrimage** Religious language
is used to describe the beginnings of a secular love. Here
Desdemona is seen to be the supplicant with a *prayer*, and
Othello's adventures are presented in terms of a *pilgrimage* as
if his travels have been undertaken for spiritual reasons.

26 **dilate** describe in detail.

27 **by parcel** in parts.

29 **beguile her of her tears** This is an interesting choice of
phrase, as on the one hand it can be read as winning or
holding Desdemona's attention with his stories and thus
coaxing tears from her. Alternatively, *beguile* can suggest
trickery, perhaps indicating that Othello calculates the
emotional effect of his stories.

33–4 What is the effect of the use of anaphora (repetition) in
Desdemona's reported response?

35–6 The fragmented sentence structure reflects the development of Desdemona's growing love for Othello, and the subtle manner in which this is conveyed.

40–41 In these lines Othello defines the way he understands their love. The audience may question how much he knows about relationships and marriage.

43 Othello's insistence that Desdemona be given the opportunity to *witness* his version of events suggests that at this point he trusts her, values her opinion and is keen that she should publicly affirm their marriage.

46 **mangled matter** This suggests the Duke regards the situation as muddled, or at least unconventional.

52–3 Brabantio's question to his daughter affirms the concept of male authority, as a woman is expected to be subservient to her father until marriage, and then to her husband.

54 Desdemona's challenging response alerts the audience to her assertive character. She goes on to offer a reasoned and logical argument to support her case. Her tone is calm, controlled and confident.

62 **bu'y** be with you.

64 **get** beget, father. Brabantio's response is decisive, and his dismissal of his paternal bond reflects his refusal to tolerate female dissent.

68 **For your sake** because of you.

70 The word *escape* suggests that Desdemona has attained some form of freedom, and his insistence that if he had another child he would turn to *tyranny* implies that he believes he has been too liberal in allowing Desdemona access to Othello.

71 **clogs** weights attached to the legs of animals to stop them roaming.

King Lear (c. 1605)

King Lear, in his old age, decides that it is time to hand over responsibility for ruling the kingdom to his three daughters. To help him decide which daughter is to rule each part of the kingdom, he fashions a 'love-test' whereby the one who can convince him, in a public declaration, that she loves him most will inherit the most land and power. His two eldest daughters are deceitful and without conscience. One after the other they make exaggerated claims about their love for him and are rewarded with large parts of his kingdom. The youngest daughter, Cordelia, truly loves her father yet is too honest to exaggerate this love for such a purpose. Instead, she modestly expresses what she feels: that she loves her father exactly as she ought to do. This is insufficient for Lear, who attempts to persuade her to construct an elaborate, rhetorical argument as her sisters have done, in order to be rewarded with even more land than theirs; because she refuses to do this, he banishes her.

Lear casts himself upon the hospitality of his two eldest daughters, between whom he has divided the entire kingdom. He soon regrets his foolishness as he finds himself thrown out of doors and his country at war, with the two daughters seeking to destroy each other. Towards the end of the play he is reunited with his youngest daughter, Cordelia, and overjoyed to see her. Their reunion is painfully brief, however, as he is imprisoned separately from her and she is murdered in her cell. This extract, from the very end of the play, shows Lear's grief. The other characters in this scene have been trying unsuccessfully to protect Lear and Cordelia; Albany is acting as temporary ruler of the kingdom.

1 sd The visual tableau represented by this stage direction is distressing: the father is carrying his child as he may have done when she was a baby, but she is dead. The topsy-turvy nature of this in terms of the cycle of life is striking: the child dying before the parent is always a tragic situation. Here, all that has gone before in the play makes the pathos even more powerful.

1 **Howl, howl, howl** There are no words commensurate to Lear's grief; instead, Shakespeare gives him this articulation of utter despair, which is also a command to those around him as to how they should respond to Cordelia's death.
you are men of stones The bereft father is unable to comprehend the apparent composure of the other characters.

3 **heaven's vault should crack** Perhaps Lear implies that the gods themselves would be forced to take pity and return his beloved daughter to him.

4–7 **I know when one is dead... she lives** Lear's anguished
state of mind alternates between disbelief in and painful
acceptance of Cordelia's death.

6 **stone** polished surface used as a mirror.

7 **the promis'd end** the Day of Judgement, promised in the
Bible at the end of time. The interjected comments of Kent,
Edgar and Albany work almost like a chorus, articulating
grief and shock.

8 **Fall and cease** let the heavens fall and everything come to
an end.

9 **This feather stirs** Lear imagines he sees a feather moving
near Cordelia's lips, indicating that she is breathing.

12 **'Tis noble Kent, your friend** Edgar's attempt to make Lear
recognize his loyal former servant shows how overcome by
grief Lear is, and also widens the tragedy to encompass the
suffering of other characters.

13–15 What is the effect of Lear's alternation between anger and
tenderness?

16 **Her voice was ever soft** Lear allows himself to remember
the voice of his child. The juxtaposition of this memory with
the sad events of the play, culminating in her violent death,
creates more pathos for the audience.

18 This sudden statement shocks the audience, as Lear has
been a rather broken, pathetic figure in recent scenes. It adds
another image to the tragedy and futility of Cordelia's death,
and perpetuates the cycle of violence in the death of the *slave*.

20 **falchion** small sword.

22 **crosses** troubles.

24–5 Kent's analogy describes a person detested by the personified
Fortune. If he is answering Lear's question *Who are you?*, he
may be referring to himself; alternatively, he means Lear.

27 **Caius** Kent, who had been banished like Cordelia, returned
to Lear's service in disguise hoping to protect him, and used
the name *Caius*.

31 **I'll see that straight** I'll deal with that in a moment. Lear is
too distracted to take in the information.

34 **All's cheerless, dark, and deadly** Kent's reflection sums up
the mood at the end of the play.

35 **fordone** destroyed.

36 **desperately**   in despair.

38 **bootless**   pointless.

39 **Edmund**   the wicked half-brother of Edgar, mortally wounded in an earlier fight.

45 **With boot and such addition**   with such additional rights and titles.

49 **And my poor fool is hang'd!**   If the word *fool* refers to Cordelia it is used affectionately, but also suggests her unwordliness. However, the line may refer to Lear's faithful Fool or jester, who has not appeared for several scenes (and may, in Shakespeare's time, have sometimes been played by the same actor as Cordelia). In this reading, the two powerless truth-tellers of the play are brought together in the same cruel fate.

54–5 Lear seems to imagine that he sees a flicker of life on Cordelia's *lips*. Does he die feeling a joyful hope that she may be living still?

56 **Break, heart**   Kent is either speaking of his own heart, or of Lear's; in either case, he wishes for an end to suffering.

57 **Vex not his ghost**   Kent begs that Lear be allowed to die peacefully. His *ghost* is his departing soul.

58 **the rack of this tough world**   To live on would be torment for Lear; in this metaphor, the *world* itself becomes an instrument of torture, the *rack*.

64 **gor'd**   damaged.

65–6 Kent hints that he will soon be joining his master in death; his *journey* is to another world.

67–70 It is Edgar, not Albany, who has the concluding speech of the play and he tacitly accepts the new role of king. He affirms that the events they have witnessed are sure to prove more memorable and tragic than any still to come in their lifetimes.

The Tempest (c. 1610)

At the beginning of *The Tempest*, one of Shakespeare's last plays, the dukedom of Milan has been seized from Prospero by his younger brother. Prospero has been banished and cast upon a magical island with his then three-year-old daughter, Miranda. They have nothing but some magic books from which Prospero has learned to cast spells. Miranda thus grows up in isolation; the only other inhabitants of the island are a monstrous creature called Caliban, whom Prospero enslaves, and Ariel, a spirit who is also in thrall to Prospero.

The play begins 12 years after his banishment, when Prospero finally sees the opportunity to take revenge on his usurping brother, Antonio. He uses his magical powers to create a tempest that shipwrecks Antonio and his travelling companions (including the King of Naples) on the island, when they are sailing home from a royal wedding. Prospero's magic ensures that no one is harmed, but he causes the party to be separated.

Ferdinand, son of the King of Naples, stumbles upon the home of Prospero and Miranda. He is the first man that Miranda has ever seen (apart from her father and the monster, Caliban). This extract shows the first meeting of Ferdinand and Miranda, brought together by Prospero's magic and destined to marry. The idea of the noble father selecting the bridegroom for his daughter is not surprising; more unusual are the methods Prospero uses to be sure of the devotion of the pair. He creates obstacles to the progress of their courtship so that they do not find love too easily and consequently value it too lightly.

The theme of love at first sight, although it is here brought about by magic, is a literary tradition well established by Shakespeare's time.

6 **passion**   i.e. grief.
21 **owes**   owns.
22 Prospero commands Miranda to open her eyes. Such imperative language is typical of Prospero's speech and demonstrates his control over his daughter. This goes beyond the realms of usual parental control: Prospero several times causes Miranda to fall asleep as it suits him, and here she wakes in accordance with his commands.
23 **What is 't? a spirit?**   Miranda's innocence is illustrated here as she does not even recognize that Ferdinand is a man. What does characterizing him as *a spirit* suggest?
25 **brave form**   handsome shape.

26 **wench**   young girl.

27 **gallant**   This term suggests an attractive gentleman. Prospero's tone at this point may be quite jovial.

28 **but**   except that.

29 **canker**   disease, or cause of decay.

32 **A thing divine**   Miranda believes him to be a god as she has never before seen a handsome young man.
natural   in nature.

33–4 **It goes on... my soul prompts it**   Prospero is pleased by Miranda's reaction to the sight of Ferdinand: it is just as he planned it.

34 **Spirit, fine spirit!**   Ariel is Prospero's spirit, who helps him in his magical work about the island. Prospero has made himself Ariel's master, yet promises to free him from enslavement in recompense for his work raising the tempest and dealing with the shipwrecked men.

35–6 **the goddess/ On whom these airs attend**   There is a beautiful symmetry in Ferdinand's first reaction to the sight of Miranda: just as she thought him a god, so he assumes her to be a goddess, and connects her with the *airs* (music) he has heard. The similarity of their reactions suggests their compatibility.

36 **Vouchsafe**   grant.

39–40 **my prime request... last pronounce**   It is not surprising that Ferdinand chooses to pronounce this *prime* request *last*, as it is clearly of a personal nature. His enquiry as to whether Miranda is a *maid* functions in two senses: at one level it is a request for clarification as to whether she is human or a goddess. In another sense of the word, it is a question about her marital status: he is inquiring whether she is unmarried (literally, a virgin), suggesting his interest in her as a potential wife.

40 **O you wonder!**   Ferdinand's exclamation doesn't simply express his admiration for Miranda, it also operates as a play on words as the name *Miranda* (which he hasn't yet learned) comes from the Latin verb *miror*, meaning to wonder at, or admire. There is a later play on Miranda's name as Ferdinand calls her 'admired Miranda'.

42 **My language!**   Ferdinand is astonished that his *goddess* speaks the same language as he does.

43 Ferdinand is mistakenly assuming that his father, the King of Naples, is dead. Were this to be the case, of course, he (as the son of the king) would indeed be *the best* surviving Neapolitan speaker.

46 **A single thing** Ferdinand's reply plays on several meanings: he is alone, unique, sincere (not 'double' or deceitful) and without help.

47 **He does hear me** Ferdinand is playing with his assumed new identity: the *he* referred to here is the King of Naples who is also (he assumes) himself.

49 **mine eyes, never since at ebb** i.e. he has been weeping ever since he saw his father shipwrecked.

51 **the Duke of Milan** Ferdinand is referring to Antonio, the usurping brother of Prospero, whom he assumes to be the rightful duke. In the following aside, Prospero claims the title for himself.

53 **control** contradict, prove wrong.

55 **chang'd eyes** fallen in love. Miranda and Ferdinand gaze so fixedly at each other that Prospero describes them in a figurative sense as having exchanged eyes.

57 **you have done yourself some wrong** you are mistaken. Prospero rebukes Ferdinand, partly for his presumption in addressing his daughter and partly hinting at the mistake Ferdinand has made in assuming that he is now King of Naples.

58 **Why speaks my father so ungently?** Miranda's question suggests that her loyalties have already shifted and now lie with Ferdinand.

59 **the third man that e'er I saw** The first was Prospero, and the second Caliban.

Early seventeenth century

The Duchess of Malfi: John Webster (c. 1613)

John Webster was born in London between 1578 and 1580, and it is likely that he attended the prestigious Merchant Taylors' School. His writing for the stage uses the genre of revenge tragedy, and in

The Duchess of Malfi he exposes the hypocrisy of the Church and the dangers that face a self-determined woman, even a powerful one.

This extract shows the Duchess, who is, as she says, *a young widow*, declaring her love for her steward, Antonio. In doing so, the Duchess is defying her overbearing brothers, who have commanded her not to re-marry. In this scene she demonstrates some of her most attractive character traits; the audience can see her as strong, passionate, sensual, courageous, independent, intelligent, and witty. All these qualities are, however, potentially dangerous in the restrictive and male-dominated society that the Duchess inhabits. She refuses to be subservient to men: she ignores her brothers' commands not to marry, and takes the initiative to woo Antonio.

The specific threat that the Duchess poses to the male-dominated order is that in marrying someone of her own choosing, for love, she passes the family wealth and status to that man (and subsequently his children), and gives him a position of power in the state. She is here placing her personal desires above her public role as Duchess. In the Renaissance doctrine of 'the king's two bodies', a ruler was considered to have both a public and private persona; when private self-interest is pursued, the state is likely to suffer. The Duchess also places herself above the authority of the Church, being rather cavalier about the official rites of marriage (see lines 48 and 51–3). In placing passion above reason, the Duchess conforms to the then common view of women as having a weaker capacity for reasoning than men, being more easily swayed by passion, and more easily deceived (as was Eve in the Garden of Eden), thus needing male leadership in matters of family, Church, and state.

It can be argued that the Duchess does show herself a poor judge of character, as she too quickly dismisses her brothers' potential for violent revenge when she says that *time will easily/ Scatter the tempest*.

4 **equivocates** uses vague or ambiguous language rather than being direct and clear.
5 **violent passions** This admission of sexual desire from a female character challenges expectations: a woman would be

expected to display *simple virtue* rather than acknowledging her *passions*.

8 **Go, go brag** The anaphora (repetition) creates an authoritative tone as befits the status of the Duchess.

9 **heartless** There is an ironic play on the word, as it may suggest that she is callous and unfeeling. This is turned on its head in the second half of the line as she insists that her heart is now in her loved one's *bosom*. Webster is subverting the idea of courtly love, as the speaker is a woman who presents herself as vulnerable and at the mercy of her lover's response, rather than the usual male voice.

11–15 The commanding tone in these lines reflects the status of the Duchess; however, the content challenges the traditional presentation of a woman. Again Webster challenges conventional attitudes and values as the male is seen to *tremble* and *fear* rather than reciprocate the desires expressed.

18 **claims you** This assertion by the Duchess reinforces the image already created of a woman insisting on self-determination.

18–19 **like a widow... half a blush in't** She is keen to assert her familiarity with marital love, and to show that she has appropriate modesty as a mature woman, but neither the innocence of a young girl nor false modesty.

19–21 **Truth speak... your good name** The formality of Antonio's reply and his use of the word *sanctuary* suggest his subservient position in relation to the Duchess. His assurance that her *good name* will not be endangered and that he will act as a refuge or safe haven for it demonstrates his awareness of her social position as a Duchess and her vulnerability as a woman. What do you make of the caution Antonio shows here?

24 *Quietus est* This expression means that a debt is 'quit' or paid. By discharging Antonio from any debt to her, the Duchess suggests he will become her equal.

29 **without this circumference** outside our small circle. An image of a wedding ring may be implied.

35 sd *Cariola* the Duchess's serving woman.

39 ***Per verba de presenti*** 'through words about the present'. This means the expression of an intention to marry in the future, which (if before witnesses) was binding. Here the Duchess insists that they can create an *absolute marriage* in secret and without the Church.

40 **this sacred Gordian** In Greek mythology, no one could untie the Gordian knot, until Alexander the Great simply cut through it with his sword. Here it symbolizes the binding together of the couple in security and unity, but it is also *sacred*. This is another example of religious ideas being appropriated to describe human passion and desire.

42 **spheres** the circles in which the stars and planets appeared to revolve, and were believed to make *music* (line 44).

43 **Quickening** coming to life; making new life.

45–7 **loving palms... bore fruit divided** It was thought that palm trees could only reproduce if they were close together.

52–3 The confidence of these words challenges the authority of the Church, and to a Jacobean audience they may suggest that the Duchess is acting recklessly.

54–5 **I now am blind... lead your fortune by the hand** The Duchess alludes to the image of blind Fortune. The Wheel of Fortune is a concept in medieval and ancient philosophy referring to the capricious nature of fate. The goddess Fortuna, sometimes depicted blindfolded, spins her wheel at random, so that some people fall and suffer great misfortune, while others rise – until the next spin of the wheel.

59 **my humorous kindred** This refers to the contemporary belief in the theory of humours or moods (see pages 95–6).

60 **'Alexander and Lodovic'** According to this *old tale*, the friends Alexander and Lodovic were so alike that they could change places without anyone noticing. When Lodovic married the Princess of Hungaria in Alexander's name, he laid a naked sword between the Princess and himself each night to maintain their chastity. Despite her earlier provocative language, the Duchess now playfully suggests she will maintain a chaste distance between herself and Antonio.

The Sun Rising: John Donne (published 1633)

This poem by John Donne (1572–1631), who is generally regarded as the greatest of the so-called Metaphysical poets, displays many of the features typical of its genre. It uses striking images and extravagant exaggeration or hyperbole. The speaker personifies the sun as a sentient being disturbing him and his lover as they lie in bed in the morning. The poem follows the tradition of the *aubade*, or love poem about the dawn, usually portrayed as a sad time for lovers as they must part for the day. Donne subverts that tradition here and the speaker, instead of being melancholy, challenges the sun in a surprisingly feisty manner.

The poem is also typical of the Metaphysical genre in that it refers to the scientific and geographical discoveries of the time. It references the spices of India and the mining of precious metals in the New World; it also alludes to the recent and radical theory of a universe with the sun at its centre, rather than the earth. Here again, however, Donne adopts an unexpected approach: where he might have been expected to embrace this Copernican theory and lay down a challenge to the old earth-centred doctrine, the poem not only has the sun travelling (as in traditional beliefs) around the earth, but creates an entirely new lovers' cosmology, with not merely the earth but the lovers' bed at its centre.

It is not known exactly when Donne, who became Dean of St Paul's Cathedral, wrote most of his poems; a collection was first published after his death.

1 **Busy old fool** This dismissive way of addressing the sun introduces the extended metaphor personifying the sun as an old busybody. How would you characterize this as an opening to a poem?

2 **Why dost thou** The speaker daringly challenges the sun and addresses it with the familiar second-person pronoun *thou*.

3 **Through windows, and through curtains** This reference to the physical features of the room imagines the sunbeams as zooming in on the lovers, first through the windows, then through the curtains that surround the four-poster bed.

us   The plural first-person pronoun for the lovers contrasts with the singular second-person pronoun for the sun, suggesting the unity of the couple contrasted with the isolation of the sun.

4   The speaker asks the age-old question: must lovers be subject to the clock, rising and parting in the morning as dictated by the sunrise?

5   **Saucy pedantic wretch**   The sun is here belittled in terms that suggest it is a rude and boring person; the description of the sun as a pedant implies it is keen to enforce its old-fashioned rules in an unnecessary way.

5–8   **go chide... harvest offices**   The speaker lists other types of people who must get up and go about their daily business, as if in an effort to divert the sun from its apparent interest in waking the lovers.

8   **country ants**   The image of people who work in the countryside as *ants* is an imaginative re-creation of how the harvesters must appear from the sun's viewpoint. The dramatic perspective here is a typical Metaphysical device, all the more surprising at a time before it became a familiar experience to see the landscape from a great height.

9–10   In another hyperbolic leap, the speaker imagines that lovers exist in a state of bliss outside time. The sun's job in marking out the passage of time is therefore dismissed as unnecessary, and its features – *season, hours, days, months* – become merely the metaphorical *rags* in which *time* clothes itself.

11–13   The speaker boldly suggests that, despite the fact that the sun regards its beams as *reverend* (worthy of great respect) and *strong*, they are insignificant when one considers that all the speaker needs to do to render them powerless is to *wink*. The verbs *eclipse* and *cloud* simultaneously challenge the sun by referring to natural elements that can dim its beams, and emphasize the pride of the speaker in claiming such powers for himself.

14   It is implied here that the power of love is stronger than the sun: the speaker could, if he chose, block out the sun's rays, but this would mean he lost the sight of his loved one. He is not prepared to do this, suggesting that his lover is far more important and thus more powerful than the sun.

15 This line continues the idea that his beloved is more powerful than the sun. Traditionally the eyes of a loved one were compared with the sun (see the first line of Shakespeare's sonnet debunking such ideas, 'My mistress' eyes are nothing like the sun'). But here, Donne takes the traditional idea further, suggesting that his lover's eyes are so dazzlingly beautiful that they could *blind* the sun instead of the other way round.

17 **both th'Indias of spice and mine** the East Indies (famous for its valuable *spices*) and the West Indies, where precious metals were mined. In an image evoking the geographical discoveries and the trading riches of the era, the speaker dismisses the excitement of exploration and goes on to suggest that the only territory he wishes to discover is the body of his lover.

20 **All here in one bed lay** His lover is the essence of all the rich, newly discovered lands and the speaker is more fortunate than all *those kings* whom the sun may see on its daily journey.

21–2 The speaker makes explicit the image from the end of the previous stanza in this simple declarative statement. There is a certainty to the tone that forestalls any challenge, compounded by the full stop at the end of the sentence. There is an undeniable sense of patriarchal possession in the metaphor naming himself as the *prince* of the woman's *state*, which echoes the colonial arrogance of the era as well as the convention of regarding women as the property of men.

23 **Princes do but play us** The speaker insists that although there are 'real' *Princes*, they merely mimic the happiness of the lovers.

24 In comparison with the joy of the lovers, all the world's titles indicating rank and respect (*honour*) are mere substitutes for the real glory of love. Similarly, all of the world's *wealth* is like artificially blended base metals, in comparison with the purity and richness of their love. There may be a play on words in the mention of *honour*, which also referred to a woman's chastity. The speaker may be suggesting that compared with the true love of the couple, worldly estimations of what constitutes honour, including female chastity, are meaningless.

25–8 Boldly, the sun is again addressed by the second-person pronoun as the speaker finishes with a neatly executed piece of logic typical of a Metaphysical poem. He argues that the lovers have made the sun's job easy by shrinking the world to its essentials – the entire world being *contracted* into the bed of the lovers – and, since the sun is in his old age, he ought to be grateful. In this argument, the old sun's only task now is to *warm* the lovers by shining upon them.

29–30 In a final twist, the reader is reminded of the cosmology suggested at the poem's outset: the lovers in their *bed* are at the *centre* of the universe, and the *walls* of their room form the *sphere* around which the sun is required to navigate.

Death and Love: Ben Jonson (c. 1637)

Ben Jonson (1572–1637) was a dramatist who is also well known for his lyric poetry, as well as for his relationship with Shakespeare. His plays were extremely popular in their time (especially *Volpone*, *The Alchemist* and *Bartholomew Fair*) and have had a lasting influence. Over the course of his career he enjoyed the patronage of the king (leading some to call him England's first Poet Laureate), became an honorary citizen of Edinburgh, and was awarded an honorary Master of Arts degree from Oxford University.

Death and Love comes from *The Sad Shepherd*, an unfinished pastoral play that he was said to be working on at the time of his death. In it, Jonson uses a regular classical form typical of Renaissance poetry, with octosyllabic (eight-syllable) rhyming couplets. The poem is brief and largely unadorned by the type of complex phrasing and conceits that typified Metaphysical poetry during the same period (see page 108). Nevertheless it does demonstrate a feature very typical of its time as it sets out to develop an apparently logical argument, just as many Metaphysical poems did.

With its 16-line form, the poem is too long to be classified as a typical sonnet, yet it does use quatrains (groups of four lines), the usual organizational structure for a sonnet. Its regular rhythm also recalls the sonnet form, as does its subject matter, love; and, as in a typical Shakespearian sonnet, the last two lines are used to provide a twist on the ideas set out in the main body of the poem.

The poem is written in the first person, using a surprisingly conversational style, with phrases such as *I have heard* and *I have been told*.

1 **Though I am young** The poem sets up an apparently logical argument signalled by this disclaimer, which suggests that the speaker's authority on such matters as Death and Love may not be entirely trustworthy because of his youth. What is the effect of this?

3 **Yet I have heard** The speaker claims to be relying on the authority of others, presumably those older and wiser than himself.

both bear darts These are the metaphorical arrows of Cupid in the case of the personified Love, and a more literal and dangerous *dart* in the case of Death. An initial comparison is established here between two apparently fatal conditions. This connection is to be explored through the course of the poem.

5 A conversational style has by now been set up, aided by references to what others have said. As the second quatrain of the poem begins, the speaker changes focus.

6 **heat, cold** The opposition of these terms suggests the difference between Love and Death, whereas the first quatrain emphasized the similarity between the two. Attributing *heat* to Love is typical of the representation of love in literature through the ages: the heat of passion is a common image. This is neatly juxtaposed with the coldness associated with Death.

8 **one thing** the same thing (presumably danger and fatality).

9–14 In the second stanza, the speaker sets up a similar pattern to the first, by initially pointing out the similarities between Death and Love. He uses a simile to explore different causes of death – notice that these also are pairs of extremes, where one may physically go either up or down into death, and perish by fire (*lightning*) or water (*wave*). He compares these to Love's damaging ways. The *wave* may also recall the chill of death (alluded to in line 6) whereas the *flash of lightning* recalls the heat of passion.

13 **Love's inflamèd shaft or brand**   This recalls the allusion to Cupid's arrows in the first stanza, suggesting a circularity to the poem's structure as it enters its closing argument.

14 **May kill**   The speaker could be alluding to death caused by a broken heart or, possibly, to the traditional characterization of orgasm as a little death. Thus, both love and death are shown to be fatal.

15 **Except**   This word signals a change in the argument of the poem.

15–16 **the virtue... the grave**   The speaker now argues that Love is the more powerful of the two forces, thus perhaps ending the poem on an optimistic note, by indicating that Love is a force for good in that it can combat the *frost* of the *grave*.

The Fair Singer: Andrew Marvell (c. 1647)

This poem by Andrew Marvell (1621–78) demonstrates several features that might be classed as typical of Metaphysical poetry (see page 108): he uses hyperbolic language to describe the loved one in extravagant terms, and the poem works through an extended metaphor as the speaker imagines his loved one being created specifically by a personified Love in order to make him subject to Love's whims. The logical force of the poem's argument is also a typical feature of Metaphysical poetry.

The poem is written in regular, six-line stanzas of mostly iambic pentameter, with four alternately rhyming lines followed by a concluding rhyming couplet in each stanza. The alternate rhymes give the poet the space to set up an argument or description, which is powerfully concluded by the rhetorical force of the rhyming couplet in each stanza.

The title calls to mind the sirens of ancient Greek mythology: mythical mermaid-like creatures with powerful, magical voices who lured sailors to their doom on the rocks.

2 **so sweet an enemy**   The oxymoron (contradiction in terms) is clear: the *enemy* is *sweet* because it is a loved woman, yet her destructive power is all the greater because she enables Love to subdue the speaker to its will (*make a final conquest*, line 1).

3 **both beauties to my death agree** The *beauties* are identified in the following lines as the *eyes* and the *voice* of the Fair Singer. The combined force of these is said by the speaker to be utterly irresistible and will conclude in his *death*. As in the Jonson poem *Death and Love* (see above), there is possibly an allusion to the traditional connection between *death* and orgasm, a reading that makes perfect sense here.

4 **fatal harmony** The metaphor of the two *beauties* is extended, and neatly refers to the voice of the loved one and its potential danger to the speaker.

5–6 The parallel structure within the couplet emphasizes the logical nature of its argument: beauty entrances the *heart*, while the *voice* (which could, by extension, be taken to refer to the wit and intelligence of the woman) *captivate*s the *mind* of the speaker.

7 **I could have fled** The modal verb suggests a possibility that did not arise in this case: an *enemy* with only beauty, or only a *voice*, could have been resisted.
but only.

8–9 The metaphor of entanglement suggests how the speaker is captured by the woman's beauty. The curls that metaphorically entrap him may be an allusion to the myth of Medusa, who had snakes growing from her head instead of hair, and could turn a man to stone with just a glance.

9 **trammels** devices that shackle animals. What do you make of this extraordinary metaphor?

10 **how should I avoid** The rhetorical question appeals to the reader to answer the dilemma posed, suggesting its unavoidable logical force.

11 **subtle art** The speaker seems to refer to the attractions of the woman here as a deliberate ploy to entrap him.
wreathe weave, twist together.

12 **fetters** chains.
the very air I breathe The speaker illustrates the unlimited power of the Fair Singer to control him, as the metaphorical chains she creates for him are made of the *very air* they both use – he to *breathe*, she to sing. Here, he seems to suggest that she is knowingly seductive, drawing him into her embraces

in a deliberate fashion. It is an image of woman as seductress that is as ancient as the Book of Genesis.

13 **had**   would have.

fighting in some plain   Love is here represented as a battle, and one in which the woman has an unfair advantage.

14 **hang in equal choice**   The idea of the scales of justice is alluded to here, with the implication being that this battle is unfair as the scales are loaded in her favour.

17 **all my forces**   The metaphor of the battle of love is extended here: the *forces* suggest armies. The speaker's *forces* are his mental and physical faculties, all of which he tries unsuccessfully to deploy against the attractions of the Fair Singer.

18 **both the wind and sun**   The Fair Singer is represented as having two of the great forces of nature (with the *sun* representing fire) on her side. She knows how to manipulate the *wind* or air as she uses it to create the voice that enslaves the speaker. The sun illuminates the beauty of her *eyes*, again causing him to fall under her spell. Thus both of these natural elements are portrayed as being *gainèd* by her, and used to entrap the speaker. Notice how Marvell has created an image of the forces of the natural world ranked against him as they might be in a military battle.

Restoration

Paradise Lost: John Milton (1667)

Paradise Lost is an epic poem written in blank verse. Traditionally, epic poems are long narrative poems telling of heroic deeds and events significant to a culture or nation. Milton originally published *Paradise Lost* in 10 books in 1667, but released a new edition divided into 12 books (the classic structure for epic poems) in 1674.

Milton bases his poem on stories of Satan's rebellion against God, and on the biblical story of the temptation of Adam and

Eve and their expulsion from the Garden of Eden (see page 7). Adam and Eve are presented as two individuals with distinct personalities, and the poem tells of their love and their tragic mistakes. This extract, which is from Book 4, begins with Eve speaking to Adam. She tells him about her first awakening into consciousness and describes her confusion about who and where she is. Interestingly it is not until Book 8 that the reader learns of Adam's awakening, and it would be useful to look at his description in parallel with Eve's.

2   **flesh of thy flesh**   This phrase is from Genesis 2:23, and alerts the reader to Eve's status in relation to Adam.

3   **without whom am to no end**   The message is reinforced by Eve's insistence that without Adam she has no purpose.

5   **him**   God.

6–9   In these lines Eve presents herself as one who has been given a greater blessing than Adam because she has him as a companion, calling him *Pre-eminent by so much odds*, while Adam has no equal to commune with. This is an interesting assertion as in Book 8 Adam relates that God made Eve after he asked for a companion to remedy his loneliness. Could Eve be mistaken in her perception of Adam's needs?

8   **odds**   advantage, superiority.

12   **Under a shade of flowers**   It is interesting to note that Eve describes her awakening as being in *shade*, possibly suggesting her distance from God's light of truth, and her need for guidance.

18   **unexperienced thought**   This phrase illustrates Eve's innocence but also presents her as vulnerable, having a mind that can be influenced. At this point in the poem the influence comes from Adam, but later it is Satan who is able to project desires upon Eve.

18–19   **laid me down... to look**   Eve's first act is to look down at the lake, whereas in Book 8 we learn that Adam first looks up to heaven.

21–5   Eve's first experience is to be captivated and deceived by an image she cannot identify – which is, of course, her own reflection. Here Milton appropriates the story of Narcissus from Ovid's *Metamorphoses*. Narcissus fell in love with his own reflection, and his story is often used to demonstrate that erotic desire is based on visual images that are deceptive and worthless. Milton suggests that Eve, and therefore all women, are in need of God's guidance to escape being ensnared by illusory images.

28 **a voice**   presumably God's voice.

31 **stays**   waits for. Eve is deceived by shadowy appearances while she remains separate from Adam.

32–3 **he/ Whose image thou art**   Eve is defined by God as an image not of God himself but of Adam.

37 **invisibly thus led**   Again this phase suggests Eve's natural tendency to follow and obey.

39 **platan**   the Greek name for a plane tree. By using the name, Milton makes a link to the Greek philosopher Plato, who argues that the ultimate reality consists of ideal forms that can only be perceived by the intellect. These forms contrast with the reflections and shadows that humans see and touch in the physical world and are deceived into thinking of as reality. Milton situates Adam *Under a platan* to suggest his close relationship with and understanding of the essences of things. In contrast, Eve is presented as being part of the world of images and reflections from which she is led away reluctantly.

39–41 **less fair... watery image**   Eve at first appears disappointed in Adam as he is unlike the image she has seen of herself. However, what she is now seeing is not the indirect image of a reflection of Adam (Eve herself) but a direct reflection of God. Once again Milton distances Eve in terms of both her identity and her sense of self.

43 The use of chiasmus (repetition with a change of structure in the repeated phrase) foregrounds Adam's authority, as the rhetorical construction suggests a voice with firm and natural confidence.

44–6 **I lent... Substantial life**   Eve was created by God from one of Adam's ribs.

47 **individual**   inseparable.

48 **thee claim**   Adam concludes his speech with an assertion of power.

52 Unlike Eve's beauty, which is mere appearance, Adam is *truly fair* because he is defined by his *wisdom*.

53 **general** shared.

54 **conjugal** associated with marriage.
unreproved innocent.

55–8 **half embracing leaned… loose tresses hid** The rich and sensual description of Eve in these lines portrays her as both offering and receiving virtuous pleasure.

58–61 **he in delight… on Juno smiles** Adam's *delight* is not only in her beauty but in her *submissive* behaviour. Milton makes it clear that what Adam offers is *superior love*, as Adam is linked to *Jupiter*, the king of the gods, smiling upon his queen *Juno*.

61 **impregns** makes pregnant. Jupiter fills the clouds with fruitful rain showers, which make possible the *May flowers*. Milton fuses biblical iconography with classical allusions, thus blurring the boundaries between the pagan and the Christian world.

The Country Wife: William Wycherley (1675)

William Wycherley was a successful playwright of the Restoration period. The return of the monarchy with Charles II in 1660 opened up a new era in the theatre, which had been repressed under Puritan rule. There was a profusion of popular comic plays for a period of about 50 years, creating the genre of Restoration comedy. The tolerance of the king in both political and social matters allowed theatres to perform risqué material, and *The Country Wife* is representative of this attitude, being concerned with sexual intrigues.

In this extract, which is the whole of Act III Scene I of the play, Pinchwife rails at his sister for being a bad influence on the innocent wife he has brought to London from the country. Throughout the play Wycherley satirizes men's concern with their wives' faithfulness and the foolishness of jealous husbands, while also exposing the superficiality of the monied classes and town life.

1 **Sister** Alethea is the sister of Mrs Pinchwife's husband.

3–5 **fluttering about abroad… in a cage** This extended metaphor (which is continued in Alethea's answering speech) suggests a sense of Alethea's freedom, contrasted with Mrs Pinchwife's position, which she characterizes as one of imprisonment and entrapment.

12 **pure** The ironic use of this word serves not only to create comedy but to reinforce the presentation of Mrs Pinchwife as naive and innocent.

13 **dancing, meetings, and junketings** The use of a list reflects the insistent tone of Mrs Pinchwife as she catalogues the pleasures she believes she is missing. *Junketings* is a general term for outings, excursions or parties of any kind.

15 **ninepins** a game that resembles skittles. Mrs Pinchwife's mention of this game demonstrates how little she knows about *London ladies*, who would be unlikely to play a game associated with country folk.

21–2 **like a confessor** Pinchwife's image of himself as his wife's spiritual adviser reinforces the status he wishes to assume in the marriage. It is, however, immediately challenged by Alethea, who undermines his status and ridicules his own view of his actions.

24 **ostler** groom who cares for horses.
grease the horses' teeth This was a trick to save hay by making it difficult for horses to eat.

26 **precepts** rules, principles.

30 **would** wanted to.

45–6 Wycherley signals a change in Mrs Pinchwife's attitude.

49 **Oh, if that be all** What do you make of this remark?

50–52 **I have not been well... in love with me** Here Wycherley ironically refers to the conventions of courtly love, where falling in love is often compared to suffering a wound or the onset of sickness. However, unlike the courtly lover, whose love remains secret (especially from the woman's husband), Mrs Pinchwife is naively frank about her emotions.

62 **receipt-book** book of remedies for common illnesses. Here it seems Mrs Pinchwife is being dismissive.

65–6 **cuckolds and bastards... own fortune** Illegitimate children were unlikely to inherit any property and were therefore obliged to secure their own position in life. Similarly it was commonly held that those whose wives were unfaithful – *cuckolds* – must accept responsibility for their own fate as their situation was often considered to be the result of their own foolishness or lack of care.

69 **'Tis just done – she comes from it**   The afternoon performance of the play has finished – Alethea has just come from the theatre.

71–2 **not that I care... player-men**   What do you make of Wycherley's humorous characterization of reasons for attending the theatre?

82–3 **that's once**   that's flat. There is a new and assertive tone from Mrs Pinchwife as she insists rather bluntly that she will have her own way. See also line 101.

93, 102 The asides allow the audience insight into Pinchwife's attitudes and behaviour and serve to reinforce the comedy through the use of dramatic irony.

113 **use her to**   let her get used to.

117 **The Exchange**   an area with fashionable shops.

Song: Aphra Behn (1676)

Aphra Behn (1640–89) was a supporter of the monarchy, and after the restoration of Charles II she worked for his government as a spy against the Dutch. However, the king refused to pay her expenses on her return to London, and despite her connections at court she was sent to a debtor's prison. After her release, and very unusually for a woman at that time, she turned to writing to earn a living.

Behn experimented with all forms of writing, including novels such as *Oroonoko*, but is mostly known as a playwright. This poem is a ballad that opens her play *Abdelazer or The Moor's Revenge*. It is a good example of the way Behn uses conventional modes to explore issues concerning love. Her poetic style recalls the lyricism of the previous century and tends to emulate writers such as Sir Philip Sidney, Edmund Spenser and Shakespeare.

In many of her poems Behn uses a dramatic voice. Here a lover describes Cupid's power to ensnare, and it is through the use of a specific voice that the poem attains a sense of immediacy. The alternating rhymes set up a series of contrasts in terms of the opposing experiences of longing for a loved one and resisting the pains of love.

1 The personification of *Love* in male form as Cupid, presented as sitting in *triumph*, sets the tone of the poem. The little god of love glories in his success; the following lines paint a picture of what his success entails.

4 **strange tyrannic power** The image is of premeditated and unrelenting cruelty – love is seen as oppressive and controlling – yet there is something *strange* about this power. Its strangeness is illustrated in the descriptions that follow, listing its constituent parts.

5–8 In the second quatrain the speaker sets up the contrast between lover and loved one. The elemental image of *fires* in the loved one's *bright eyes* suggests a destructive attractiveness, intensity and energy. In contrast, the speaker has only *desires*, a perpetual longing for fulfilment in love.

9–10 The second stanza begins with a contrast between the lover's experience of love, *sighs and tears*, and the loved one's *pride and cruelty*.

11 **languishments** Notice how this word seems to echo with the unattainable longings of the first stanza.

13–16 The poem concludes with an image of the suffering of unrequited love as Cupid is presented as able to wound at will. The rhyming of *armed* and *harmed* suggests misery and anguish for the speaker, while the pairing of *deity* and *free* – the latter given prominence by being the last word in the poem – leaves the reader in no doubt that the loved one is the *victor* whose heart maintains its independence and liberty.

The Rover: Aphra Behn (1677)

See the headnote on page 120 for information on Aphra Behn. *The Rover* is her best-known play, first performed in 1677 to great acclaim. As noted on page 118, Restoration comedy is notorious for its sexual explicitness, a quality that was encouraged by the carefree, licentious character of Charles II's court. Behn's work is concerned with the relations between the sexes, but should also be read in the light of her political opinions. As a royalist, she frequently portrays Puritans in a bad light. The subtitle of the play, *The Banish'd Cavaliers*, refers to the years of exile that the Cavalier forces experienced during the period of parliamentary and military rule by Oliver Cromwell, which ended with the restoration of Charles II to the throne in 1660.

The *Rover* of the play's title is Willmore, a rakish naval captain. Despite his womanizing ways he falls in love with a young woman named Hellena, who has set out to experience love before her brother sends her to a convent. Complications arise when Angellica Bianca, a famous prostitute, becomes obsessed with Willmore and swears revenge on him for his betrayal.

The secondary plot explores the attempt by Hellena's sister Florinda to marry Colonel Belvile rather than the man her brother has selected for her. As the passage opens Florinda, wearing nightclothes, is waiting in her garden for a secret meeting with Belvile. Willmore enters, having been drinking, and mistakes Florinda for a prostitute. He tries to persuade her to have sex with him, and when she resists he attempts to rape her. This is only prevented by the arrival of Belvile and his friend Frederick.

> 2 **Callis** Florinda's governess.
> 3 **cabinet** small apartment.
> 4 **garden** Behn uses the image of the garden to suggest the possibility of temptation, as in the Garden of Eden, and this is developed in Willmore's speech.
> 16–17 **a garden!... sent us here** The extended metaphor of the garden now becomes more explicit as Willmore suggests God has sent him a woman. Biblical iconography is used to describe illicit sexual desire.
> 20 Humour is here created through bathos.
> 21–6 The drama becomes increasingly farcical through a stock dramatic technique of this type of comedy, mistaken identity.
> 24–6 The use of anaphora (repetition) in Willmore's appeals to Florinda serves to present him as both inebriated and insistent. Her vulnerability is emphasized by the way he refers to her as a *child*.

33 **honest**   Willmore feigns nobility as he insists Florinda's secret will be safe with him.

34 **disguised**   i.e. drunk. Why do you think he points this out to her?

35–6 **I'll not boast who 'twas obliged me**   Here Behn satirizes contemporary attitudes to women and chastity, while also alluding to the masculine propensity to *boast* about sexual matters. A feminist reading would suggest that Behn is exposing female vulnerability and powerlessness in a predatory male-dominated society.

39–47 **there will be no sin in't... deny me nothing**   Willmore's argument echoes the type of logic seen in earlier Metaphysical poetry (see page 108), particularly that of John Donne and Andrew Marvell. Many Metaphysical poems use complex logical arguments and far-fetched imagery as a means to persuade lovers into bed. Once again the language of the Bible, such as *sin* and *fornication*, is subverted as Willmore asserts an outrageously twisted view of Christian obligations.

50–52 **a judge... first provocation**   Willmore's statement echoes the sentiments often expressed in earlier medieval writing in terms of the power of a woman's *eyes* to lure a man, and alludes to the biblical image of Eve as the wicked temptress of Adam. He deploys the age-old justification for rape: that men are powerless to resist the *provocation* of women's beauty.

63–4 **Why, at this time... but to catch flies**   The rhetorical nature of this question, and the metaphor of a *spider* catching *flies*, emphasizes the arrogance of Willmore and also the hypocrisy surrounding male obsession with supposed female promiscuity. Here Florinda is presented as the predator while Willmore paints a picture of himself as one who has been lured into a trap.

65 **coil**   turmoil, disturbance.

68 **pistole**   gold coin. The offer of payment clearly determines Florinda's supposed status in relation to Willmore.

77–9 The violence of Willmore's language and his aggressive behaviour creates a dark moment in the comedy. The scene comes to a crisis as Willmore moves from linguistic harassment to a physical attack.

84 Florinda's cries for help are not simply focused on the physical assault but on the threatened damage to her reputation, without which she will be *ruined*. Once again Behn underlines the critical importance for a woman of maintaining her public status as one who is chaste and virtuous.

86–7 **A man!... that lady** These words return the play to comedy and farce, while reinstating Florinda as a respectable woman. Order – although of an unstable kind – can be restored as the mistaken identities are cleared up.

Eighteenth century

Letter: From George Farquhar to Anne Oldfield (c. 1699)

George Farquhar is best remembered for his comedies *The Recruiting Officer* (1706) and *The Beaux' Stratagem* (1707). He was an actor before becoming a playwright, and a lively young man who had a propensity for causing trouble. He was much struck by the beauty and abilities of Anne Oldfield; after hearing her reading aloud from a play in a tavern, he introduced her to his theatrical friends. She was engaged as an actor and had a highly successful career, appearing in Farquhar's own comedies.

In the following letter, written on first seeing her, Farquhar protests that he has been completely captivated by both her *wit* and her *beauty*. However, the final sentence is interesting as it changes the whole tone of the letter from a celebration of the young woman's qualities to a sudden attack on her ability to bewitch him.

Their relationship does not appear to have developed into a love affair. By 1703 Farquhar had married a widow called Margaret Pemell.

1 **I came... was conquered** Farquhar appropriates the words attributed to Julius Caesar after a Roman victory. However, the final word in the triplet is altered to the passive, so that

the speaker presents himself not as the conqueror but as the vanquished.

2 **yet can I say nothing** This echoes earlier writing on love (such as Shakespeare's *King Lear*, in which Cordelia is challenged to declare how much she loves her father, see page 98) in suggesting that love can make the lover inarticulate because it transcends language.

2–3 **where others go to save their souls** i.e. church. As with many writers through the ages, Farquhar blurs the boundaries between the sacred and the profane by alluding to the loss of his soul to love rather than finding it through religion.

3 **Divinity** The use of a capital letter again signals the fusing of the sacred and the secular; the divine in this context is an admired woman.

5 **raptures** ecstasy of emotion.

7 **charm** This word implies that the woman is enchanting or captivating, and there is the suggestion that the man is being lured or entranced against his will.

7–11 **after this… break my heart** The tone becomes reflective as the speaker develops a logical argument to justify his love.

13 **a liking or an aversion** The woman's response is all-important. Some aspects of courtly love are recalled here, as she is empowered to judge and therefore can cause the man to suffer.

your sense is above your sex This rather back-handed compliment reinforces gender stereotypes by implying that women are generally foolish, so she is *above* them. Setting this woman apart from her sex in this way puts her on a pedestal, just as in the courtly love tradition.

17 **such a face** As is traditional in the representation of a woman, Farquhar comments on her physical appearance, but he softens this in the following line with his reference to her *smile of good nature*.

20–21 **retire again to my desert** This implies that his life will be empty unless his love is requited; once again this image echoes the ideals of courtly love.

22–3 **receive my sentence from your own mouth** Here, Farquhar reinforces the idea of the woman as both judge and jury; the fate of the lover is balanced in her hands.

26–8 What do you make of these lines? There is a sudden change
of tone from humble, flattering and passionate to dismissive
and authoritative as the writer re-empowers himself. He
asserts that he has been bewitched. The setting in church
makes these final lines even more shocking. It is also notable
that he does not put his name to the letter, nor does he use
any of the usual complimentary phrases as a way of signing
off. Instead, he chooses to berate the young woman, perhaps
to present his desires as being beyond his control.

Pamela: Samuel Richardson (1740)

Samuel Richardson wrote *Pamela* at a time when the novel was
only just becoming established as a literary genre. Its epistolary
form (it is written as a series of letters) suggests the infancy of the
novel at this time, as does the alternative title, *Virtue Rewarded*,
which reflects its alleged aim: to instruct and edify readers through
the moral example presented in the text. Novels had little literary
prestige at the time, and Richardson had originally conceived of his
text as a 'conduct book', which gave moral and social instruction
to its readers. However, over the course of writing it he decided
that the moral of the story was sufficiently strong for the text to
stand or fall on its literary merits, and it was finally published as a
novel in two volumes. Its reception was mixed, with some praising
its scope and the immediacy gained from the epistolary form, and
others criticizing it for its sexually explicit content.

The story concerns a young girl, Pamela, who has been the
servant of a wealthy woman since the age of 12 but finds herself
in a compromising position when the woman dies and her son,
Mr B, becomes master. He quickly makes clear his sexual interest
in Pamela, which she describes with horror to her parents through
the series of letters that make up the narrative. The story tells
how she is continually subjected to his advances but manages
to protect her virginity; she is even at one point abducted and
imprisoned by him. In accordance with the expected course
of courtly love, the more she refuses him, the more his ardour
becomes inflamed.

Although he professes love for Pamela, Mr B feels unable to offer marriage because of her lowly status. Over the course of the first volume of the novel, however, his admiration and respect for Pamela's virtue (demonstrated by her refusal to bow to his persuasions and his bullying) and her intelligence (seen in the letters to her parents, which he intercepts) grow to the point where he can no longer deny his genuine feelings for her. He finally proposes marriage to her, despite their difference in social status.

The fact that Pamela's marriage to Mr B was to be considered as *Virtue Rewarded* in 1740, although he had previously abducted and imprisoned her, demonstrates the importance of a socially advantageous marriage to a young woman at this time; but it also reflects the belief that 'virtue' can be taught by the humble Pamela to a man such as Mr B, and can earn his genuine love and respect.

This extract details the beginning of the process that will lead to his marriage proposal. Although it is in letter form, the prose style is very similar to a first-person narrative and relies heavily on direct speech.

3 **Give me your hand**   The use of the imperative is typical of the speech of an older, high-status male to a younger, low-status female. The hand is often used symbolically in the literature of love to signify a pledge, as in the marriage vows when bride and groom hold hands as they make their vows. The hands are also often the first point of lovers' physical contact, and are therefore imbued with significance. Here, the reader is alerted that the speech that follows is to be serious.

5–6 **I will now talk to you in a serious manner**   Once more Mr B addresses Pamela in a commanding way.

7 **prudence, penetration**   Mr B comments on Pamela's careful approach to life and her sharp intellect: he clearly admires these qualities in her, yet does not let that change his assumption of superiority over her. This is not surprising in the depiction of relationships between men and women at this time, and shows Mr B's expectation that she will remain subservient to him.

9–10 **open, frank, and generous mind**   Note that Mr B places these qualities before the reference to her appearance (*in person* *you are so lovely*), suggesting that he has come to appreciate her virtues above her physical attributes.

11 **All these accomplishments**   all of Pamela's personal and physical qualities. The noun later came to signify a woman's achievements in skills such as singing, dancing, drawing and reading, all of which were deliberately practised in order to make a woman a more attractive wife for a potential suitor.

13 **I cannot live without you**   The hyperbolic phrase is a commonplace in the literature of love and echoes the sentiments of courtly love.

13–15 **I would divide... my own terms**   Mr B refers to earlier offers he has made to Pamela of a financially attractive but dishonourable arrangement whereby she would become his partner but not his legal wife.

15 **offering**   attempting.

18–19 **in such a manner... admire you the more**   This is a response typical of the courtly lover, whose ardour would traditionally be inflamed when he is rejected by the object of his desires. However, Mr B is impressed by the *manner* of Pamela's rejection.

22–4 **so watchful ... increased by it**   Mr B is more open here in his discussion of Pamela's refusal of a sexual relationship with him, clearly showing that he simultaneously admires and regrets her *virtue*.

25 **I will make you my adviser**   Mr B alludes to the type of relationship to which women have always aspired. Compare Chaucer's Wife of Bath (page 19), who maintains that all women desire *maistrie* (the upper hand) in relationships. Interestingly, Mr B withholds real power from Pamela, however, going on to say that he will be the *definitive judge* in the course of their relationship.

27–9 **You cannot believe... *very* enormous actions**   Mr B attempts to justify his actions in abducting Pamela and imprisoning her in the house, as well as his various attempts to violate her honour.

32–3 **I should before now have gratified them**   He uses the fact that he has not yet raped her to excuse his many crimes against her.

37 **I cannot endure the thought of marriage**   The rejection of or fear of marriage is not uncommon in literature about

love from the male perspective, where marriage is often seen as a trap and the wife is represented as a burden upon the husband.

40 **the distance between us**   Mr B refers to Pamela's lowly social position. This speech is reminiscent of Mr Darcy's first proposal to Elizabeth Bennet in Jane Austen's *Pride and Prejudice* (1813), where he claims that he is forced to propose to her against his better judgement, his head being overruled by his passion.

44 **Williams**   the man who has been suggested as a suitable husband for Pamela.

48–50 **your eyes... your bosom**   Mr B's observations of Pamela linger on these sexualized physical features, which he claims the power to interpret as holding significant meanings.

51–2 **what you would have me do**   Mr B once more seems to empower Pamela in this situation, although as mentioned above (see Note to line 25), such power is merely an illusion as he will make the final decision.

53–4 **the agitations of my mind**   Pamela is deeply disturbed by Mr B's speech.

55 **condescending**   polite, showing a proper degree of respect for a person who is socially inferior.

59 **O sir**   Pamela's way of addressing Mr B casts her in the role of supplicant to him (begging favour), but also reflects the fact that he intrigues her. Her behaviour appears to show the virtues that would be hoped for in a young woman in her position at that time, but it is interesting to consider whether Pamela's stance is to be accepted as entirely genuine or whether it would be read by a contemporary audience as unconsciously flirtatious.

66 **approbation**   approval.

69 **As to *my* poor thoughts**   When pushed for a more *explicit answer* to his queries, Pamela appears to be even more self-deprecating.

81 **tell me still more explicitly**   It seems that Pamela's advice to Mr B to focus his attention upon others is not satisfactory to him: his insistence that she be more explicit thinly veils the fact that he wishes her response to focus on their own relationship.

84–5 **were I the first lady in the land**   Pamela's response is
oblique and seems to deliberately obscure its true meaning:
she implies that she is too lowly for her advice to be worth
hearing, but also suggests that if she felt in a position to do
so, she would tell him something that would reveal her *free
and open heart.*

88 **O my dear father and mother!**   This is a reminder that
Pamela's parents are, of course, the audience for the letter.

91–2 **the reason why… would not let me hate him**   Pamela hints
at her growing love for Mr B. The fact that she is afraid of
this emotion is not uncommon in literature about love: the
powerful sway of emotions can produce fears of a loss of
self-control, which is presumably what Pamela is experiencing
here.

93 **be assured still**   The direct address to her parents is
touching in its bravery and helps to illustrate the appeal of
the epistolary novel: it places readers in the position of the
recipient of the letter, so that they feel they too are being
addressed directly.

95 **appearance of true love**   With this phrase Pamela reassures
her parents that she will be on her guard against any
deception, but also introduces the idea of accepting that Mr
B may genuinely care for her.

The Art of Coquetry: Charlotte Lennox (1747)

Charlotte Lennox, who was born in 1729 or 1730, was a writer who
enjoyed a varied career as an actor, poet, playwright and novelist.
She married and had two children, but was estranged from her
husband for many years before separating from him permanently.
She was known for her associations with famous people including
Samuel Richardson (see headnote on page 126) and the painter
Joshua Reynolds, but most notably Samuel Johnson, who is
alleged to have contributed to her most famous novel, *The Female
Quixote*. This was a clever inversion of Miguel de Cervantes'
classic early seventeenth-century novel, *Don Quixote*.

   The Art of Coquetry is her most famous poem, published
in her first collection, *Poems on Several Occasions*, in 1747, and

later in the *Gentleman's Magazine*. A term only ever applied to women's behaviour, not men's, *coquetry* means flirting or making teasing, romantic approaches to the opposite sex. The meaning is made very clear over the course of the poem, as Lennox sets out some rules or methods by which an *artful* woman (see line 1) can bring a man under her spell.

This extract is from the end of the poem. *The Art of Coquetry* begins with the speaker defining the different types of women who might be trying to find love, such as the 'haughty beauty', the 'witty fair', and the 'languid nymph', and describes the different strategies that each should use in order to attract and secure a lover. In the lines preceding this extract, the speaker advises that if a woman encounters resistance from a 'stubborn soul', she should 'have recourse to art' in order to gradually woo the object of her affections.

It is an interesting and revealing poem in its open adoption of the 'arts' that women have always been accused by men of using in order to win them over. Although writers as early as the Roman poet Ovid in his *Ars Amatoria* (*The Art of Love*, written in approximately 2 CE) had instructed men on ways to win women, this sort of apparently instructional tract written for women is fairly rare. When one puts it alongside Ovid, it also holds interesting parallels with Lennox's novel *The Female Quixote*, in its subversion of the kind of writing that was previously produced for and about men. What do you make of the teasing tone and tongue-in-cheek humour that Lennox employs here?

1 The speaker advises the woman to carefully compose and practise her *artful looks* so that she will be able to produce them at will as circumstances demand them.
3 **careless youth** inattentive young man.
   dart The verb reminds the reader of the arrows of Cupid.
6 **soft confusion** According to the expected behaviour of a coquettish woman, she is advised not to be too direct, in case she should be considered too easy a prize. The apparent *confusion* (embarrassment) and downcast eyes are intended to suggest that her *glances* were involuntary.

9 **Caught** This adjective suggests the man is a *victim* (line 10) of the woman's wiles.
   elate elated.

11 **pursues** This verb moves the man back into the more usual position, in the role of the pursuer. His *imagined victory* over her heart places him in this *pleasing* position.

13 **her shape, her air, her face** The triad recalls the traditional poetic blazon, a list of the desired features of the loved one.

14 **each feature wears an added grace** The woman's supposed interest in him has increased her value in his eyes. What does this suggest about the man?

15 **proves** tests.

16 **sublimed** transformed. His gratitude is slowly transformed into love.

17 The reader is alerted to a change in the focus of the poem with this line: having attracted the attention – even love – of the man, the harder task will be to maintain (*fix*) it.

18 **art** A man may weary of a lover, no matter how beautiful she might be, and thus it requires deliberate effort and devices to maintain his affections.

19–20 The speaker warns the woman to beware of extremes of behaviour: be neither too kind nor too cold.

19 **cloys** sickens through excess.

22 **ill-requited pains** unrewarded efforts. Also, the *pains* of unrequited love are suggested.

23 **sway** control, power.
   break his chains What connotations does this metaphor have?

25 **alarm your pride** The speaker warns the reader that she may experience resentment from the man as he attempts to puncture her self-possession.

26 The reader is advised not to react to the man's resentment, and to pretend to view his behaviour as merely *chance*.

27 **to seek new conquests range** look elsewhere for other men to attract (in order to awaken jealousy, see the next line).

29 Such volatile and changeable behaviour is typical of a lover, often portrayed in literature about love as a person whose emotions are unpredictable and out of control.

30 **weak deceit** i.e. his former attempt to defy her power.

31 What does the verb *bears* suggest about the measure of control the man has over himself?

32–3 The speaker suggests that there are special considerations that must be taken on board if the lover is jealous, because men, that *haughty sex*, do not cope well with that emotion. Notice that these and the following lines suggest men are a type apart from women.

35 **distrust** The literature of love is full of examples of men who have a jealous disposition: consider Othello, or Pinchwife (from William Wycherley's *The Country Wife*, see page 40) or the case of January and May from Chaucer's *The Merchant's Tale*.

36–7 There is clear irony in the fact that the speaker is advocating an appearance of openness and sincerity in a poem that encourages the use of artfulness in love.

41 The *rising blush* is the supposed result of revealing the hidden love without apparently meaning to, as advised in the previous line; paradoxically, by pretending to *anxiously conceal* it, the woman will draw attention to it.

44 **But** The conjunction signals another change in direction for the poem.

45 **fatal passion** This is a common idea in literature about love, as in Ben Jonson's poem *Death and Love*, page 36.

46 The reader is advised to check any natural impulses towards love before they become too powerful; they should be regarded as unwanted intrusions in the game of courtship.

47 **sweet invader** What is the effect of the oxymoron here?

48 The speaker warns that those who wish to employ the art of coquetry must be firm and resolute in matters of the heart, not *tender*.

49 The woman who wishes to practise coquetry must be able to keep her true emotions from showing in her face.

50 **native languishment** natural propensity to pine with love or grief.

52–7 The type of woman who can benefit from *these rules* is described, in contrast to the *tender* type depicted in lines 48–51.

52 **nymph who liberty can prize** beautiful young woman who values her freedom and independence.

53 **vindicate**   justify and maintain.
   eyes   i.e. beauty.
55 This type of woman can use her intelligence to control the man who is won by her *beauty*.
56 **empire**   What does this noun suggest about the ambitions of those women who can effectively employ the art of coquetry? Compare Chaucer's *The Wife of Bath's Tale* (see page 19).
57 **controul the world**   The poem ends by promising women that their ambitions for this type of power can be rewarded bounteously.

The Rivals: Richard Brinsley Sheridan (1775)

Richard Brinsley Sheridan was born in Dublin in 1751. As a young man he took part in two duels defending the honour of his wife, a famous singer with whom he had eloped. In the second duel he was badly injured. The notoriety he earned by these escapades was not unhelpful to him in his theatrical career; in 1775 he wrote his first play, *The Rivals*, and the following year took over management of the Theatre Royal Drury Lane. Although he wrote other successful plays and later became an MP who was admired for his speeches in the House of Commons, throughout his life he was extravagant and in debt. He died in poverty but was buried in Poets' Corner, Westminster Abbey, next to the great actor-manager David Garrick, his predecessor as manager of the Theatre Royal.

In this extract from *The Rivals* there is a discussion between Sir Anthony Absolute and his son Captain Jack Absolute. The father is making plans for his son's future, and it becomes apparent that these involve a marriage. However, unbeknown to his father, Captain Absolute has already sworn undying love to a young woman, Lydia Languish, whom he hopes to marry.

1–2 **the income of your commission**   your army pay.
   3 **but a small... of your spirit**   The tone of Sir Anthony's opening remarks appears measured and reasonable as he acknowledges that a gentleman, especially one of *spirit* like Jack, must have more than a mere *pittance* to live on.

4, 8–10 Jack's responses are formal, in keeping with the expected codes of behaviour between father and son at this time.

14–15 Jack is presented as a young man who now sees independence and liberty opening up before him.

18 Sheridan subverts traditional representations of the paternal role, in which a father chooses a husband for his daughter, as it becomes clear that Sir Anthony has chosen a wife for his son.

28 **The fortune is saddled with a wife** Sir Anthony's representation of marriage at this point suggests that it is no more than a business arrangement.

37 **with the livestock on it** A wife is presented as nothing more important than a domestic animal.

38, 39 **price, purchase** The idea of marriage as a monetary arrangement is reinforced through the use of this language, but Jack is rejecting this in favour of *happiness*.

40–41 **give me your promise** Sheridan brings out the humour of Sir Anthony's character by showing the unreasonable and illogical way he appeals to reason and logic.

51–2 **my vows are pledged... let her foreclose** Sir Anthony picks up the term *pledged*, which is used in cases of monetary debts, to suggest that the arrangement can be terminated like a legal contract. When a creditor *forecloses* he takes possession of the property that has been pledged by the debtor in return for the loan; this happens when it is clear the debt is unlikely to be repaid. Sir Anthony is suggesting that vows made to women can easily be broken if circumstances change.

58–62 Sir Anthony appears to be speaking firmly and authoritatively, while simultaneously revealing himself to be childish and bad-tempered.

65 **if ever I call you Jack again** What do you think the use of the name *Jack* signifies to Sir Anthony?

73 **Zounds, sirrah** *Zounds* is a mild swearword (meaning 'God's wounds'). *Sirrah* is a disrespectful version of 'sir', used in addressing an inferior person.

75 **Crescent** the Royal Crescent in Bath (the setting for the play).

76 **the bull's in Cox's Museum** James Cox exhibited mechanical toys in London in the 1770s.

82 **jackanapes** a monkey, hence a naughty child. Notice the play on Jack's name.

88–90 Humour is developed in these lines by the way Sir Anthony projects his own emotions onto his son. The rant that follows serves to increase the comic effect as Sir Anthony describes himself as a calm and reasonable man while showing that he is possessed by violent anger.

113 **unget** unconceive.

115–121 Jack's ironic response after his father's departure develops the comic effect while also encouraging the audience to sympathize with his predicament. This is compounded by the revelation that his father married *for love*, and *was in his youth a bold intriguer* (lover, seducer) thus making Sir Anthony appear an even greater hypocrite.

The Romantics

Journal: Dorothy Wordsworth (1802)

Dorothy Wordsworth, sister of the poet William Wordsworth, began her 'Grasmere Journal' on 14 May 1800, after William left on a short journey:

> I resolved to write a journal[...] and I set about keeping my resolve, because I will not quarrel with myself, and because I shall give Wm pleasure by it when he comes home again.

She continued to write her Journal, which was a popular activity in this period, until January 1803. It was intended not as a private diary, but as a means of recording events and impressions that could be shared with those she was close to, above all her brother. Throughout his poetic career, Wordsworth is believed to have taken inspiration from his sister's writing, and this is seen particularly in his poem *The Daffodils*: she had recorded the experience described in the poem in her Journal on 15 April 1802, and it was only in 1804 that Wordsworth returned to it and composed the now famous poem.

The passage shown in the extract records William's marriage to Mary Hutchinson and the early part of their honeymoon. What is notable is Dorothy's description of her own reactions to the marriage and her account of the journey the three undertake together.

1–3 **On Monday... in the morning**   The tone in the opening sentences is matter of fact and betrays none of the emotion that is revealed in the rest of the entry.

5 **William had parted from me upstairs**   This is on the one hand a literal statement of fact, but on the other seems to imply that his marriage is to be a form of separation from his sister.

6 **Sara**   Mary's sister, who ultimately became the focus of Samuel Taylor Coleridge's affections and is the woman referred to in his poem *Dejection: An Ode*.

8–9 **it was over**   This unexpected phrase would be more suitable to something like an execution having taken place, rather than a wedding.

9–11 **I could stand it... neither hearing or seeing anything**   Her behaviour after receiving the news is even more unexpected; it seems as if her nerves have been overstrained.

12–15 **This forced me... fell upon his bosom**   The jerky rhythm reveals the tension and confusion of Dorothy's emotions. The language is characterized by images of being compelled to act, and the tension seems only to be defused by the appearance of the *beloved William* and her falling *upon his bosom*. It might be suggested that this description reads not like that of a sister greeting a brother on his wedding day but more like a lover reunited with one whom she believes is lost to her.

15–16 **led me to the house**   The need for her to be *led* again suggests a situation that goes against her real desires.

17–18 **we had breakfasted... we set off**   The focus on *we* clearly links Dorothy to the newlyweds as they all depart together for the honeymoon.

21–2 **sunshine and showers... chearfulness**   The listing creates a picture of a comfortable relationship, but the reader is reminded that it is now a group of three that are to enjoy the delights of the early days of marriage rather than simply the bride and groom.

27–34 **There was one... recollect their own frailties** This part
of the entry focuses on the type of individuals who had
traditionally not become the subject of poetry or literature:
the poor, the isolated and those who remain on the fringes
of society. William Wordsworth took inspiration from the
people they encountered in their local area for many of his
characters in *Lyrical Ballads*, a collection of his and Coleridge's
poetry first published in 1798 and generally considered to have
marked the beginning of the Romantic movement in English
literature. The idea had been to write a new kind of poetry that
could be read and understood by everybody.

35–41 **There is not much variety... Helmsley Castle** This
description of the setting and landscape is characteristic of
Dorothy's writing, and it is the freshness and immediacy of
her accounts that often provided her brother with inspiration
for his poetry.

42 **gay** high-spirited.

49–51 **My heart danced... gavel-ended front** The use of colour
and detail in these lines creates not simply a picture of the
inn but also of Dorothy's emotions as she recalls her earlier
visit with William.

56–60 **the old ruin... chiefly ashes** The images used here recall
those of Romantic poetry, but her account is fresh and of
the moment, offering the reader a sense of her personal
engagement with the beauty of the view.

61–2 **We left Mary sitting by the kitchen fire** This sentence re-
focuses the reader on Dorothy's relationship with William,
and all the implications of the new marriage.

So, We'll Go No More A-Roving: Lord Byron (1817)

Lord Byron (1788–1824) was a notable poet in the British Romantic
movement, although the satirical style of much of his poetry
recalls earlier writers such as Alexander Pope and John Dryden.
Byron's most celebrated work was an extended narrative poem,
Don Juan, which ranges across international borders giving a
humorous picture of contemporary societies, politics and morals.

Byron was famed for his personal excesses: he was often in
debt and was a notorious womanizer (he was even thought to have

had a sexual liaison with his half-sister). He was also a passionate believer in certain political causes, for which he was willing to fight. In Greece today, he is still considered a national hero because he fought in the Greek war of independence against the Ottomans. Byron succumbed to a fever while fighting in Greece and died at 36 years of age.

Such passions, both sexual and political, are exactly the subject matter of *So, We'll Go No More A-Roving*, where the speaker seems to accept that passion cannot be sustained, and resigns himself – perhaps sadly – to fatigue. Byron sent the poem in a letter from Venice to Thomas Moore, an Irish poet and entertainer. The speaker seems tired of life's excesses and wishes to settle to a quieter life. Byron explained his motivation for writing the poem in the letter that accompanied it:

> At present, I am on the invalid regimen [diet] myself. The Carnival – that is, the latter part of it – and sitting up late o' nights, had knocked me up a little. But it is over – and it is now Lent, with all its abstinence and sacred music... [T]hough I did not dissipate [indulge in excess] much upon the whole, yet I find 'the sword wearing out the scabbard,' though I have but just turned the corner of twenty-nine.

The poem's three simple quatrains allow the poet to develop its theme through a lyrical, repetitive structure. The poem's metrical scheme begins with a striking anapaestic foot (two unstressed syllables flowed by one stressed syllable). This is repeated at the beginning of each new stanza. The interlaced rhyme scheme links alternate lines, and they are carried along with a driving trimester (each line has three beats) that seems to generate its own energy with a force almost at odds with the subject matter of the poem. There is a strange irony that it is a work of such power.

1 **So** The poem begins in a conversational style. What is the effect of this?
no more a-roving There is a deliberately archaic tone to this expression, with the dialect form *a-roving* recalling a

Scottish song called *The Jolly Beggar*, which uses the same refrain.

3 Is there a sadness to this line, as if impediments have been placed in the way of lovers? The speaker will go on to outline what these might be in the following stanza. On the other hand, there are positive aspects to the assertion that the *heart* is *still as loving*.

3, 4 **as, as** This repetition suggests that nothing has changed in the outside world, nor in their love for each other, perhaps setting up a mystery as to why the pair must no longer be together. See also lines 9 and 10.

4 **the moon** Often used as a symbol of love, the moon was sacred to the virgin goddess Diana; young virgins were traditionally associated with the moon and the goddess. The moon also represents the night, a time for lovers to meet. Symbols from both nature and ancient mythology were important in Romantic poetry.

5 This can be taken as a metaphor for struggles within relationships, or other challenges in life. There could also be a bawdy play on words here, suggesting sexual exhaustion.

6 This line suggests emotional or spiritual fatigue.

8 The speaker seems to suggest that the process of loving itself has worn out the lover's capacity for love.

9 The speaker calls upon the traditional romantic associations of the *night*.

10 The unwelcome return of daylight is another traditional theme for love poetry: see John Donne's *The Sun Rising*, and the headnote on page 108.

11 **Yet** The conjunction suggests the conclusion to a logical argument: although the world is unchanged, they must part for the reasons given in stanza 2.

12 The poem ends with another reference to moonlight, reminding the reader of the romance that is being lost. There is a sense of the speaker recognizing that life cannot always be fully savoured: there must be periods of rest and recuperation, like the period of Lent after the Carnival to which Byron alludes in his letter to Thomas Moore (see headnote).

La Belle Dame sans Merci: John Keats (1819)

La Belle Dame sans Merci, which translates as 'The beautiful lady without pity', is the title of an early fifteenth-century French poem by Alain Chartier, which belongs to the tradition of courtly love. John Keats's poem using the same title was included in a letter that he wrote to his brother George dated 21 April 1819. A revised version was published in the *Indicator* on 10 May 1820, and it has become one of Keats's most celebrated poems.

Keats was among the second wave of Romantic poets, part of a philosophical, literary, artistic and cultural movement that stressed an empathetic relationship with nature and a desire to engage with the supernatural.

The poem takes the form of a ballad and is set in a mysterious, barren wasteland where a knight-at-arms is found looking *haggard* and *woe-begone*. In the first three stanzas, a speaker asks the knight why he looks this way, and it is the knight's reply that forms the main body of the poem. Realistic and familiar details are woven into a strange and mysterious tale; thus the poem moves beyond the simple form of a folk ballad or traditional love poem and enters the world of dreams and visionary experience.

1–2   The question offers the reader an image of the physical condition of the knight; he is depicted as one who is drained of colour and listlessly waiting, in complete contrast to the idea of the gallant, brave and noble warrior normally associated with a medieval soldier of such high rank.

3–4   The description of the landscape mirrors the knight's mental condition, as all is bleak and desolate.

3   **sedge**   a marshland plant.

5   The repetition of line 1 (repeated lines are a feature of the ballad form) re-focuses attention onto his emotional state.

7–8   These lines present an autumnal image, and depict a more fruitful world than lines 3–4, but one where summer has passed.

9   **lily**   The flower imagery suggests extreme paleness. Lilies were associated with purity and death.

10   The misery the knight endures is like a *fever*.

11–12   The *rose* is a symbol of love and beauty, but here it is *fading*. This adjective and the verb *withereth* reinforce the idea of the sapping of the knight's vigour and youth.

13   The knight's narrative begins. At first the knight seems dominant as he describes his action: *I met*.

14   Through this description the *lady* is distanced from reality as she is presented as mysterious and magical.

15–16   The triadic structure of the description concludes with a reference to her *eyes*, which are *wild*. Eyes are traditionally considered to be the windows of the soul, so the reader is alerted to the suggestion that this woman is not easily tamed but rather free and unconventional.

17–18   Once again the knight appears empowered as he describes his actions, creating for the woman a *garland*, *bracelets* and a *zone* (girdle or belt). All are circular in shape and can be seen as attempts to contain and control the woman.

19   **as**   as if. The conditional term creates a slight tension between the knight's perception and the woman's real intentions.

20–22   The suggestions of suppressed sexual energy in these lines reveal the passion and desires of the knight.

23–4   The *sidelong* posture and the *faery's song* suggest a lack of communication between the knight and the lady, as clearly he is mortal and unable to understand this magical voice.

25–8   There is now a shift in power as the woman becomes active, and speaks for the first time. Her *language* is *strange* to the knight, reinforcing her mysteriousness.

26   **manna-dew**   According to the Bible, when the Israelites were wandering hungry in the wilderness, God sent down a dew that solidified into a food, manna.

29   The setting now becomes magical as the knight is taken to her *elfin grot*, a place that exists in the world of dreams and the imagination. The word *elfin* suggests enchantment or a visionary experience, and *grot* is a grotto or small cave.

33   The knight is disempowered as he falls into a reverie.

34–6   The world of the dreamer changes from one absorbed in the pleasures of the imagination to one of a more sinister kind.

37–8   The knight's dream is filled by images of men of high rank
        who are *death-pale*. The repetition of *pale* returns the reader
        to the opening description of the knight himself.

39–40 This exclamation, which seems like a sentence of doom, may
        be read in two ways. On the one hand the woman can be seen
        to belong to the tradition of the seductress who enthrals the
        knight with her beauty and protestations of love. The vision
        of the pale *kings and princes* suggests that she is deliberately
        destructive, a theme commonly found in folk ballads.
        Alternatively, the lady can be seen to represent an impossible
        ideal of love, and as the knight embraces the world of his
        dreams he rejects reality, in consequence being destroyed by
        his delusions. Which reading do you prefer?

41   **gloam**   half-light.

45–8   The final stanza echoes the opening of the poem, creating a
        circular structure which suggests there is no escape for the
        knight.

45   **sojourn**   stay.

To... : Percy Bysshe Shelley (1822)

Percy Bysshe Shelley (1792–1822) was one of the major figures of the
English Romantic movement. Although he also wrote some prose
fiction, pamphlets and drama, his best-loved work is his poetry.

He had a brief, eventful life. He was educated at Eton College
and Oxford University, although he was sent down from Oxford
for publishing a pamphlet called 'The Necessity of Atheism'. He
held several viewpoints that were radical for his time: he was known
to advocate vegetarianism and non-violent political resistance. He
became infamous for abandoning his pregnant first wife to elope
with the 16-year-old Mary Godwin, who went on to write the
gothic novel *Frankenstein*. Shelley married Mary after the suicide
of his first wife (it is thought that she believed herself to have been
abandoned by a new lover). Shelley drowned in Italy when his small
boat sank between Livorno and Lerici. He was just 29 years old.

This poem is written in two 8-line stanzas. It alternates
lines of tetrameter (with four metric feet per line) with lines of
trimeter (three metric feet per line). This produces an uneven

effect, suggesting an imbalance of parts. Shelley uses this form to compare a variety of emotions in the first stanza. The second stanza expands the focus of the poem from the concerns of ordinary human love to the more exalted version of devotion that the poet feels he can offer.

Title   The fact that the addressee of the poem is unnamed makes the poem seem like a Valentine greeting.
1   **One word**   Presumably, the word is 'love'.
profaned   debased or disrespected. The speaker therefore suggests that the word 'love' is too often lightly used, so he will not offer this debased token of affection to his loved one.
3   **One feeling**   Again, the speaker seems to refer to love. The repetition of *One* adds rhetorical force to the argument.
disdained   treated with contempt. There is a suggestion that the emotion of love is often dismissed or disregarded. The poet seems to urge his lover not to do likewise.
4   **thee**   Throughout the poem, the speaker addresses his loved one with this informal, familiar, second-person pronoun.
5   The fragility of the *hope* that love will be requited appears to be implied here: the speaker suggests that there is a fine line between *hope* and *despair* for a lover.
6   **prudence**   caution.
smother   Although *prudence* might destroy feelings of *hope*, it could not destroy *despair*. Thus the poem sets up a natural affinity between despair and caution, and places hope on the opposite emotional axis.
7   **pity**   Pity from the loved one is often hoped for in courtly love: the lover traditionally requests that the object of his affections pities him in his distressed state and rescues him from his love-sickness by returning his love.
9   **what men call love**   Notice the change in direction at the opening of the second stanza. The speaker moves from defining qualities typically associated with love to examining what he can offer to his loved one. He rejects the feeling that *men call love*, presumably in favour of a more exalted quality or feeling.
10   **But**   This conjunction forms the hinge of the poem as the speaker makes his counter-offer.

wilt thou accept not   What effect is created by the
construction of this question?

11 **worship**   This is one of the things that is offered in place of
what men call love.

12 The speaker suggests that even the *heavens* approve of his *worship*
of her, thus justifying and authenticating the quality of his love.

13 As a *moth* is naturally drawn to a light, the speaker chooses
the greatest and highest of natural lights, the light of a *star*.
The star suggests something to be aspired to, an unattainable
goal which is nonetheless infinitely desirable.

14 A similar metaphorical structure is set up here, to suggest
that just as the *moth* longs for the *star* and the *night* longs for
the morning, so does the speaker long for his loved one. The
comparisons operate on an apparently logical level, using
natural imagery typical of the Romantic poets.

15 **something afar**   The speaker suggests the apparently
unattainable quality of the loved one, a sentiment often
expressed in courtly love poetry.

16 **sphere of our sorrow**   This phrase works in conjunction
with the cosmic imagery of the poem to suggest the world of
sorrows that humanity is subject to. However, this worldly
sorrow can be transcended by *devotion to something afar*. The
word *sorrow* echoes the *despair* of the first stanza. The poet
ends on a conciliatory note, however, suggesting that even
if the lover must worship from a distance, this is not only
natural but transfigures human experience.

The Victorians

To Marguerite: Matthew Arnold (1852)

Matthew Arnold (1822–88) is, along with Robert Browning and
Alfred, Lord Tennyson, considered among the foremost poets
of the Victorian period. His work has sometimes been said to
bridge the gap between Romanticism and Modernism. William
Wordsworth was a neighbour and frequent visitor when the
Arnold family occupied their family home in the Lake District.

Arnold's poem *Dover Beach* (1867) is often hailed as one of the earliest modernist poems, yet he described himself in a preface to a volume of Wordsworth's poems as 'Wordsworthian'. In a letter to his mother in 1869, he described his work as representing 'on the whole, the main movement of mind of the last quarter of a century', suggesting that he personally viewed his work as very much a product of the Victorian era.

Arnold worked as a school inspector for many years, which involved travelling widely around England, and he became something of an expert on a variety of social customs. Possibly as a result of this experience, his work has sometimes been considered to instruct its readers in the ways of society and to criticize perceived faults in that society.

To Marguerite was first published in *Empedocles on Etna and Other Poems* (1852). In the 1857 volume and in later collected editions it is printed as a second part of the poem *Isolation*.

To Marguerite could be considered as a partial response to John Donne's famous statement that 'No man is an island entire of itself' (in *Meditation XVII*). Whereas Donne states unequivocally 'I am involved in mankind', however, Arnold explores the idea that the Victorian human condition is one that isolates individuals. The extended metaphor of humans as individual islands surrounded by life could be seen as similar to Metaphysical poetry in spirit, as is the poem's concern with geography. Its use of nature as a central uniting image, however, seems to owe more to the Romantic movement and especially to Wordsworth's idea of nature as a teacher. Its final bitter cry that *a God their severance ruled* might be seen as a more Victorian complaint to God about the nature of the world.

The poem is written in regular sestets of iambic tetrameter: six lines per stanza, with four metric feet (or beats) to a line. Each sestet begins with four alternately rhyming lines, possibly suggesting the isolation of the individual, and concludes with a rhyming couplet. This could be read as ironically alluding to the unity of the poetic form.

1 **Yes** The poem begins in a conversational style that suggests an ongoing discussion with an unseen speaker. It could be read as the continuation of his poem *Isolation* (see headnote above) in which the speaker discusses the difficulty of being parted from his lover. In this interpretation, he moves from the specific subject of the love of two individuals to the human condition of isolation in general.

   sea of life This metaphor is to be extended throughout the poem to suggest that each individual human being is isolated on a separate island adrift in an *estranging sea* (24).

2 **echoing straits** A *strait* is a narrow channel of water that separates land and connects larger bodies of water. The adjective *echoing* suggests the emptiness of the space between the islands. This emptiness could be seen as metaphor for lovelessness or godlessness, as well as a physical description.

   thrown The verb suggests the malicious action of an uncaring force acting deliberately to separate humans. This force is identified in the final stanza of the poem as *a God*.

3 **Dotting** This suggests the miniscule size of the (human) islands compared with the *shoreless watery wild*.

4 The vast number of individuals makes it all the more ironic that they should be isolated from each other. There is a paradox here: how can so many *live alone*?

5 **enclasping** There is another bitter irony here: the adjective *enclasping* suggests a warm embrace, but it is the isolating water that embraces, suggesting only loneliness. The word takes on another meaning, suggesting complete isolation.

6 **endless bounds** The water, which goes on for ever, serves to separate them from each other eternally.

7 **But** The new stanza suggests a change in the direction of the poem. The reader may anticipate a more hopeful tone.

   their hollows The features of the individual dwelling place of each person, as represented by the separate islands, are suggested. Perhaps nature seems kinder here, providing a more pleasant dwelling place.

8 **swept** This verb suggests not just winds, but possibly the encircling water.

balms   The healing properties of the *spring* are suggested by this term.

10 **nightingales**   These birds are often associated with love, as they are in Shakespeare's *Romeo and Juliet*, because they sing during the night as well as the day. It is the male bird that sings, often in an attempt to attract a mate. The song of the bird can therefore in itself be taken to be a love song.

11–12 **from shore to shore,/ Across**   The love song of the birds can transcend the boundaries between the individual islands. This serves to increase the pathos, as the islands themselves apparently cannot be united.

12 **pour**   What does this verb suggest?

13 **Oh!**   Just as the second stanza began with the conjunction *But*, indicating a change in direction, this stanza begins with a similarly striking exclamation. Instead of suggesting hope, the natural beauties of the previous stanza have only served to highlight the isolation of the individual islands.

15–18 These lines express the collective thoughts of the islands (signalled by the words *they feel*). It could be suggested that the islands are at least united in their lament at their isolation: they use the collective pronoun *we*.

18 **Oh**   The repetition of this word, now in the voice of the islands themselves rather than the speaker, suggests how heartfelt this plea is.
marges   margins, edges.

19 **Who order'd**   The rhetorical question is forceful and bitter as the speaker demands to know who has forced this condition upon humanity.

19–20 **fire... cool'd**   The metaphor suggests passion and its frustration.

21 **Who**   The repetition introducing another rhetorical question deepens the tone of anger.
deep desire   Alliteration emphasizes the idea that it is human passion that is regulated and stifled.

22 **A God, a God**   What is the effect of the repetition here?
severance   separation, parting. What connotations does the noun have?

23 **bade**   commanded or ordered.

24 **unplumb'd** unmeasured. The depth of the *estranging sea* has not been, or cannot be, measured. The structure of the final line serves to further emphasize the idea of individual isolation, as each adjective seems to stand separately. **estranging** The separation seems to be not only physical but emotional.

The Lost Mistress: Robert Browning (1845)

Robert Browning (1812–89) was one of the most influential poets of the Victorian period. He is famous for his use of the dramatic monologue form, in which the speaker of the poem is a character who reveals more and more about himself as the poem progresses. Browning is also well known for his love affair with the poet Elizabeth Barrett, which met with the implacable opposition of her father. The two poets married in 1846, moving to Italy to begin a new life together.

The Lost Mistress is concerned with coming to terms with the transitory nature of relationships, but also looks at what remains of emotions and feelings when lovers part.

1–2 There is a stark sense of shock in the opening brief assertion that *All's over*, which is developed in the rhetorical question highlighting the pain of this acknowledgement.

3–4 The speaker distances himself from the pain by focusing on the natural surroundings, suggesting perhaps that the birds sing despite human suffering. However, their song is also a farewell, a *good-night twitter*.

5–8 In the second stanza the speaker continues to detail the beauty of the natural world, referring to the promise of spring with the *buds* that are about to *burst*. It is as if he is acknowledging that life goes on with no regard for his pain, yet there is a hint of decay or loss of beauty in the phrase *turns grey*.

9–10 These two questions directed to his lover reveal tentativeness and humility as he introduces the possibility of friendship.

11–12 How do you feel the tone changes in these lines, as the speaker contemplates what he must now *resign*?

13–16 The inner struggle of the speaker is shown here as he catalogues what he cannot bring himself to *resign* but will always keep in his *heart* and *soul*. Browning is suggesting the complexity of a relationship and the boundaries that must be accepted when it becomes nothing more than friendship.

17–20 In the final stanza, the speaker affirms his inability to redefine the relationship completely, and by suggesting that he may speak very slightly more ardently (*a thought stronger*) and hold her hand *so very little longer* than a friend would, he indicates a lack of resolution and a reluctance to renounce all the claims he may have had. The reader is left with the sense that the speaker has managed to achieve only a painful compromise.

Far From the Madding Crowd: Thomas Hardy (1874)

Thomas Hardy was born near Dorchester on 2 June 1840. Although he worked for several years as an architect, his main interest was always writing. Hardy lived to the age of 87 (well into the twentieth century), but his intellectually formative years, that is the years that came to determine the mood of his writing, were in the late 1850s and 1860s. This period was the high point of Victorian industrialization and commercialism; Hardy was very critical of the materialism of the Victorian middle classes and their obsession with 'progress'. To Hardy this was symbolized by the coming of the railway, pushing its way into Dorset and destroying forever the ancient ways of country life.

In 1874 Hardy married Emma Gifford, but by 1892 their relationship was deteriorating, and the rift was never repaired. Emma's death in 1912 came as a great shock to Hardy, and he wrote a flood of poems about her and their relationship. In 1914 he married his secretary, but continued writing about his first wife. When the First World War broke out, he joined a group of writers who pledged to write for the Allied cause. Hardy died in 1928 and his ashes were buried in Westminster Abbey, but his heart was placed in his first wife's grave in Stinsford churchyard.

Far From the Madding Crowd was Hardy's fourth novel, and its success enabled him to pursue a literary career full time. It illustrates his growing interest in tragedy, as well as his long-standing passion for farming and rural communities. The title is taken from Thomas Gray's poem *Elegy Written in a Country Churchyard* (1751) and seems to extol the virtues of country life: it alludes to those who live their lives quietly, away from the noisy throngs of the cities. Although the pastoral setting of the text may suggest quietness, however, the characters with whom the story concerns itself are impassioned and their lives are eventful, which may suggest an ironic juxtaposition with the title.

This extract shows the beginning of the romance between Bathsheba Everdene, an independent young woman who has inherited her uncle's fortune and is running her own farm, and Sergeant Troy, a young soldier. In the novel, the character of Troy is contrasted with Bathsheba's two other suitors, the reliable and sincere farmer Gabriel Oak (whom she eventually marries, after a disastrous marriage to Troy) and Farmer Boldwood, an aloof local farmer who becomes obsessed with Bathsheba after she playfully sends him a Valentine card.

The extract has become a famous and oft-quoted piece of writing about sexual attraction and seduction.

2 **Bathsheba's adventurous spirit**   The heroine is in an unusually independent position for a woman of her time: she manages a busy farm and is the head of a sizeable household. Her *adventurous spirit* is celebrated but also questioned in the novel.

4 **as directed**   Troy is used to being obeyed.

5 **pluck**   courage.

6 **preliminary test**   Troy's language is deliberately teasing: his intention is to show off his skills of swordsmanship in order to impress Bathsheba. The flirtatious overtones are clear.

7–11 **flourished, darting, emerging**   What is the effect of the abundance of active verbs related to Troy? Consider their juxtaposition with the stationary figure of Bathsheba.

12–13 **passed through her body**   The movement of the sword (itself a phallic symbol) appears to physically penetrate Bathsheba, in an image of sexual possession.

Notes

16–17   **quick as electricity**   What does this simile imply?

18   **she cried out in affright**   Compare this reaction with Troy's reply: his control of the situation is clear, just as Bathsheba appears to lose control.

32–41   **Beams of light... close at hand**   The scene is suffused with elemental imagery of light and sound in these lines, seeming to suggest that Troy's manoeuvres transport Bathsheba into a different world. The images build up to a crescendo with *a sky-full of meteors*. The description suggests the power of Troy's swordsmanship from Bathsheba's point of view.

46–7   **evening sunshine among the ferns**   Notice the way that natural imagery is used to suggest that nature itself supports the union of these two people.

51–2   **almost a mould of Bathsheba's figure**   Hardy suggests that Troy's sword has metaphorically caressed Bathsheba's body. The image is a sexual one but also implies the danger of his embraces.

53   *aurora militaris*   Hardy is playing on the name for the northern lights, the *aurora borealis*. This light is 'military' because it is created by Troy's swordsmanship.

55   **scarlet haze**   The scarlet jacket of the military uniform is often described as attractive to young women in literature about love (see, for example, Lydia in Jane Austen's *Pride and Prejudice*).

56   **twanged harpstring**   This could suggest angelic or heavenly music.

58–9   **keenly measuring her breadth and outline**   Troy's intense gaze is made to sound like a caress, but also calculating.

67   **The lock dropped to the ground**   The audacious removal of Bathsheba's lock of hair recalls Delilah's cutting of Samson's hair in the Bible (though here the genders are reversed and the male has all the power), or the stealing of a woman's lock of hair in Alexander Pope's mock epic poem *The Rape of the Lock* (1712). Notice that Bathsheba has no time to either consent or object. There is a foreshadowing of the kiss at the end of the extract.

75   **that caterpillar settling on you**   The shape of the caterpillar may remind us of the snake in the Garden of Eden. Its *settling* upon Bathsheba may suggest that sexual urges are being created in her.

80   **seemingly enter it**   This is another image of penetration. It also suggests the arrows of Cupid entering the heart of Bathsheba.

86, 87 **magic, dexterity** The opposing viewpoints emphasize the difference between the characters: Bathsheba's innocence is highlighted here, with her exclamation sounding almost naive. Troy's logical rebuttal shows him to be in control of the situation and of Bathsheba's reactions.

102 **force me to tell you a fib** Troy's choice of the verb *force* suggests both that it was difficult for him to tell a lie, and that she is responsible for his doing so. As the reader will see in the course of the novel, he is in fact inclined towards both deceit and blaming others.

106 **More precisely speaking** Troy speaks with the voice of authority again, subjugating Bathsheba and appearing more knowledgeable.

113–14 **a hundred tumultuous feelings** Has Hardy successfully shown what many of those conflicting feelings might be?

116 **I must leave you now** Troy quickly abandons Bathsheba when he has overcome her, a pattern that foreshadows their eventual marriage.

117 **take and keep this** The lock of hair was shorn without first obtaining consent, and is taken without properly requesting permission.

121–2 **She felt powerless to withstand or deny him** Bathsheba is portrayed as completely in thrall to Troy at this moment. This is a dramatic reversal in her usual position of authority in the text. It is significant that this moment of powerlessness leads to Troy's kiss.

126 **He drew near** The structure of the extract's last three paragraphs is significant: the reader does not find out until the end that the momentous kiss has occurred. Hardy deliberately withholds the information, creating an element of surprise for the reader, but also reflecting Bathsheba's confused perceptions of what happened.

129 **like a brand swiftly waved** What does the simile suggest about Troy's personality, or the consequences of the pair's meeting?

131 **set her stinging as if aflame** Notice how Hardy extends the metaphor of fire and flame here to suggest the passion of Bathsheba's response.

134 **Moses in Horeb** According to the Bible (Exodus 17), Moses struck a rock upon Mount Horeb and a stream of

water poured out of it to quench the thirst of the Israelites.
The comparison suggests the great volume of Bathsheba's
stream of tears.

136 **sinned a great sin**   Bathsheba's shame contrasts clearly with
Troy's sense of impunity.

137–8 **gentle dip of Troy's mouth downwards upon her own**   The
kiss itself is described in romantic terms and, notably, the
responsibility for the action is Troy's, not Bathsheba's.
Her sense of shame and guilt can be taken as a typical
representation of the woman suffering for either a shared act
or, as in this case, the acts of the man.

138 **He had kissed her**   Note the simple declarative sentence.
Its lack of drama effectively suggests the significance of the
event, assisted by its position at the end of the chapter, where
it acts as a cliffhanger.

Letter: From Oscar Wilde to Lord Alfred Douglas (1895)

Oscar Wilde (1854–1900) was an Irish poet and playwright who
became one of London's most famous personalities in the early
1890s (see page 11). He wrote several successful plays that are still
popular today, and he is also remembered for the circumstances
of his imprisonment and his early death.

Wilde's final and perhaps most famous comedy, *The Importance
of Being Earnest* (1895), was still on stage in London when his
dispute with the Marquess of Queensberry came to a head.
Queensberry was the father of Wilde's lover Lord Alfred Douglas,
and violently opposed to their relationship. Wilde unwisely decided
to prosecute him for libel, but the trial unearthed evidence that
caused his own arrest. He and other men were tried for gross
indecency (a charge that covered homosexual acts), and Wilde
was imprisoned for two years' hard labour. After his release from
prison he left the country for good, and he died isolated and
broken in Paris three years later at the age of 46.

The letter below was written to his lover Lord Alfred Douglas,
known as Bosie, at the time he was on trial, and in it he expresses

his unwavering love despite public humiliation and the possibility of imprisonment. The sentiments expressed reveal a man who is prepared to make any sacrifice for 'the love that dare not speak its name' (the phrase comes from one of Bosie's poems).

Wilde begins the letter by addressing Bosie as *My child*. This form of address reveals Wilde's definition of the relationship, suggesting he feels the responsibility of a parent, and perhaps indicating a belief that at all costs Bosie must be protected.

1 **the verdicts**   The context of the letter is made clear here, thus setting the tone of despair but also resignation as Wilde awaits judgement and possible imprisonment.

2 **Taylor**   Alfred Taylor, one of his co-accused.

3–4 **My sweet rose... lily of lilies**   The triplet of flower images used to address his lover associate him with beauty through the allusion to the *rose*, and with innocence or purity in the *lily*. However, lilies are also associated with death, which may suggest a sense of foreboding.

6 **make the bitter waters sweet**   The metaphor reveals both Wilde's engagement with the reality of what he faces and his affirmation that love can be transformative. The idea of love having transformative qualities is seen in literature through the ages. Consider what else you have read that explores this idea.

10–11 **mutilated my life... a perfect soul**   In these lines Wilde presents Bosie as his muse or inspiration, and once again he uses the rhetorical device of the triadic structure to express the strength of his passion. The image of the *broken musical chords* also serves to present the idea of the harmony his love creates.

11–16 **Even covered with mud... the image of you**   The extreme, emotive language reveals the depth of Wilde's commitment and his belief that love can conquer all suffering or humiliation.

14 **accept every outrage**   An almost Christ-like sacrifice is suggested in this phrase.

18–19 **Pleasure hides... in its essence**   Wilde's contemplation of *pain* and *pleasure* echoes earlier writers who explore the

fusion of these two conflicting experiences. Wilde argues it is
pain that offers the greater insight into love.

19–22 **O dearest… restore his soul**   The religious imagery is
extended as Wilde portrays Bosie as having Christ-like qualities.

29 **white narcissus in an unmown field**   According to ancient
Greek myth, the vain youth Narcissus was turned into a
flower after becoming obsessed with his own reflection in a
pool. The narcissus flower is, therefore, often a symbol of
vanity. Is Wilde using it as an image of irresistible beauty, or
suggesting that Bosie is (rightfully?) proud of his own power?
Or both?

33–4 **weeps in hell… heaven in his heart**   The paradox in these
lines reinforces the complexity of this love, one that society
condemns and punishes, but is in fact transformative in
nature (see Note to line 6).

34–40 **I love you… the cassia tree**   Wilde's protestations of love
and the imagery used to describe it create vignettes in which
his lover is seen as the catalyst to his creative spirit.

39 **myrrh**   one of the gifts given to the baby Jesus by the three
wise men; a fragrant resin or gum obtained from trees found
in the Near East. An exotic, eastern perfume is suggested.

40 **cassia**   cinnamon.

41 **love me always**   The repetition suggests a pleading tone.

44 **to stay**   Wilde's friends had urged him to flee the country.

50–53 In the concluding lines of the letter Wilde defines himself
solely through his relationship with Bosie. There is a sense
that he has negated himself and can only affirm his identity
within the boundaries of this love, insisting *my life is your life*.

Early twentieth century

A Room with a View: E.M. Forster (1908)

A Room with a View is a romantic novel that can be read as something
of a *bildungsroman* (a novel charting the development of a young
person). It tells the story of Lucy, who is a privileged young
English girl on holiday in Italy, chaperoned by her much older
cousin Charlotte Bartlett. The young Englishman in the extract

is a fellow tourist, George Emerson, who is staying at the same hotel, along with his father. The Emersons come from a lower social class than Lucy and Charlotte, so in obedience to the class restraints of the day the women have tried to avoid socializing with them up to this point. This is despite the father's generous but embarrassing offer to swap hotel rooms with the ladies so that they can enjoy a beautiful view, an offer to which they were eventually persuaded to agree.

Here, they are enjoying an outing to the hills overlooking the town of Florence. It is a large, mixed party and Lucy has gone for a walk after lunch. On encountering the Italian driver of their carriage, she inquires in broken Italian after the whereabouts of the clergymen who are leading the expedition. It seems that the driver – whom we have previously seen engaged in a romantic liaison of his own – has spotted something no one else has: there is an attraction between George Emerson and Lucy. The driver misinterprets her request and instead of taking her to the clergymen takes her to George. Ecstatic over the beauty of the hillside, George kisses Lucy in excitement.

In the extract we therefore see the beginning of a passionate relationship that is to lead Lucy to reject her socially acceptable fiancé in favour of George. The novel shows the couple experiencing a force of feeling for each other that shapes the course of their lives.

Set at the beginning of the twentieth century, the novel is of the Edwardian era, and its characters and concerns are typical of this age. The rigid adherence to doctrines of class, as shown by Lucy's chaperone Charlotte, is typical of this time. In this sense, *A Room with a View* can be seen as a critique of the rigid social constraints of its day. Social changes were beginning to have an effect, as we can see from the fact that the Emersons are staying in the hotel at all. Nevertheless, it took the First World War to really challenge an entrenched social system. This novel works partly as a challenge to such entrenchment. The theme of love that crosses class boundaries is one that has often been seen in literature through the ages.

1 **Lucy departed**   Lucy leaves her tiresome chaperone in search of diversion.

2 **Mr Beebe and Mr Eager**   Two clergymen. In seeking out the churchmen, Lucy is looking for more agreeable company that would also be deemed socially acceptable for a young woman.

5 **miscreant**   person who behaves badly. The Italian driver of one of the carriages has already been firmly chastised by Mr Eager for bringing a girlfriend (whom he claimed, unconvincingly, to be his sister) on the drive. He is thus identified by Forster as a man of passion.

8 *Dove?*   Where.

16 *buoni uomini*   good men. Lucy's broken Italian leaves much to be desired, but the driver interprets it in the way he feels is appropriate.

19 *Uno – piu – piccolo*   one – more – small.

22–6 **He tied the horse... to conduct her**   Forster creates humour through the business-like and rapid preparations the driver makes before offering to direct Lucy.

26–30 **Italians are born... gift from God**   This authorial interjection seems to cast light on differences between the English and the Italians. Italians accept and are ready for love, it is hinted, juxtaposing Lucy's naivety with the driver's worldly knowledge.

31–2 **some great blue violets**   The offering of *violets* recalls an earlier gift of violets that old Mr Emerson had made to some of the women at the hotel: the friendly and romantic gesture thus links to the Emersons. The mention of the violets also looks forward to the end of this extract.

33 **this common man**   This reference to the driver also suggests the subordinate position of the Emersons in society, and can be seen as foreshadowing Lucy's response to George Emerson's romantic gesture at the end of this extract.

38–9 **Certainly... violets afterwards**   In responding to Lucy's insistence the driver seems to agree that even in the pursuit of love there must be purpose. Forster renders the thoughts of the driver as they apparently come to him without expressing them as direct speech, creating humour in the simplicity of his intentions, especially bearing in mind the far-reaching consequences of his actions.

42–3 **the brown network of the bushes** As they approach the viewpoint the *brown* bushes impede their passage. Thus brown comes to be associated with frustration and the obscuring of beauty. See lines 82–3 and Note.

48 **What is that?** There is a note of caution in Lucy's sharp question. Although it is *shrugged* away by the driver, it is a hint that Lucy is not being led towards the meeting she expects, and perhaps a warning that there may be an intrusion upon this perfect scene.

53–4 **The view was forming at last** The *view* seems to stand for enlightenment and growth, as it does throughout the text. It is something to be worked towards. Lucy recognizes this pursuit of beauty as a welcome *escape from dullness* (lines 45–6) and savours every moment.

54–5 **she could discern… other hills** There is a hint of rewards at last.

56 *Eccolo!* there he is, or there it is. The driver feels he has fulfilled his duty. Once more, there is humour in the fact that his aim and Lucy's have been at such cross-purposes.

57–9 **the ground gave way… enveloped her** Lucy is suddenly made to appear alone, out in the open. She is immersed in and by the view, becoming part of the beauty of the natural landscape. Forster makes this a pivotal moment of being transported outside mundane everyday existence.

62 **Courage and love** The driver's tone here is one of infinite hope.

64–7 **violets ran down… azure foam** The metaphor of water emphasizes the blueness of the flowers and their abundance. Water is often a symbol of fertility.

69–70 **the well-head… to water the earth** The reader is reminded of the sea as the source of all life.

71 **like a swimmer who prepares** Notice George's relation to the metaphor of the sea of life that has been established. His behaviour – the wordless kissing of Lucy – is natural and spontaneous, but also courageous. He does not ask her permission: that would be to acknowledge the possibility of rebuttal. Instead he hopes for the best and plunges in *like a swimmer*.

72–3 **But he was not the good man that she had expected** What meanings can you find in this comment?

159

73 **he was alone**   The reference to George's isolation reminds the reader of the social constrictions of Edwardian society, where a young woman should not be in the company of a man without a chaperone.

76 **He saw radiant joy in her face**   This suggests George sees his emotions being reciprocated by Lucy.

76–7 **the flowers beat against her dress**   This image suggests that her heartbeat has become one with nature. The natural beauty of the landscape seems to nurture human love. George is transformed by the beauty around him and he sees Lucy as part of this natural landscape.

77–8 **The bushes above them closed**   The driver has left them together, and nature seems to form a cocoon around them, facilitating the kiss.

80 **almost before she could feel**   Charlotte Bartlett's untimely entrance demonstrates that she represents all the social impediments to Lucy's emotional development.

82–3 **stood brown against the view**   Charlotte's entrance at this point, breaking the *silence of life*, is a reminder of obstacles to happiness, like the bushes that delayed Lucy's approach (see lines 42–3 and Note). The preposition *against* clearly shows that Charlotte is in opposition to the growth and fulfilment symbolized by *the view*.

The Going: Thomas Hardy (1912)

See the headnote on page 150 for Thomas Hardy. As described there, his wife Emma died suddenly in 1912, and her death resulted in Hardy writing many poems about her and regretting their estrangement, of which *The Going* is one. The poem concerns itself with the shock of Emma's death and it is one of Hardy's first attempts to reconcile himself to the situation.

The form the poem takes is rather unusual. Lines 5 and 6 of each stanza are couplets of five or six syllables per line, with feminine rhymes (the final syllable unstressed). In consequence they sound rather light and tripping, but also yearning and unresolved. In what ways do you feel that this form creates a poignant effect for the reader?

The poem makes various uses of the verb 'to go'. What effect do you feel this has?

1–4 The tone in these opening lines is one of complaint and of questioning. The simple masculine rhyme scheme reinforces the suggestion of the grievance he maintains on finding she has *gone* from him forever.

5–6 The couplet of short lines changes the mood to one of sorrow and lament. The feminine rhyme of *follow* and *swallow* creates a mournful tone.

8–11 The poem now moves back to a tone of reproach, but although the rhyme scheme echoes the first stanza's, the line structure has changed. The first two lines create a sharp staccato rhythm, which may be regarded as producing an accusatory tone, but the following two lines develop the argument in less severe terms. Is there a hint through the use of the word *harden* that Emma's going has left him alone in a world that is harsh and uncompromising?

14 **that moment** Hardy focuses on the instant of her death, and alerts the reader to two of his major themes: the workings of fate and time.
altered all The internal rhyme emphasizes the enormity of the loss.

15–18 Once again the tone is one of blame as Hardy reverts to the rhetorical-question style of the first stanza. Now he is questioning why she continues to have such a hold over him.

19–20 The imagery is dark, almost threatening in the couplet. The word *dankness* suggests a murky and chilling atmosphere.

20–21 **yawning blankness/ Of the perspective** Her death has left a *yawning blankness*, suggesting a future whose emptiness *sickens* the speaker.

22–8 The change to the past tense in this stanza creates a change in tone as the speaker is reminded of the elation he felt when he first met Emma, in Cornwall. This meeting is celebrated in the poem *When I Set Out for Lyonnesse*. In these lines Hardy presents Emma as one who is in harmony with the romantic landscape she inhabits. The active verbs such as *rode* suggest her youthful vitality.

25 **beetling** jutting, overhanging.

Beeny Crest Beeny Cliff in Cornwall.

29–32 **Why, then... time's renewal** The poem returns to the recent past with the word *latterly*, and to rhetorical questions, but the tone has changed again, this time to one of self-reproach. We are given a picture of the estrangement that had come to characterize their relationship.

31 **ere** before.

32 **We might have said** The conditional tense creates pathos by considering what *might have* been.

36–8 The final stanza opens with a sense of resolution and acceptance that *All's past amend* and *Unchangeable*. The speaker seems to be accepting that we have no control and are at the mercy of time and fate.

39–42 **O you could not know... undo me so** There is a sense of forgiveness and tenderness here, although the fragmented lines and broken syntax reflect the despair that is such a feature of this poem.

Leda and the Swan: W.B. Yeats (1923)

William Butler Yeats (1865–1939) was a poet and playwright born and educated in Dublin, who is credited with being the motivation behind the Irish literary revival. He was awarded the Nobel Prize for Literature in 1923, the first Irishman ever to win this accolade.

Yeats was fascinated by Irish legends, explorations of Irish identity, and the occult, and such themes characterize his earlier work. For this poem, first published in the American magazine *The Dial* in 1924, he turned to Greek mythology. It describes the rape of Leda by the god Zeus, in the form of a swan. Such tales of gods pursuing young girls in a variety of forms were found in the Roman poet Ovid's *Metamorphoses*, written in 8 CE.

The union of Leda and Zeus in the form of the swan was said to have resulted in the births of Helen and Polydeuces. The abduction of Helen (of Troy) would later be the cause of the Trojan War. The two offspring were born at the same time as Castor and Clytemnestra, children of Leda's husband, the King of Sparta. The poem seems to suggest that their origins disturbed

Clytemnestra so much that this led to her eventual murder of her husband, King Agamemnon, who commanded the Greeks in the Trojan War.

The poem is written in the form of a sonnet divided in Petrarchan fashion into two quatrains and a sestet. It is interesting that Yeats chose to use this form, so often associated with love, to depict a violent and forceful encounter between woman and god.

Title Notice that the title does not refer to Zeus by name. This is maintained throughout the poem, creating an air of mystery.

1 **A sudden blow** Yeats shows the young girl to be stunned and physically dominated, so as to make her less able to resist the god's assault.

great wings beating still Her powerlessness against the swan's wing span is emphasized. The *beating* may suggest both violence and the speeding up of the girl's heartbeat in fear.

2 **Above** What does this preposition suggest?

staggering The adjective connotes surprise, but also a response to the *sudden blow*.

thighs caressed The sexual overtones make the intentions of the descending creature clear.

3 **dark webs** the swan's webbed feet.

caught in his bill Leda's physical capture is depicted here.

4 **helpless breast upon his breast** The animal and human forms seem to be less differentiated here, with the repetition of the noun *breast*. The line suggests their close physical proximity as well as her inability to free herself from his clutches.

5 **terrified vague fingers** The girl's terror makes her movements uncertain as she attempts to extricate herself.

6 **feathered glory** The poet suggests the masculinity and the divinity lurking beneath the swan's covering.

loosening thighs There is no indication as to whether the *loosening* is willed by the girl or the swan.

7 **how can** The phrase, repeated from the beginning of line 5, suggests the girl's helplessness. The cumulative effect of the two rhetorical questions is interesting as one seems to lead to

the other: because the *fingers* cannot *push* away the *feathered glory*, the girl is forced to feel the creature's *strange heart beating*.

9 **A shudder in the loins** the swan's ejaculation. This leads to the conception of the children Helen and Polydeuces.

engenders The verb has a double meaning here. The two children, Helen and Polydeuces, are literally conceived. Metaphorically and psychologically, Yeats suggests that this act led to the Trojan War (see headnote), which is evoked in line 10, and to the murder of the Greek commander *Agamemnon* by his wife Clytemnestra on his return home (line 11).

11 **Agamemnon dead** Notice the caesura that dramatically breaks the line after these words, making the reader pause to consider the magnitude of these events.

11–12 **so caught up/ So mastered** Leda's lack of choice is emphasized. The word *mastered* is especially rich in connotations, suggesting the subjugation of the female to the male's will, or the subjugation of the mortal to the god's.

12 **brute blood** What effect does the alliteration of these two monosyllabic words have here?

13 **Did she put on his knowledge** The question seems to ask whether the girl felt what it was like to be a god as she was physically joined to him.

14 The final line shows Zeus's cold detachment once he has completed the act of rape. The *drop* returns Leda to earth in an undignified fashion, further emphasizing the god's superior position. The apparent indifference of the gods, who seem to abandon human beings in their time of need, has interested writers across the centuries.

Post Second World War

In a Garden: Elizabeth Jennings (1986)

Elizabeth Jennings (1926–2001) was born in Boston, Lincolnshire but moved with her Roman Catholic family to Oxford when she was six. As a child, Jennings found religion to be a source of terror and misery, and she had a difficult relationship with her father. She was frequently physically ill, and her anxieties manifested themselves in the insomnia and nightmares that she termed from the age of seven her 'neuroses'.

Jennings was based in Oxford for the rest of her life and studied English literature at St Anne's College from 1944 to 1947, attending lectures by famous scholars such as C.S. Lewis. She later became a librarian and a publisher's reader.

In a Garden is a variation on a sonnet, and the poem concerns itself with a sense of loss. It is left to the reader to explore the ambiguity of who or what is lost. It can be read as a loss of innocence, of a golden age of childhood, as the loss of a lover or, as in the reading below, loss of faith.

1–3   The *garden* can be read, as line 3 suggests, as a *metaphor* for the Garden of *Eden*. There is a sense in which these lines allude to the fall from grace of Adam and Eve. The image of *waiting an event* suggests perhaps the idea of a second coming of Christ (who redeems the sin of disobedience committed in the Garden of Eden).

3   **spruce**   elegant, trim, smart. The garden has perhaps lost its natural, free and effortless beauty and is now formalized, controlled and limited, constrained by the human desire to contain and restrict.

5   **Quietly godlike**   This suggests it was the *gardener's* decision to leave, just as God leaves humankind to deal with life.

6–7   **Not made me… tempting me**   These lines recall the biblical story of the Garden of Eden, where Adam and Eve had been commanded by God not to eat the fruit of 'the tree of the knowledge of good and evil', but were tempted into doing so (Genesis 2 and 3).

7–8   **bad/ Choice**   The speaker has free will and can avoid evil.

8   **Yet I still felt lost**   The feelings of loss, perhaps spiritual loss, are intense.

9–11   The change in the stanza structure from four lines to three reinforces the sense of loss.

10   **threat**   The speaker's sense of self and her relationship with nature are both blighted and have become almost a kind of menace.

11 **Everything was too neat** This is an echo of the sentiment expressed in line 3.

11–12 **someone cares/ In the wrong way** The enjambment across the stanza break creates a sense of hope that is immediately dashed. Here the speaker seems to allude once again to the idea that there is control rather than nurture. The *someone* is distant but nevertheless a kind of threat that seems to create order rather than opening up the possibilities of being cherished.

12 **I need not have stood long** This assertion suggests a choice, but one that leads only to pain.

13 **Mocked by the smell of a mown lawn** The word *Mocked* highlights the sense of loss again, as all that remains is a *smell* appropriate to a cultivated garden – one that is *mown*, perhaps unable to blossom.

14 **Sickness for Eden** The final line of the poem foregrounds the image of *Sickness* and there is a sense of nostalgia as the speaker seems to yearn for a lost world of innocence or faith, or a world uncomplicated by human desires.

Possession: A.S. Byatt (1990)

A.S. Byatt, born in 1936 in Sheffield, is a prize-winning novelist and poet. Her novel *Possession*, written in 1990, is a complex interweaving of two time periods. There is a modern love story set in the 1990s, concerning a couple who are brought together over their shared interest in the works of the (fictional) Victorian poets Randolph Henry Ash and Christabel LaMotte. The poets are the couple in the extract, who are travelling in the year 1860. Their romance is therefore set against the backdrop of Victorian England. It is not too far distant in time from George and Lucy's romance in *A Room with a View* (see page 72).

Ash is married and it appears unthinkable that he would leave his wife. One can sense the careful regulation of the lovers' public behaviour, such as on this train journey. The fact that they are pursuing their forbidden relationship shows that the couple have decided to ignore some of society's strict rules. They are aware that their transgressions will have serious implications and that LaMotte, at least, will *regret* (line 86) their actions. She has led a sheltered life but their friendship, sparked by shared literary interests, has clearly grown into a passion that has overpowered them both and led them to plan the weekend away together which this extract sees them embarked upon. The intention to consummate their passion weighs heavily upon them and both are clearly nervous about the possible outcome.

In this episode, Byatt prefaces the interaction between the lovers with a carefully balanced description of both. Each is described in turn, in isolation, as if to emphasize their separate identities. Before the beginning of this extract, Ash has been described in similar detail.

2 **grey-striped** Notice the many references to colours in this descriptive paragraph. What effect do they have?

27 **proper modesty** The description of LaMotte ends by emphasizing this, as if to juxtapose the inappropriate behaviour with the appropriate appearance of this lady.

28 **well beyond York** Ash is shown to wait until they are well beyond any area in which a person who might know either of them is likely to observe them talking.

31 **earnestly** Ash's demeanour is doubtless intended to reassure LaMotte of the sincerity of his intentions towards her. The reader will be aware of a discrepancy between his behaviour towards her and his circumstances as a married man.

38–9 **not in a state of mind that allowed of tiredness** What does this suggest? Is LaMotte tense and nervous as well as being excited?

40–41 **possessed himself of one of the little gloved hands** The verb *possessed* echoes the title of the novel and takes up one of its recurring themes. Here it suggests the male taking control of the female in a symbolic way. The possession of the hand acts as a precursor to the possession of her body that is soon to take place. The fact that the hand is *gloved* suggests Victorian restraint, or at least the appearance of it.

41–2 **lay still and then clasped his** LaMotte's initial lack of response suggests that she is guarded and careful. The focus here is on active verbs, small details and the symbolism of the clasping of hands. This lends intensity to the narrative.

42–7 **There were matters... could overcome** How does Byatt suggest Ash's delicacy in broaching the most indelicate subject?

52 **curled and crisped** LaMotte gradually becomes more animated.

53 **We are travelling together** Ash begins with a simple declaration of fact, avoiding the more difficult matters yet to be raised.

53–4 **We decided – you decided** The back-tracking and hesitation in his speech suggested by the fragmented structure here clearly demonstrates Ash's embarrassment.

60 **a wife** The use of the indefinite article shows Ash's hesitation to attribute the status of *wife* to LaMotte in case she is unwilling to accept this.

68 **I want to be with you** LaMotte's response is simple and declarative: she does not resort to the evasions often adopted by women in love, but speaks with the kind of forthright simplicity that is so marked in Miranda in Shakespeare's *The Tempest* (see page 30).

71 **I – we – had decided** LaMotte's speech becomes hesitant like Ash's, but her transition from the singular to the collective pronoun is significant in illustrating the changing way in which she is considering their relationship.

76 **This is necessity** Her description of their approaching sexual union as a *necessity* turns it from an act of indulgence or weakness into a natural requirement, like eating or drinking, as though the pair have embarked on a course that must end in consummating their relationship.

87 **you must not speak nonsense** Ash's imperative is quickly brushed aside by LaMotte's similarly imperative rejoinder, which highlights their difference in status: as a single woman whose reputation is dependent upon her chastity, she feels it is inevitable that she will live to regret their sexual relationship. As a married man, he may suffer pangs of guilt but no material consequence as a result of the transgression.

95 **I too have brought a ring** There is a meaningful symmetry in the fact that both have, without prior discussion, brought rings to take the place of a wedding ring. Both rings have

significance for the owner: his belonged to his *mother*, hers to her *great-aunt*. Ash describes his as a *plain gold band*, although it is *engraved with daisies*. LaMotte's is a *simple stone* yet carved with an engraved initial. Byatt seems to suggest that her protagonists are attempting to reduce the huge symbolic significance of the rings by describing them in reductive language.

100 **I shall be happy to wear your ring** This assertion seems remarkably composed, thus echoing the behaviour expected of a lady at this time. It does not express the kind of emotion one might expect to be associated with this highly symbolic action.

106–7 **Their unspoken presence hung in the air** Both characters are clearly aware they are parodying the marriage service. Their circumstances dictate that the placing of the ring on her finger is carried out in silence.

107–8 **He seized the little hand and carried it to his lips** The 'ceremony' is concluded with a kiss, as is traditional at weddings. Here the kiss is of her hand, not her lips. The act is nevertheless imbued with eroticism by the way that he has *peeled off* her glove, and the very restrained nature of the exchange so far.

109–10 **pushing its soft leather pockets back into shape** Ash's caress of the glove could be seen as a displaced symbolic caress of LaMotte's body. The passion between the two is expressed not in the language used to address one another but in the touching of hands and the symbolism of the glove.

114–15 **possessed by the imagination of her** There is a suggestion that Ash is like a courtly lover here, carried away by the thought of the forbidden but desired love so that his imaginings have become almost sufficient for him. Note again the use of the verb *possessed*. What connotations does it have here?

115–16 **a princess in a tower** Byatt reinforces the idea of Ash's romanticism with this reference to fairy tales.

121–2 *only* **to be imagined** The author reinforces the sense of the forbidden here.

122–3 **engaged in observing** The lover weighs up the reality of his lover as compared to *the woman he dreamed*.

A *Pink Wool Knitted Dress*: Ted Hughes (1998)

Ted Hughes was Poet Laureate from 1984 until his death in 1998. Also a children's writer, he is considered to be one of the best poets of the twentieth century.

Hughes was married to the American poet Sylvia Plath (see page 13), and they had two children. After they separated, she committed suicide in 1963 at the age of 30. His conduct in that relationship has remained controversial, particularly to admirers of Plath. In his last collection of poetic work, *Birthday Letters*, published after his death, Hughes explores their complex relationship.

A Pink Wool Knitted Dress is from the *Birthday Letters* collection. It describes the day of his marriage to Plath on 16 June 1956. It is the bride's unconventional pink outfit that acts as a catalyst to Hughes's recollections of the day.

2 **smudged** This verb suggests their life together beyond this day would somehow be soiled and complicated. It sets the tone for the underlying feelings of guilt and perhaps remorse that characterize the poem.

3 **Bloomsday** the annual celebration of the life of the Irish writer James Joyce, commemorating the events of his novel *Ulysses* (which is set on 16 June 1904). The name alludes to Leopold Bloom, the protagonist of *Ulysses*. Clearly Hughes makes the connection between his wedding date and that of the Bloomsday celebrations, but the term *Bloom* also creates an image of blossoming and coming to fruition, thus creating an image of Plath as a flower in bloom as she *stood at the altar*. The image is bold and celebratory, as well as a reminder of the pair's shared love of literature.

4 **Rain** The allusion to the weather perhaps ominously suggests the coming storm clouds in their future together.

7–10 The bridegroom's shabby appearance could suggest either that he is unworldly and not concerned with conventional appearances, or emphasize his relative poverty, or imply that this is a hurried, makeshift commitment, one that has not been planned or thought through. The unconventionality of his attire also lends an almost ridiculous air to the ceremony.

12 **Frog-Prince**   a fairy-tale character made famous by the Brothers Grimm. In the tale, a spoiled princess reluctantly befriends a frog, who then magically transforms into a handsome prince. In modern versions of the story the transformation is triggered by the princess kissing the frog.

Swineherd   another fairy-tale character, this time by Hans Christian Andersen. A prince disguises himself as a swineherd to woo an arrogant princess. The allusions to fairy tales suggest the speaker is one who conceals great possibilities, but perhaps that there is a lack of realism in the commitment required for marriage. The bridegroom could be regarded as self-deprecating for seeing himself as a shabby *Swineherd* or ugly *Frog*, or alternatively rather conceited and condescending if he is attributing these fairy-tale dreams to his bride (or, given the use of the term *son-in-law*, to her mother, mentioned in line 25).

13 **Stealing**   What do you make of the idea of theft that is introduced here? See also line 32.

pedigree dreams   There is a self-conscious sense of class difference here.

14 **watchtowered searchlit future**   This suggests that his bride has been perhaps isolated and protected from life, again like a fairy-tale princess in a tower, and that he is robbing her of all the unfulfilled expectations of her future.

15 **conscript**   The military imagery here brings in suggestions of battle and conquest.

18 The use of the personal pronoun *My* creates a self-consciousness here that excludes the bride and focuses on the emotions and feelings of the speaker. In so doing it distances the reader from the sense of two people committing themselves to a life-long relationship, as does the verb *to hide*.

20–21 **Why not?... why not**   The understated humour in these lines reveals a lack of realism or understanding about how to organize a wedding.

24 **squeezed into marriage** This suggests the idea of being constrained or limited.

26 **gamble** The element of risk and chance involved in this coupling is emphasized.

29–30 The placing of *My family* on a line of its own suggests (perhaps ironically) how important they are, but their status is undermined by the statement that they had *heard nothing about it*. Once again there is perhaps the suggestion that the speaker takes the whole occasion lightly.

32 **theft** Does this create an ominous tone that echoes the foreboding imagery of the first part of the poem?

34 The construction of this line, with the adverb *meanwhile* turned into an adjective, suggests that the commitment symbolized by the *rings* is only temporary and transient.

35 **sexton** person who looks after a church and churchyard.

38 **prison animals** The image, linked to the moment of marriage, implies that like the creatures in the zoo these two individuals are being robbed of their liberty and self-determination.

39 **You were transfigured** The sudden change of mood after the caesura or break in this line seem to signal that the speaker suddenly feels a sense of the magic of the moment as he looks at his bride.

40 The triplet of adjectives suggests the vulnerability of the bride.

42–3 The structure of these lines echoes the complexity of emotions experienced by the bride. The tone becomes awed as the stanza fills with religious references.

44–5 This is an allusion to Shakespeare, 'The clouds methought would open, and show riches/ Ready to drop upon me' (*The Tempest*, III.ii). Once again the literary reference reflects their shared interests. This image is in direct contrast to the suggestions of poverty and restriction earlier in the poem.

46 This line acts as a balance to the first part of the poem. Here it seems the speaker is both elevated (*Levitated*) and powerless (*subjected*).

47 **spellbound future** On the one hand this suggests something magical, but on the other there might be the idea of a threat or menace.

50 How do you read this description? Does he now see her differently? The image of *flames* suggests passion and her awesome, elemental power.

51–4 The vulnerability of the young bride is stressed. The imagery may suggest that the woman is a prize or a commodity *like big jewels*, and that marriage is the ultimate gamble where she is *Shaken in a dice-cup* and offered to him. Her eyes, however, draw him in with their power and conflicting emotions, conjured up with the oxymoron *tear-flames*.

Interpretations

This section will examine different interpretations of the poems and extracts presented in this book. The texts will be considered in pairs by highlighting a particular theme that links two pieces. Of course, you will be able to find other themes and ideas that can be explored in different pairings of texts.

The interpretations below illustrate a variety of the different types of love that have been written about through the ages. Love can take many forms, and responses to it are infinitely varied.

Strife in love

Throughout the ages the struggles and strife of love have been presented in many different types of literature. In Chaucer's *The Knight's Tale* we are shown the anguish that rivalry in love can create between two sworn friends. In the extract from *Othello*, Shakespeare similarly depicts rivalry between two men over a young woman, but rather than both being lovers, one is the husband and the other the father. The two passages explore the complexities of love in different ways, and both offer an image of love that involves conflicts between men because of the competing claims they make on women's love.

Activity

Compare the ways the extracts from *Othello* and *The Knight's Tale* present strife in love. In your answer you should explore links through form, structure and language as well as themes and ideas, and attempt to make at least three wider reading links: one from drama, one from poetry and the other from prose.

Discussion

Both passages explore the issue of divided loyalties. However, Chaucer presents this through the fraying relationship between two knights who suddenly become rivals, whereas Shakespeare includes the voice of the woman, who considers the complexities of dividing her love and duty between a father and a husband.

In *The Knight's Tale*, love strikes the two imprisoned men as a kind of injury, as Palamon asserts he has been *hurt right now thurghout myn ye / Into myn herte, that wol my bane be* (lines 5–6). Similarly Arcite, on seeing Emelye, insists that *The fresshe beautee sleeth me sodeynly* (line 27). Thus love is presented in the courtly tradition as a torment; both men suffer and are driven to utter eloquent complaints to describe their anguish.

In contrast, Desdemona's experience of falling in love is described by Othello himself. Othello relates that she would *with a greedy ear / Devour up my discourse* (lines 22–23). The allusions to physical appetite here suggest Desdemona's overwhelming desire to listen to Othello's stories. Unlike the lovers in *The Knight's Tale*, Othello is able to communicate directly and powerfully with his loved one, who is given a right of reply. Desdemona is presented as one who pities her lover's past sufferings, offering *a world of sighs* and asserting that *'Twas pitiful, 'twas wondrous pitiful* (lines 32, 34). The use of anaphora (repetition) here reinforces the image of Desdemona as one who is full of compassion. This contrasts with the presentation of Emelye in *The Knight's Tale*, a young woman who by simply being in the garden *romen to and fro* is the cause of all Palamon's *criyng* and *wo* (lines 8, 9), and causes Arcite to be equally distraught. Palamon, although he has never spoken to the young woman, insists to Arcite that she is *my lady, whom I love and serve,/ And evere shal til that myn herte sterve* (lines 52–53). The use of the possessive pronoun emphasizes the fact that both

Eamonn Walker as Othello and Zoe Tapper as Desdemona at Shakespeare's Globe, London

men see Emelye as a prize to be owned. In the extract from *Othello*, it is the way Desdemona moves from being Brabantio's dutiful daughter to being Othello's wife that is the cause of conflict.

Literature through the ages has shown women being considered as possessions of either their fathers or husbands. This is illustrated elsewhere in Shakespeare, for example in *Much Ado About Nothing*. During the first wedding scene Claudio demands 'Will you with free and unconstrained soul / Give me this maid, your daughter?' and the father Leonato replies 'As freely, son, as God did give her me' (IV.i.24–6). Brabantio has not consented to Desdemona's marriage, but has been unable to prevent it, so his response is a paradox:

> I here do give thee that, with all my heart,
> Which, but thou hast already, with all my heart
> I would keep from thee.

(lines 66–68)

Here Shakespeare shows a father breaking the paternal bond because he refuses to accept female dissent. In contrast to *The Knight's Tale*, Shakespeare gives the young woman a voice; Desdemona is able to articulate her feelings and justify her decisions. Her tone is calm but firm as she acknowledges her *divided duty* (line 54) and openly professes the love *Due to the Moor my lord* (line 62). In the extract from Chaucer's tale, Emelye has no voice and has not chosen to arouse passions in the two knights; they regard her as a *goddesse*, the personification of *Venus* (lines 10–11), rather than a person with her own will. Later in the Romantic period, the poet Keats presents in *La Belle Dame sans Merci* a woman who not only causes suffering as with Arcite and Palamon, but becomes an active destroyer. The fate of the knight-at-arms is pointed out by his fellow sufferers: *La Belle Dame sans Merci / Thee hath in thrall!* (lines 39–40). By the late Victorian period we see a woman insisting on self-determination: Sue Bridehead in Thomas Hardy's *Jude the Obscure* asserts that she wants to choose the way she conducts love relationships, 'how I'll live with you, and whether I'll be married or no' (Part 5 Chapter 1).

Strife in love can be seen in many contexts in literature, but the two passages from Chaucer and Shakespeare display a contrast between the representations of male and female experiences of love, and give a sense of how attitudes were beginning to change towards women and their duties to men.

Women in love

The extracts from *The Wife of Bath's Tale* and *Paradise Lost* are very interesting in terms of their representation of women. Chaucer, writing at the end of the fourteenth century, depicts the Wife of Bath as a self-determined, sexualized woman who certainly carves a space for herself in a male world. In contrast Milton, writing in the seventeenth century, looks back to the biblical story of Genesis to create a picture of ideal womanhood that is subservient, innocent, vulnerable and clearly in need of male guidance.

Both passages explore ideas about female identity and the true meaning of beauty. In *The Wife of Bath's Tale* the knight is rewarded with a beautiful and loving young wife because he has been prepared to relinquish control in marriage. In contrast, in *Paradise Lost* Eve is ignorant of her own identity, and God urges her to look away from her own reflection whereas Adam is permitted to gaze at her; it is her beauty and submissiveness that Adam finds so desirable.

Activity

Compare the representations of women in love in the extracts from *The Wife of Bath's Tale* and *Paradise Lost*. In your answer you should refer to form, structure and language as well as themes and ideas, and include three wider reading links from poetry to illuminate the texts.

Discussion

The narrative voice of the two poems presents the reader with an interesting contrast; although both passages are written by men, Chaucer uses the female voice of the Wife of Bath as a narrator. She adopts a commanding tone throughout and exposes the limitations of relationships based on masculine *maistrie*. In contrast, Milton maintains the male perspective and through the use of an omniscient (all-knowing) narrator describes a relationship characterized by a traditional hierarchy – Adam is placed above Eve in intellect, knowledge, relationship to God, and even in physical *grace*; Eve is made to acknowledge that female *beauty is excelled by manly grace / And wisdom, which alone is truly fair* (lines 51–52).

In *The Wife of Bath's Tale* it is the old woman who challenges the knight's preconceptions about love, marriage and beauty. She offers him the choice of being married to a woman who is *foul and old*, but who will always be a *trewe, humble wyf*, or one who is *yong and fair* but who may betray him (lines 8–11). The tale hinges upon the knight's reply, and Chaucer maintains suspense as he is seen to prevaricate: *This knyght avyseth hym and sore siketh* (line 16). However, his response reveals a man who has come to accept that marriage is about partnership, and he tells his wife he will *put me in youre wise governance* (line 19). The old woman does not accept this concession at face value and insists on clarification: *Thanne have I gete of yow maistrie... Syn I may chese and governe as me lest?* (lines 24–25). The direct tone and uncompromising language suggest a woman who is insisting on self-determination. Married love, it can be argued, is shown by the end of the extract to be an equal partnership that works best if neither partner insists on control. This contrasts with the situation described by Aphra Behn in the final lines of her poem *Song*, where the speaker reveals that her *poor heart alone is harmed / Whilst thine the victor is, and free!*

In *Paradise Lost* Eve describes herself as one whose first memory is of being *reposed / Under a shade* (lines 11–12), so from the first she appears distanced from the clear light of God. Her words to Adam present her as subservient and unable to direct herself:

> O thou for whom
> And from whom I was formed flesh of thy flesh,
> And without whom am to no end, my guide
> And head...
>
> (lines 1–4)

In contrast to the knight in the extract from *The Wife of Bath's Tale*, Adam responds to Eve by making claims on her: *I seek thee, and thee claim / My other half* (lines 48–49). Eve's description of the moment clearly illustrates the balance of power in the relationship: *with that thy gentle hand / Seized mine, I yielded* (lines 49–50). The active verb *Seized*, though its effect is modified by the adjective describing the *hand* as *gentle*, suggests a measure of force as if Eve is at first detained against her will, and the image of her *yield*ing implies a surrender or capitulation. The narrator moves on to create an image of their love-making that presents Eve as the compliant woman who offers *meek surrender* and modesty in *half embracing* Adam. He is enamoured of her *beauty and submissive charms* and smiles *with superior love* (lines 55–60).

Elizabeth Jennings alludes to Adam and Eve's Garden of Eden in the opening lines of *In a Garden*. This poem explores love as dependency and as spiritual commitment, and the opening adopts a mournful tone: *When the gardener has gone this garden / Looks wistful and seems waiting an event*. Like Milton's Eve, the speaker appears to define herself in terms of love and its absence: *Sickness for Eden was so strong* (line 14).

In the two narrative poems *The Wife of Bath's Tale* and *Paradise Lost*, the reader is presented with contrasting representations of women in love. The tone of the concluding lines of Chaucer's tale reveals a strong, determined woman who is clear about what she requires in a man if he is to maintain her commitment. The Wife of Bath, like Eve, sees herself as subservient to God and ends the narration of her tale by calling on *Jhesu Crist* to *sende / Housbondes meeke, yonge, and fressh abedde,/ And grace t'overbyde hem that we wedde* (lines 46–48). In her prayer the Wife fuses worldly concerns with the sacred, and her sexuality is clearly self-determined. In contrast, Eve is sexualized through the male narrative voice, and it is Adam's response to her *swelling breast / Naked* and *loose tresses* that is important. The reader is not given a physical description of Adam; it is only Eve whose body is presented for contemplation.

Defining women by their sexual attractions is a characteristic of literature through the ages; Keats's description of *La Belle Dame sans Merci* is similarly sensual, despite her ethereal nature. She is described in stanza IV as:

Full beautiful – a faery's child,
Her hair was long, her foot was light,
And her eyes were wild.

Like Eve she is a temptation to men, but Keats suggests the *Belle Dame* acts like a siren who deliberately lures men to their destruction, whereas Eve's beauty is not used consciously and Adam's subsequent fall from obedience to God can be seen to be more a result of his vulnerability than something willed by Eve.

Love and the pressures of society

Both Samuel Richardson's *Pamela* and the Paston letters show couples experiencing great difficulties in negotiating the terms of their prospective unions. Margery Brews's letters to her beloved John Paston were written at a time when she was uncertain about the course of their future together: she could not know whether they would marry, because of the negotiations with her father over her dowry. The letters, as described in the Notes on page 91, are among the earliest surviving examples of love correspondence in English.

Pamela was written much later, in 1740, yet it addresses a similar problem regarding the terms of a union between a man and woman, this time of two very different social classes. The divide between Pamela and Mr B is obviously larger than that between Brews and Paston, but nevertheless the wrangling over money and social position is comparable, as are the terms in which the lovers express themselves.

Activity

Compare the ways Richardson and Brews explore the conflict between love and the pressures of society in the extracts from their texts. In your answer you should refer to links through form, structure and language as well as themes and ideas, and attempt to make wider reading links with other prose texts.

Discussion

The forms of these pieces create interesting comparisons, as both are letters giving a voice to young women: Brews's prose is obviously non-fiction, while Richardson's is a novel in epistolary form (see page 126). One difference between the forms is shown by the fact that Richardson makes much use of dialogue, both to further the plot and to develop characterization.

Both extracts have an open-ended structure: resolution is desired by the writer / narrator of each, but both are powerless to bring about an end to negotiations. This power lies in the hands of the men in each case.

The letters show several interesting differences between the characters of the women who are (apparently, in the case of Pamela) writing them. One might expect from the time of composition that the letters of Margery Brews would show a more retiring and deferential character, appropriate to the stereotype of the obedient woman in medieval times. However, it is evidently the voice of a forthright, candid young woman who states her feelings with refreshing honesty. When in the second letter she straightforwardly tells her beloved that if he thinks he *could get more money* elsewhere he should *not take the trouble to visit any more on this business* (lines 25–28), the reader can detect the resolution of a strong, determined woman. Furthermore, there is no apparent bitterness here: her claim that their possible marriage need never be *spoken of again, on condition that I may be your faithful friend and petitioner for the duration of my life* (lines 29–30) sounds heartfelt and genuine. Brews does not characterize herself as the spurned lover.

In his characterization of Pamela, however, Richardson portrays a much more reticent woman who begs her master to *spare your poor servant's confusion!* (lines 59–60). Pamela's self-deprecating language is rather surprising in a character who has shown herself to have rather acute perception of the behaviour and motivation of those around her. Pamela may be seen as disingenuous, especially as she clearly profits from her apparently artless demeanour by winning the esteem of Mr B. But there is no reason to doubt that she genuinely accepts the reality of class barriers and respects Mr B's social position. Pamela claims that *It is impossible for me to express the agitations of my mind* (lines 53–54), whereas Brews's sparse, forthright prose gives her views and expresses her feelings very clearly. However, Pamela's careful comment, *were I the first lady in the land, instead of the poor abject Pamela Andrews, I would, I could tell you* (lines 84–86) gives clear hints as to her true feelings for Mr B and confidence in her own views, while indicating that she is not free to speak plainly because of the social gulf between them. The different degrees of social separation between Brews and Paston on the one hand, and Pamela and Mr B on the other, go further towards explaining the confidence of the one and the reticence of the other than do issues of gender.

In both of these relationships, the nature of love is clouded by practical and financial considerations. Brews is anticipating difficulties in bringing about the marriage because of her father's reluctance to increase her dowry. Pamela is shown to be hesitant about expressing her feelings because of her lowly social status. Both texts characterize the women as feeling sincere regard for the men. Yet Brews repeatedly refers to a prospective match between herself and Paston as *the business* and is not shy about going into details on the financial transactions that will determine their relationship. Mr B tells Pamela: *I would divide, with all my soul, my estate with you, to make you mine upon my own terms* (lines 13–15). The use of the word *terms* also clearly suggests the business-like nature of the transaction.

Both Pamela and Brews are intimately involved in the *business* of arranging their marriages: they are not merely bystanders in the negotiations. Brews appears to have clear opinions on how negotiations should progress, and expresses her own reactions to these, even if she is powerless to increase the size of her dowry. Pamela is an active participant in the negotiations over her future and some might argue that she skilfully manoeuvres her master and achieves an impressive negotiating position by guarding her chastity, the only bargaining chip at her disposal. Her master defers to her opinion, and allows her to become *my adviser in this matter* (lines 25–26) despite her gender and *the distance between us, in the world's judgment* (line 40).

In modern texts, it might be considered unusual to see lovers openly discuss the financial terms of their relationships; the connection between money and love has become a taboo subject. Marriages today are seldom arranged by others, and the idea of dowries can be seen as an affront to a woman in a society that claims equal rights for men and women. But it is not unusual in modern texts to see depictions of loving relationships that are not the conventional marriages so determinedly sought in *Pamela* and the Paston letters. In *Enduring Love* by Ian McEwan (1997), the narrator and protagonist, Joe Rose, says of his relationship with his girlfriend, 'We were seven years into a childless marriage of love... there was nothing that threatened our free and intimate existence'. The use of the adjective 'free' and the qualifying phrase 'of love' suggest that this is not a marriage that has been formalized by Church or state. The actual state of their union is never clarified by the text and, given the modern context of the writing, it does not appear to matter.

In contrast, the unsanctified union of Sue Bridehead and Jude Fawley in Thomas Hardy's Victorian novel *Jude the Obscure* is shown to ultimately destroy both parties and their children, as a result of society's condemnation and Sue's inability to live with its pressure. Today, in Western culture, a situation such as Jude and Sue's is considered perfectly normal and a relationship such as that in *Enduring Love* brooks no disapproval. This is in stark contrast to the situation in the works of Jane Austen, Charlotte Bronte, Thomas Hardy, E.M. Forster and many other earlier writers who depict the efforts required to bring about appropriate, socially approved marriages between loving couples.

The art of love

Throughout the ages, methods of wooing and the art of love have frequently been the subject of discussion and the focus for poetry, prose and drama. In the extract from *As You Like It*, we see a dramatic representation of a 'cure' for love-sickness, presented rather duplicitously by a disguised woman to a man who is love-sick for her. In *The Art of Coquetry*, on the other hand, Charlotte Lennox presents her 'art' rather differently, in the form of a poem addressed apparently to young women, yet printed in the *Gentleman's Magazine*. Interestingly, therefore, both passages – though separated by hundreds of years, by genre and by their apparent purpose – explore elements of deception in love. They each feature a presentation of love as something that can be deliberately engendered (as in *The Art of Coquetry*) or destroyed (as in *As You Like It*) by careful adherence to a set of rules.

Charlotte Lennox had a varied writing and acting career; *The Art of
Coquetry* is her best-known poem

Activity

Compare the ways the extracts from *As You Like It* and *The Art of
Coquetry* explore methods of wooing and the art of love. In your answer
you should make links through form, structure and language as well as
themes and ideas, and attempt to make at least three wider reading
links: one from drama, one from poetry and the other from prose.

Discussion

Both passages explore the issue of artifice in wooing. Shakespeare
presents this primarily through the conventions of the dramatic form;
Rosalind's disguise as a young man results in many dramatic ironies.
This artifice allows Shakespeare to present one half of his loving couple
as completely unaware of the manipulations of the other. Lennox's
poem, on the other hand, is apparently intended for a young, naive,

female audience with the purpose of advising them about methods of attracting and entrapping a man, though its real audience and purpose may be very different. Just as Shakespeare employs dramatic irony, there is a gently mocking irony in Lennox's poem as she portrays the calculating and duplicitous behaviour men have suspected in the female sex for so long.

Shakespeare's presentation of the knowing female advising the naive male lover involves a delightful piece of gender role-reversal. A more typical presentation at this time of a young woman in a courtship situation might be seen in Miranda in *The Tempest*; her behaviour towards her would-be lover is circumscribed by her father. Shakespeare creates humour in the situation in *As You Like It* by having Orlando unknowingly seek advice about wooing from his loved one, to the point where he swears *by the white hand of Rosalind* to Rosalind herself (lines 33–34).

Lennox's poem also presents the female as a teacher about love, and the speaker adopts a tone of authority on the subject. The advice of a wiser, more experienced female is not uncommon in the literature of love through the ages. In Jane Austen's novel *Pride and Prejudice*, for example, the Elizabeth Bennet's Aunt Gardiner gently advises and guides her niece to a more accurate interpretation of the character of Mr Darcy.

The art of wooing is discussed in Lennox's poem in a practical and outspoken fashion, as the speaker presents a set of rules to be followed by young women who wish to be successful in love. The imperative tone is used throughout, as the poem takes the form of a set of instructions, using a direct, second-person mode of address: *First form your artful looks with studious care* (line 1). Shakespeare gives Rosalind a similarly decisive tone as she sets out to give Orlando *some good counsel* in the ways of love (line 6). As she examines him for the *marks* of love, she is, like the speaker in Lennox's poem, forthright and unequivocal, telling him he shows none of the signs of unrequited love.

Both extracts have carefully delineated structures. Rosalind first seeks to ascertain the extent of the love-sickness experienced by Orlando before outlining her manner of 'curing' him by persuading him to woo her as *his love, his mistress* (line 46). Their business is concluded with the practical details of where and when this 'cure' will be begun. Lennox describes the course of wooing to be pursued, delineated by such markers as *First, Then* (line 8), *'Tis harder still…* (line 17), each introducing the next stage of advice to be followed.

Shakespeare has Rosalind argue that love is merely a *madness* that can be cured *by counsel* (lines 39–43), undercutting the idea of love as a romantic ideal. Ironically, she speaks in this way to conceal her own vulnerability as one who is deeply in love with Orlando. Similarly, Lennox's poem turns love into a contest where the woman chooses to entrap by such means as *glances* (line 3) and *a soft sigh* (line 7); this manipulative behaviour also robs the idea of love of its romance. Such calculation in matters of love may also be seen in *The Tempest*, where Prospero chooses Ferdinand for his daughter and uses his magical arts to ensure their devotion to each other. Prospero's behaviour echoes the advice in Lennox's poem that *What's won by beauty must be kept by art* (line 18) and *Too kind a treatment the best lover cloys* (line 19). The difference here is obviously that it is the father not the young woman who subjects the lover to a series of hardships to test his love. Keats also presents a woman whose behaviour may seem to be in accordance with Lennox's rules, in *La Belle Dame sans Merci*; the knight-at-arms relates that *She looked at me as she did love* (line 19) and her 'arts' soon entrap the knight so that he is *in thrall* to her.

Rosalind humorously outlines the behaviour of a woman who has a man *in thrall*, telling Orlando that in order to cure someone of love-sickness, she behaved in all manner of unpredictable ways: she would *be effeminate, changeable, longing and liking, proud, fantastical, apish, shallow, inconstant... would now like him, now loathe him* (lines 48–53). Thus, she declares, she *cured him* of his love. With gentle irony, Lennox has the speaker of her poem present just such *inconstant* behaviour as the best way to *fix... a heart* (line 17). Both writers appeal to the natural human desire to gain control over the loved one and over one's own feelings, bringing out the humour of such attempts – usually doomed to failure – to control the workings of love.

Love as transaction

The Tempest, one of Shakespeare's last plays, shows the revenge of Prospero, the rightful Duke of Milan, upon his usurping brother, whom he causes to be shipwrecked on the magical island to which Prospero has been banished. A romantic offshoot of this plot, however, is that it brings the young Prince Ferdinand of

Naples to the island and Prospero has, without the knowledge of his daughter Miranda, selected him as her husband.

In Sheridan's play *The Rivals* (1775), the audience is treated to the spectacle of a very different father, Sir Anthony Absolute, arranging a marriage for his son, again without the son's knowledge or consent (see the photograph of a production of *The Rivals* on page 8). The plays, although separated by over 160 years, both show fathers regarding marriage as a transaction to be arranged on behalf of their children.

Activity

Compare the ways Shakespeare and Sheridan explore the presentation of love as a transaction in the extracts from *The Tempest* and *The Rivals*. In your answer you should refer to form, structure and language as well as themes and ideas, and attempt to make wider reading links with other drama texts.

Discussion

The extracts are taken from early parts of the plays and show the development of a complex situation that is to be worked out over the course of the play. The comedic form of *The Rivals* leads its audience to expect a plot that develops complicated impediments to the course of true love, and they are not disappointed. Shakespeare's play is sometimes considered to be a comedy, and the love plot between Ferdinand and Miranda fits this categorization because they overcome difficulties to reach their happy ending.

Several similarities can be seen in the characters of the fathers in these two plays. Prospero is a commanding, imperious figure as he addresses Ferdinand with *A word, good sir* (line 56), demanding that Ferdinand transfer his attention from Miranda to her father. Indeed, his tone is so abrupt that Miranda is prompted to ask *Why speaks my father so ungently?* (line 58). Sir Anthony is similarly imperious in his conversation with his son: *Come, give me your promise to love and to marry her directly* (lines 40–41). As the scene goes on and Jack Absolute continues to resist, Sir Anthony becomes increasingly irritated; he is clearly unused to such disobedience. He threatens all the punishments he can think of if Jack does not consent to the marriage he wishes to arrange.

The fathers are both presented as considering themselves completely in control of the marriages they are proposing for their children. In both cases, however, the children do in fact wish to marry the partner selected for them. In *The Rivals*, Jack is humorously unaware of the fact that the selected wife is the very *angel* to whom he has already *pledged* his *vows* (lines 48, 51). In *The Tempest*, Miranda and Ferdinand fall in love at first sight and are more than willing to marry: it is Prospero who puts impediments in their way, in case love too easily found is insufficiently appreciated. The working out of these misunderstandings or impediments is important to the plot of each play and leads to the final union of the couples.

The idea of marriage as a transaction is common to both Prospero and Sir Anthony: they view it as their duty to arrange advantageous marriages for their offspring. The language used by Sir Anthony clearly illustrates this unromantic view; he offers his son financial independence, which is gladly accepted by Jack until he discovers that *The fortune is saddled with a wife* (line 28). The metaphor *saddled* dehumanizes the woman involved: she is merely an encumbrance, a necessary burden that accompanies the fortune. Sir Anthony's description of the wife as *livestock* in line 37 goes even further in using animal imagery to describe her role. Absolute's response to this, *If my happiness is to be the price, I must beg leave to decline the purchase*, continues his father's imagery of financial transactions.

In *The Tempest*, Ferdinand's *prime request* (line 39) to be assured of Miranda's virginity emphasizes the fact that this is a requirement of their union. Such an insistence is unsurprising, considering that he intends her to become *Queen of Naples* (line 63) and presumably to produce heirs to the throne. It nevertheless illustrates the idea that for love to lead to marriage, certain requirements must be met. In the case of *The Rivals*, the marriage is the price that Sir Anthony wants his son to pay for his fortune. In *The Tempest*, Miranda's virginity is the price required for her to become *Queen of Naples*. Even in modern plays such as *A Streetcar Named Desire* (1947), clear expectations of female chastity are attached to a marriage proposal. In *Streetcar*, the fading Southern belle Blanche du Bois seeks a marriage with Mitch, the uninspiring friend of her brother-in-law, in order to gain financial security. She sees marriage not as a romantic attachment but as a 'cleft in the rock of the world' in which she can hide. Although Mitch initially contemplates marriage to Blanche, he is deterred by tales of her chequered past. He rejects her, accusing her of being 'not clean enough' to marry. Miranda in *The Tempest* can attest to the fact that she is *certainly a maid* (line 42) and thus her relationship with Ferdinand can continue.

In *The Tempest*, Ferdinand is keen to assert his own value: *myself am Naples* (line 48). There is the underlying suggestion that he can prove he is worthy of Miranda. Although in later scenes Prospero makes Ferdinand perform menial tasks in order to prove his devotion to his daughter, here the first instinct of the young prince is to assert his worth in terms of status. In *The Rivals*, it is in order to acquire status that Jack Absolute is urged to submit to the marriage proposed by his father. In both cases, marriage is clearly connected with social position.

In William Wycherley's *The Country Wife*, the audience is also treated to the spectacle of love as a transaction, as the recently married Pinchwife secures a marriage for his sister Alethea by paying her potential suitor a dowry: 'I must give Sparkish tomorrow five thousand pound to lie with my sister' (I.i.330–332). The blunt terms used to characterize this transaction, and the insistence upon the financial details of a union, recall the language of *The Rivals*, where Sir Anthony orders his son to *foreclose* (line 52) on his previous vow to a loved one, and Absolute is horrified and begs to *decline the purchase* (line 39).

The presentation of love as a transaction in the extracts from *The Tempest* and *The Rivals* contrasts with the romance elsewhere in these plays. The terms that Absolute uses to describe the woman he loves are hyperbolic and extravagant: she is described as *an angel* to whom his *heart is engaged* (lines 47–48). In *The Tempest*, Ferdinand describes Miranda as a *goddess* and exclaims *Oh you wonder!* (lines 35, 40) at his first sight of her. Jack Absolute also notes that his father married *for love* (line 120), despite apparently expecting his son to marry for a fortune. Both plays resolve these tensions by ensuring that the romantic aligns with the practical; the love choices of the young people coincide with the more hard-headed preferences of their parents.

The pain of loss

The extract from *King Lear* and Hardy's poem *The Going* both deal with the suffering that occurs after the death of a loved one. Hardy's poem explores his complex reaction to the sudden death of his estranged wife, and the pain is made palpable by vivid imagery. In contrast the misery of Lear over the murder of his daughter is depicted through means such as inarticulate cries and physical gestures, as well as eloquent language. In this dramatic scene we see not just Lear's individual response but that of the onlookers who serve to reinforce the impression that this is an apocalyptic moment.

Activity

Compare the ways Hardy and Shakespeare present the pain that results from the loss of loved ones in their texts. In your answer you should explore links through form, structure and language as well as themes and ideas, and attempt to make wider reading links with other drama and poetry texts.

Discussion

The extract from *King Lear* opens with the spectacle of Lear entering with his dead daughter in his arms, and the sounds of his misery as he literally *howls*. The suffering of the individual is elevated to a universal level as Lear insists that *heaven's vault should crack* (line 3).

Alan Howard as King Lear in a production at London's Old Vic

In contrast Hardy's poem focuses on one human being and one relationship. The tone of the first stanza is more one of complaint than lament, as Hardy asserts that his wife Emma left the world calmly, *as if indifferent quite* (line 3). The rhyming couplet that precedes the final line of the first stanza creates a haunting effect as, unlike Lear, Hardy alludes to a past event and in consequence the pain appears softened.

Browning in *The Lost Mistress* adopts a similarly understated, conversational tone but one that like Hardy conveys the sense of shock at an abrupt ending to a relationship: *All's over, then.* Browning also uses a similar interrogative style as he asks *does truth sound bitter / As one at first believes?* (lines 1–2). The loss depicted in Browning's poem is not through death, but nevertheless the intensity of the pain of separation is revealed. There is also a tone of finality in Browning's poem that is echoed by Hardy as it is made clear to the reader that he accepts the finality of Emma's death; he knows that he will be unable to *gain one glimpse of you ever anon* (line 7).

In contrast, Lear repeatedly raises the possibility that his daughter may still be alive, demanding a *looking-glass* to ascertain whether she is breathing (line 5), and fleetingly asserting that *This feather stirs; she lives!* (line 9). When he addresses Cordelia directly it is to beg her to *stay a little* (line 15). The sense of desolation and self-delusion is echoed in an understated way in Hardy's poem, as in stanza 3 he describes moments when he thinks *for a breath it is you I see / At the end of the alley of bending boughs.* The moment is as transitory as Lear's hope, and what Hardy is left with is a *yawning blankness* (line 20). The sense of despair, loneliness and isolation is captured in this image as the future seems to hold nothing but an ever-widening void.

This mood of despair, where the world is perceived as a wasteland, is echoed in *La Belle Dame sans Merci*, where Keats describes a knight-at-arms *Alone and palely loitering* in an empty wilderness where *no birds sing.* Similarly Kent in his reply to Lear asserts that *All's cheerless, dark, and* deadly (line 34). In contrast to Hardy, as noted above, Shakespeare extends the imagery to include the wider world; the death of Cordelia and ultimately the death of Lear are seen as a catastrophe that affects the entire society depicted in the play, whereas for Hardy it is the suffering of one man and the story of a particular relationship that the reader is invited to engage with.

The fusing of the past and the present is a feature of both texts as Lear, despite the horror of the moment, recalls that *Her voice was ever soft,/ Gentle and low* (lines 16–17). Similarly Hardy recalls Emma as *the swan-necked one who rode / Along the beetling Beeny Crest* (lines 24–25). The images of movement and action associated with Emma are in contrast to the presentation of Cordelia, who is remembered for her gentleness. It might be suggested that these two very different presentations reflect the attitudes to women at the time of writing. Cordelia, a creation of Renaissance England, is celebrated for her mild, calm temperament, as shown in her voice, whereas Emma, a woman of the late Victorian period, is remembered as an active woman whose vitality caused *Life to unroll… its very best* (line 28). A third approach is seen in *Romeo and Juliet*, as Romeo's lament over Juliet's apparently dead body is mostly concerned with her beauty; in addressing Juliet he assures her that because of her continuing beauty she has gained a victory over death: 'Thou art not conquer'd' (V.iii.94).

Throughout the Hardy poem there is a tone of regret at the estrangement that characterized the relationship up to the point of her death. In the first line of the penultimate stanza, Hardy questions *Why, then, latterly did we not speak…?* This suggests perhaps the remorse he feels in the wake of his loss, but he reflects in the final stanza that he cannot change what has passed: *All's past amend,/ Unchangeable. It must go*. In contrast, Lear speaks tragically of what might have been: *I might have sav'd her; now she's gone for ever!* (line 14). His grief is unbearable, and just before he dies the extraordinary line *Never, never, never, never, never* reflects the universal horror of the finality of loss. It is Kent who is left to comment on the relief from torment that death offers to Lear.

In contrast, pathos is created at the close of Hardy's poem by the suggestion of continued suffering, as he describes himself as *but a dead man held on end / To sink down soon*. It is clear he has no relief from his misery, as what he is left with is a *perspective* that *sickens me* (line 21).

Unrequited love

The pain of unrequited love is another frequent theme in writing about love. Andrew Marvell and Aphra Behn were writing at a similar time: Marvell was born only 20 years before Behn, so their social and historical contexts are comparable, which may in part account for the many similarities in their poems about unrequited love. Both of the poems by these two writers featured in this book explore the concept of unrequited love in a largely symbolic way. Marvell, as a Metaphysical poet, would be expected to use highly figurative language, possibly featuring conceits (far-fetched comparisons) and logical argument. Behn was better known for her plays than her poetry (it is from one of her plays that this short poem is taken), yet uses similar language and imagery.

Activity

Compare the ways Behn in *Song* and Marvell in *The Fair Singer* present the experience of unrequited love. In your answer you should explore links through form, structure and language as well as themes and ideas, and attempt to make wider reading links with other poems.

Discussion

Both poets use a regular, alternating rhyme scheme, which seems suitable as it assists in the comparisons that will be explored in the poems, although Marvell ends each stanza with a rhyming couplet that seems to clinch his argument. Behn chooses to organize her poem into two octaves (stanzas of eight lines). This balanced form allows her to create a comparative structure as she compares the different traits that *Love* has taken from her and from her lover. Marvell writes his poem in three sestets (six-line stanzas). The subject matter is largely self-contained within each stanza, and each one begins a new phase of his argument.

Each poem presents an involved first-person narrator, and a personified *Love*. The striking feature of this love is its power to enslave even (or especially) where the speaker's feelings are unrequited. Marvell's speaker is attempting to withstand the forces of *Love* but unable to do so: *how should I avoid to be her slave…?* (line 10). Behn's speaker suggests that *Love* takes qualities from her and her loved one, combining them into an invincible force; from her he takes *sighs and tears* (line 9), from her lover *pride and cruelty* (line 10).

It is interesting to compare the actions of the personified *Love* in each poem. Marvell opens his poem by claiming that *Love* created *so sweet an enemy* (his loved one) in order to *make a final conquest of all me*. Behn opens by stating that *Love in fantastic triumph sate*, unconcerned about the *bleeding hearts around him*. Both poems characterize this *Love* as a powerful, uncaring figure, keen to exercise *tyrannic power* (*Song*, line 4).

The poems both use elemental imagery in order to illustrate the extent of *Love*'s powers: Behn refers to the *fires* that *Love* takes from *bright eyes* (line 5), while Marvell claims that *Love* makes *fetters of the very air I breathe* (line 12). The idea that *Love* controls the elements suggests that it is an all-powerful force, against which we have little hope of prevailing. Robert Graves (1895–1985) uses similar imagery of elemental power in his poem *Full Moon*, where the moon forms a backdrop to the meeting of lovers. The moon is personified as the 'tyrannous queen above,/ Sole mover of their fate'. Here, the moon seems to be controlling the earth and the lovers upon it.

The power of love is illustrated by the use of military imagery in both Behn's and Marvell's poems: Behn states that she is *harmed* by *Love* as her *heart* is subdued completely to its forces (line 15). At the end of the poem her lover is pictured as *the victor... and free!* as if the relationship has been a military battle that he has won. Marvell also uses imagery of battles, suggesting that *Love* creates *an enemy* (line 2) that must be fought *in some plain,/ Where victory might hang in equal choice* (lines 13–14). Such imagery is effective in suggesting the sheer power of love and how futile it is for mere mortals to attempt to withstand it.

The two poets also both illustrate the paradoxes of love by using comparative structures that yoke together sets of opposing ideas or images. In Behn's poem, as noted above, *sighs and tears* are contrasted with *pride and cruelty*. All of these, she suggests, make up a part of the experience of love. In Marvell's poem, the *heart* and the *mind* (lines 5–6) are both made subject to the power of *Love*. Marvell combines the idea of the *wind and sun* in the final line to suggest that love has control of both. Similarly, in Graves's poem *Full Moon*, the contrasting states of night and day are brought together, as the moon 'Stood beaming like the Sun'. As the lovers come together, Graves declares 'And now cold earth was Arctic sea,' once more demonstrating how, through the power of love, opposites become one.

George Herbert, a clergyman who wrote mainly religious poems and lived from 1593–1633, was also linked to the Metaphysical school of poetry and writing only a little earlier than Marvell. He created a very different impression of love in his poem called simply *Love*, where he also uses personification as he writes 'Love bade me welcome; yet my soul drew back'. In his poem love is a benevolent force, 'sweetly questioning/ If I lack'd anything'. This love invites the speaker of the poem to 'sit down... and taste my meat', generously sharing its bounty, instead of forcing the speaker to succumb to its powers. The love Herbert is describing is a sacred and spiritual love, whereas Behn's and Marvell's *Love* is secular and sexual. Nevertheless, it has a similar effect in that this speaker is also vanquished by love and succumbs to its will: his poem ends 'So I did sit and eat'. Throughout the ages many poets have created images of love as an unstoppable power, subduing us either by stealth, as in Herbert's poem, or by outright force, as Behn and Marvell describe.

Definitions of love

Much of the literature about love through the ages has sought to define love in various ways. Ben Jonson's poem *Death and Love* begins by admitting that the speaker does not know what love truly is, and seeks to explore some of its qualities. Written later, in the Romantic period, Shelley's poem *To...* seeks to avoid the word 'love' altogether, deeming it too clichéd and therefore meaningless. Both poems therefore seek a new definition of the experience of love.

Activity

Compare the ways Shelley and Jonson explore definitions of love in *To...* and *Death and Love*. In your answer you should refer to form, structure and language as well as themes and ideas, and attempt to make wider reading links with other poems.

Discussion

Both poems explore ideas about the meaning of love. Jonson's extended sonnet (see page 111) is a variation on the classic form used to express love. Interestingly, Shelley also chooses a 16-line form to present his ideas. Whereas Jonson writes in rhyming couplets to explore the similarities between death and love, Shelley uses an alternating rhyme scheme to compare and contrast classical ideas about love with his own definition. Both poems are divided into two stanzas to explore the relationship between, in Jonson's case, *Death* and *Love*, and in Shelley's case, a debased type of love and the poet's own version.

Both poets write in the first person, presenting an almost confessional style of narrative. The tone of Jonson's speaker is conversational and discursive, as he opens by admitting *I am young, and cannot tell / Either what Death or Love is well*. While Shelley's poem begins in a more detached, philosophical tone, his second stanza introduces a comparably confessional tone when the speaker says *I can give not what men call love...* There is a difference, however, in the implied audience. Whereas Jonson seems to be addressing an unspecified general audience, who are included in his discussion through the use of the plural second-person pronoun *we*, Shelley appears to address one specific woman, to whom the poem is anonymously dedicated. This can be seen in the direct invitation to this unnamed woman: *wilt thou accept not / The worship the heart lifts above* (lines 10–11).

The difference in audience also helps to suggest the difference in the ways in which love is presented in the two poems: while Jonson seeks to come to a general understanding of the nature of love, Shelley's speaker explores his own personal feelings, which he attempts to define over the course of the poem. As Jonson explores the *Extremes* (line 8) of love and death, in the second stanza Shelley's speaker offers *not what men call love*, but *worship*, *desire* and *devotion*, which he presents as being purer and more heartfelt than the general idea of *what men call love*.

Both poems seem to present language itself as a theme and subject worthy of consideration. In comparing *Death* with *Love*, Jonson comments about the use of language: *in a ruin we it call / One thing to be blown up, or fall* (lines 9–10). Shelley explores the misappropriation of the word 'love', which he declares in his opening lines is *too often profaned / For me to profane it*. The overuse of the word causes him to avoid it and seek to define his feelings more specifically.

As part of their linguistic explorations, both poems examine opposites in an attempt to reach a closer definition of love. Jonson's comparison of *Death and Love*, promised by his title, develops into a consideration of *heat* and *cold*, and different types of *wounds* (line 6). Shelley examines the paradox that in love, *hope is too like despair*, and yokes together the *moth* and the *star*, the *night* and the morning. This bringing together of opposites appears to help the poets to reach a better understanding of the often contradictory nature of love.

Having worked through their paradoxes, however, both poets end in optimistic terms, or at least on notes of acceptance. Jonson affirms that love has the power to *fight the frost out of the grave*, and Shelley hopes that his mistress will accept his *devotion* in order to raise them both above *the sphere of our sorrow*. This idea that love can transcend pain and death and raise the true lover above the mundane is examined by John Donne in his poem *A Valediction: Forbidding Mourning*. He dismisses the love of 'Dull sublunary lovers' who are plunged into despair upon parting. He defines his love as something transcending the physical so that, when parted, he and his lover will 'Care less eyes, lips and hands to miss'. Similarly in his poem *The Ecstasy*, Donne describes lovers' souls as leaving their bodies in order to commune with each other, 'hung 'twixt her and me'.

Andrew Marvell also writes in the first person in his poem *The Definition of Love*, as he sets out on a similar task to Jonson and Shelley. Like Shelley, he links hope and despair to love, arguing that his love was 'begotten by Despair / Upon Impossibility'. He too yokes together opposites such as 'the distant poles'. Just as Shelley invokes the *heavens*, writing of the *desire of the moth for the star* (line 13), so Marvell invokes the 'giddy heaven' before concluding that his ill-fated love is 'the conjunction of the mind,/ And opposition of the stars'. Poets often invoke these lofty comparisons in an attempt to explain the inexplicable; the heavens and the stars represent the unknown and the unattainable, their very mystery symbolizing for the poets the mysterious, infinitely desirable quality of love.

Forbidden love

Both Oscar Wilde's letter and the extract from *The Duchess of Malfi* explore the pains and pleasures of forbidden love. In Wilde's letter to Lord Alfred Douglas he reveals his moments of hesitation in terms of commitment, acknowledging that it would have been wiser to end the relationship, but he makes it clear that his love is passionate and unconditional; moreover it is a necessary part of his artistic life, so that in some ways he defines his lover as his muse. Webster's *Duchess of Malfi* presents a different type of forbidden love, one that is based on a disparity of social position. It is the woman who reveals how much she is prepared to sacrifice for her lover, and the unconditional nature of the love she is declaring for him. Both of these texts therefore explore the offering of unconditional love within a framework of forbidden relationships.

Activity

Compare the ways Wilde and Webster present forbidden love in their extracts. In your answer you should explore links through form, structure and language as well as themes and ideas, and attempt to make at least three wider reading links, one from drama, one from poetry and the other from prose.

Discussion

At the beginning of the extract from *The Duchess of Malfi*, the Duchess bewails her status in society, which causes *misery* in that – unusually for a woman – she is *forced to woo, because none dare woo* her. Moreover Webster shows that the Duchess's situation raises an issue not only of class but of gender, because despite her status she is not at liberty to choose her own husband. In the Renaissance period a single woman was expected to be subservient to her father or in his absence (as in the Duchess's case) her brothers, especially in such matters as selecting marriage partners. The Duchess's social position reinforces this because her husband and any sons will gain positions of power.

The Duchess is presented as self-determined, strong and passionate in her dialogue with Antonio, not admitting any claim upon her right to choose him as her husband: *Sir, be confident;/ What is't distracts you?* (lines 12–13). She alludes to her *violent passions* (line 5) and insists *You have left me heartless: mine is in your bosom* (line 9). Her tone is uncompromising and the audience are left in no doubt about the strength of her commitment.

Eve Best as the Duchess of Malfi and Tom Bateman as Antonio in a 2012 production

Wilde identifies a difference between himself and his lover in the greeting of his letter, as he refers to him as *My child*. In so doing he reveals a hierarchical separation between himself and Bosie, not as in the Duchess's case one of social status, but one of age and experience. The intensity of Wilde's love is revealed through an explosion of flower imagery in the letter. His lover is described as *My sweet rose, my delicate flower, my lily of lilies* (lines 3–4). The use of the possessive pronoun *my* suggests not only a sense of ownership but also of responsibility. The idea of claiming a lover as one's possession is echoed in Milton's *Paradise Lost*, as Adam describes Eve as *Part of my soul I seek thee, and thee claim / My other half* (lines 48–9). This echoes the Duchess's description of herself as *a young widow / That claims you for her husband* (lines 17–18). Like Wilde and Webster, Milton defines love in terms of acquisition, but also as a fusing of two halves that come together to create one whole. The Duchess also illustrates this idea when she alludes to losing her heart to Antonio and finding it in his breast.

Webster's presentation of the Duchess can be regarded as a challenge to Renaissance attitudes and values concerning women, and the nature of marriage among dynastically powerful rulers. In a similar way the gender of Wilde's lover confronts Victorian ideas of morality, and the refusal to accept the possibility of sexual love between two men. Wilde begins his letter by acknowledging the danger of his love, but embraces the imminent likelihood of being imprisoned as a *test* of *the power of love* (line 5). In a similar vein of defiance the Duchess replies to Antonio's fears about the retribution of her brothers by dismissing them, insisting that *All discord, without this circumference,/ Is only to be pitied, and not feared* (lines 29–30). Both authors suggest the power of unconditional love to confront any opposition with strength and fortitude.

In his letter Wilde defines his love in terms of spiritual and artistic harmony, asserting that to deny it would have *ruined my art, broken the musical chords which make a perfect soul* (lines 10–11). Similarly Webster uses musical imagery to describe the love between the Duchess and Antonio, as the latter utters his hopes, *may our sweet affections, like the spheres / Be still in motion*, and the Duchess completes his thought in her reply: *Quickening, and make / The like soft music* (lines 42–44). Thus both authors present love as a unifying emotion, one that creates harmony and concord.

Both writers however, acknowledge that love, even if it is of an unconditional nature, is characterized by pain as well as pleasure. Wilde suggests that it is through suffering that love is made stronger, as he asserts: *Pleasure hides love from us but pain reveals it in its essence* (lines 18–19). The image of suffering for love is also presented in an uncompromising manner in the letter of Margery Brews, as she reveals the pain she endures while separated from her loved one. In the first letter she declares: *there wottys no creature what pain that I endure* (line 10).

The Duchess, who speaks of the *misery* and *violent passions* of her love, refuses to acknowledge that she can be made to suffer after her longed-for marriage, and remains firm in her belief that *time will easily / Scatter the tempest* (lines 31–32). She, unlike Wilde, sees no immediate peril and defies even the Church to deny her the right to marry as she chooses. Like Wilde, she revels in the glory of her love and she describes the marriage as a *sacred Gordian*, but the audience are given a hint of all that she faces even as she dismisses its possibility: the *violence* that can *untwine* their bonds of love (lines 40–41). Similarly, Wilde's confidence in his passion entails an unbending faith in the power of love to lessen the *burden* that must be endured (line 30). Ideas about the joys of love and the pain of persecution are brought together in a paradox, the image of himself as *a man who now weeps in hell, and yet carries heaven in his heart* (33–34). A tone of pathos is created throughout the letter, which evokes feelings of compassion in the reader for a man who, like Orlando in *As You Like It*, remains *love-shaked* and *would not be cured*. This is despite the possibility that his lover may not maintain his commitment, an idea hinted at in the repetition and pleading tone that opens the brief second paragraph of Wilde's letter: *Love me always, love me always.*

In contrast, the extract from Webster's play concludes with a sense of future possibility as the couple are seen united and approaching their *marriage bed* (line 56). Despite, or perhaps because of, the Duchess's playful remark that they will *Lay a naked sword between us, keep us chaste* (line 61), there is a sensual link between them. However, Wilde is facing physical separation from his lover, and expresses his passion in the celebration of his love and commitment. This requires a strength that will transcend separation as he asserts, in a final outburst of emotion: *my soul clings to your soul, my life is your life, and in all the worlds of pain and pleasure you are my ideal of admiration and joy.*

Love at first sight

Both George Farquhar in his letter and William Wycherley in *The Country Wife* explore the idea of temptation and love at first sight. Farquhar celebrates the effects of instantly discovered desire, whereas Wycherley considers the dangers such emotions can bring. The idea that love can begin in an instant is explored in many different ways in literature, and as we have seen from Chaucer to the present day the image of Cupid, the winged cherub, wantonly firing his arrows has been adopted by a variety of authors.

Activity

Compare the ways Wycherley and Farquhar present the experience of temptation and love at first sight in their extracts. In your answer you should explore links through form, structure and language as well as themes and ideas, and attempt to make at least three wider reading links, one from drama, one from poetry and the other from prose.

Discussion

The Farquhar letter opens with a subversion of the words attributed to Julius Caesar after a Roman conquest. Rather than echo the idea of being the victor, Farquhar modifies the final term of the triplet to suggest that he is the defeated one: *I came, I saw, and was conquered*. His subjugation is not of course a military one but one in which he has lost his heart, or rather his *soul*. Farquhar alludes to the idea that resonates throughout literature of the union of two souls through love. He ironically and rather humorously asserts that having first seen his love in church he finds that *where others go to save their souls, there have I lost mine* (lines 2–3). This blurring of boundaries between the sacred and the profane is a common technique used by many writers who appropriate sacred and biblical language to describe passionate love.

The idea of losing a part of oneself on falling in love is also seen in the extract from Webster's *The Duchess of Malfi*, when having declared her love for Antonio she asserts: *You have left me heartless: mine is in your bosom,/ I hope 'twill multiply love there* (lines 9–10). The idea of hearts and souls fusing to make one is a common image in the literature of love and it is used to symbolize the unity and harmony that love can create. In a similar vein to the Duchess when she refers to her love creating *soft music* (line 44) like the music of the spheres, Farquhar describes his emotional state as being in *raptures* (line 5), suggesting an ecstasy or euphoria that reverberates with the idea of a religious epiphany.

In contrast, Mrs Pinchwife's experience of temptation and love at first sight in *The Country Wife* is presented as one that creates misery and the consciousness of physical restriction. Wycherley gives her the simile of feeling like a *bird in a cage* (lines 4–5). Unlike Farquhar she does not have the experience or the liberty to celebrate her sudden desire for the *gallant at the play* (lines 51–52) or to enjoy the other temptations of town life. She is confined at home, in keeping with contemporary attitudes and values, at the whim of her husband, who has complete control over her movements. Thus she may, on the one hand, be seen as disempowered, but her robust responses to her husband's commands offer an alternative view.

Debra Gillett as Mrs Pinchwife and Robin Soans as her jealous husband in a Royal Shakespeare Company production of *The Country Wife*

In contrast Anne Oldfield, the addressee of Farquhar's letter, has no voice within the text and the comments at the end of his letter surpass anything that Pinchwife threatens in his attempts to control his wife. Farquhar's sudden, vitriolic attack on the lady, in which he implies she has bewitched him – *you may go to the devil, for I'm sure you're a witch* – alters the tone from one of humility, flattery and elation to a dismissive attitude towards a woman whose only crime is her beauty. Thus both Wycherley and Farquhar reveal the darker side of men's possessive desires, and the cost of their attempts to maintain a powerful and superior position in matters of love.

Farquhar's letter begins, however, in the style of courtly love as, like Arcite and Palamon in Chaucer's *Knight's Tale*, he celebrates the *beauty*, *charm* and *wit* (line 7) of a woman he has never spoken to. Palamon asserts that having seen Emelye roaming in the garden he has been *hurt right now thurghout myn ye* (line 5), just as Farquhar claims that at first sight he has been *conquered* and has to struggle to *talk calmly* (line 6). Chaucer uses hyperbole (exaggeration) and classical allusion in presenting Palamon's love as overwhelming: *I noot wher she be womman or goddesse,/ But Venus is it soothly, as I gesse*, he says (lines 10–11), as he falls to his knees. Similarly Farquhar speaks of his *humility* (line 16) and insists that *not to love you would proclaim me a fool* (line 8). Like Palamon, Farquhar places himself at the mercy of his lover, insisting that her word on his fate, whether he is to *be happy or retire again to my desert* is like a *sentence* that offers either life and possibility or gloom and a metaphorical death (lines 20–22). Thus both Chaucer and Farquhar present love at first sight to be enervating and to some extent incapacitating. Chaucer's style remains within the tradition of courtly love as Palamon worships only from afar, but although Farquhar adopts the style of the courtly lover his approach is more direct, addressing his lover in a forthright letter and seemingly expecting a response.

The expression of love in a courtly style, even in the face of adversity and in the most unconventional circumstances, is also seen in Oscar Wilde's letter to Lord Alfred Douglas. Wilde insists that he is prepared to *accept every outrage through devotion to love*[...] *so long as my soul may always keep the image of you* (lines 14–16). Like Farquhar, he insists that the loss of love would cast him into a spiritual and emotional wilderness. However, the tone of Wilde's letter is more intense and reflects an established relationship, whereas there appears an underlying confidence bordering on arrogance in Farquhar's letter that suggests he does not expect rejection.

The tone of the exchanges in *The Country Wife* is quite different from that of courtly love. Pinchwife's responses to his wife's naively expressed desires to see the man who loves her are peremptory and dismissive. His main concern is to prevent her from making him a cuckold, and Wycherley therefore presents the issue of temptation and the possibility of falling in love through the rather coarse perceptions of a jealous husband. Although Mrs Pinchwife's responses may echo those of Farquhar and to some extent touch on the courtly love tradition as she asserts *I have not been well since you told me there was a gallant at the play in love with me* (lines 50–52) – echoing the traditional idea of love as a sickness – love is seen as a competitive arena in which men jealously guard women as possessions. As the play is a comedy, the more menacing aspects of Pinchwife's controlling behaviour are distanced and the humorous asides prevent the tone becoming as venomous as that which concludes Farquhar's letter. Both Wycherley and Farquhar, however, reveal that although love at first sight may offer the possibility of *raptures* or the innocent desire to gaze on a loved one, in the real world the temptations of love lead to contentious issues and can be a catalyst for cruelty and suffering.

Non-consensual love

Both Aphra Behn's *The Rover* and W.B. Yeats's poem *Leda and the Swan* depict non-consensual love – a male forcing himself upon a female. However, although there is darkness to the scene in Behn's play it is understated, no harm is done and the general tone is one of humour. In contrast, Yeats's poem depicts violence and is sexually explicit; it is characterized by plain diction, rhythmic vigour, and allusions to ancient myths and mystical ideas, such as the relationship of the human and the divine, and cycles of history. It can also be read as a poem about the way a single event is to be understood as part of a larger scheme, since the result of the god's assault on Leda is the birth of Helen of Troy and the subsequent destruction of the Trojan civilization. Given Yeats's background and other writings, it can be read within the context of Ireland's struggle for independence and the metaphorical rape of that country by the English ruling classes.

Activity

Compare the ways Behn and Yeats present non-consensual love in the extract from *The Rover* and in *Leda and the Swan*. In your answer you should explore links through form, structure and language as well as themes and ideas, and attempt to make at least three wider reading links, one from drama, one from poetry and the other from prose.

Discussion

Willmore's first sighting of Florinda in *The Rover* elicits a series of rhetorical questions from him, as if he is using his powers of deduction to ascertain his position with regard to this woman. In his first speech to her he parodies the courtly lover as he begs to be allowed to *salute thy shoe-string* (line 20). This pretence is soon dismissed in favour of a more assertive approach. He refuses to answer her questions, insisting that it is enough that he is in the garden, and follows this almost immediately with the command *Come, come kiss me* (lines 25–26). The boldness of his approach and his shameless arrogance, with which the audience are already familiar, create a humour that distances the audience from the true implications of the situation. Similarly, although Yeats's poem is far more explicit in its opening description of the assault on Leda, the horror of the act is distanced by Yeats's choice of setting (classical mythology) and the fact that the perpetrator is a swan not a man.

Yeats's tone is terse and uncompromising; the poem opens with *A sudden blow* and continues with a description of the swan above the young woman, *the great wings beating still*. This creates a striking image of the bird beating its wings yet remaining *still* as it hovers above the woman. The suddenness of the attack makes it appear to have come upon Leda by chance, just as in *The Rover* Willmore insists that his meeting with Florinda is a matter of *good luck* (line 28). The drunken Willmore describes himself as one who is *a little disguised at present* (lines 33–34), just as the swan is the god Zeus in the guise of a beautiful white bird.

The description of Leda as *the staggering girl* (line 2) illustrates her physical and perhaps psychological state as she struggles under the weight of her assailant. Leda is not given a voice, and her struggle is a physical one in which she is seen to be overpowered by his strong grip and *caught in his bill* (line 3). The image of a trapped and vulnerable young woman is developed through the voice of a narrator who asks *How can those terrified vague fingers push / The feathered glory from her loosening thighs?* (lines 5–6). In contrast, Willmore's approach is at first verbal rather than physical as he taunts Florinda for being coy and insists *thou mayst be free with me* (lines 34–35). The humour of his banter prevents the scene from becoming dark and menacing, unlike *Leda and the Swan* where the physical act of rape is described in simple but shockingly graphic detail. The sestet opens with the image of *A shudder in the loins* and the woman remains silent and helpless. In contrast, Florinda is presented as assertive and challenging; she exclaims *what a filthy beast is this!* (line 37). By describing Willmore as a *beast* she reduces him to the level of a savage animal, whereas Leda has no voice, so the swan maintains its image of *feathered glory*.

The idea of male dominance is also addressed by Milton in *Paradise Lost* as Eve is made to see that although she is more beautiful than Adam, once he has claimed her as *My other half*, she must *yield* and *from that time see / How beauty is excelled by manly grace / And wisdom* (lines 49–52). Unlike Leda, Eve consents to the sexual union but it echoes the defeat of Leda as Eve gives herself to Adam with *meek surrender* (line 55). In contrast, although Florinda's cry *Oh, I am ruined! – Wicked man, unhand me* (line 49) illustrates the imminent possibility of Willmore forcing himself upon her, unlike Leda and Eve she continues an effective resistance, insisting *I'll cry murder, rape, or anything, if you do not instantly let me go* (lines 58–59). Mrs Pinchwife in *The Country Wife* is equally assertive with her over-protective husband, and like Florinda has a determination that enables her to leave the metaphorical cage created by Pinchwife and to exert her will: *Come, pray, bud, let's go abroad before 'tis late – for I will go, that's flat and plain* (lines 100–101). Although not physically threatened, Mrs Pinchwife is nevertheless constrained by a controlling male and, like Florinda, is able to construct a route for escaping this subjugation by verbal means.

Leda, as the vulnerable silent woman, has no opportunity to escape. She is *mastered by the brute blood of the air* (line 12). The plosive alliteration here denotes the violence of the attack, and the verb *mastered* reinforces the idea of complete subjugation to the male will. The narrator asks whether the act of union with a god allows Leda, just for a moment, to experience what it is like to be a god (line 13). However, her empowerment, if any, is only transitory as the poem ends with an image of the young woman being allowed to *drop* to earth in an undignified fashion. The god's cold unconcern for her fate is captured in the image of *the indifferent beak*.

Willmore is similarly unconcerned for Florinda because he wilfully mistakes her for a prostitute who is haggling over her price. Florinda's refusal serves only to anger him rather than to alert him to the true situation, and his response is to become abusive, referring to her as a *baggage* (line 60) and threatening her. A sudden and abusive verbal attack on a desired woman is also seen, surprisingly, in George Farquhar's letter to Anne Oldfield. After declaring his love for her and celebrating her beauty and wit, he concludes with the remark: *If you are not the lady in mourning that sat upon my right hand at church, you may go to the devil, for I'm sure you're a witch.* This seems quite at odds with the overall tone of the letter, but nevertheless it reveals an aggressive attitude towards women – a readiness to categorize them as witches or prostitutes – that also characterizes Willmore in *The Rover*.

Willmore's attempts at mastery are defeated by Florinda's verbal responses and eventually the intervention of her chosen lover. As is appropriate for a comedy, Behn develops the scene only to the point of crisis before any lasting harm is done, so the tone is lightened and the exchange between the characters remains in the realms of farce. In *Leda and the Swan* however, Yeats turns a mythical scene into one of real horror, and the tone and mood are menacing as well as reflecting the far-reaching consequences of the attack on Leda.

Aphra Behn, in a portrait by her contemporary Mary Beale

Lost love

The pain associated with lost love is explored in many different ways in literature, and in the two poems *The Lost Mistress* and *So, We'll Go No More A-Roving* the speakers offer a contrasting view of the loss of love. In *The Lost Mistress*, Browning focuses on the sorrow experienced when lovers part. *So, We'll Go No More A-Roving* is Byron's contemplation of emotional and spiritual fatigue; the speaker seems unable to pursue happiness in love any longer. Both poems are characterized by an ambiguity of tone, and a rhythm that creates powerful effects at odds with the speakers' insistence on their powerlessness: both speakers seem to be accepting defeat by the demands of love.

Activity

Compare the ways Browning and Byron present lost love in these poems. In your answer you should explore links through form, structure and language as well as themes and ideas, and attempt to make at least three wider reading links from poetry.

Discussion

The conversational tone that Byron adopts in the opening line, especially the word *So*, implies an acceptance of the fact that he will *go no more a-roving*. The long 'o' sounds may suggest mourning, reflecting the speaker's weariness and regrets. In line 3 the speaker reflects that his heart is *still as loving*, yet he appears to acknowledge that love is now beyond him. A similar tone is found at the opening of Browning's poem; his use of the conversational term *then* has a similar effect to Byron's *So*. The statement that *All's over* seems unambiguous, but it is slightly undercut by the next word *then*, which seems to call for a response, and by the following rhetorical question: *does truth sound bitter / As one at first believes?*

Like Byron, Browning's speaker conveys the melancholy feeling that remains when passions have receded. The allusions to nature echo the speaker's mood; although the *leaf-buds* suggest the coming of spring, this image of new growth is qualified by the direct address to the loved one, *You know the red turns grey* (line 8). Thus, through an allusion to the natural cycle of life, the speaker acknowledges the transitory nature of relationships. The speaker in Byron's poem, however, suggests his emotional state is at odds with the natural world as he asserts that *the moon* is *still as bright* (line 4). The speaker here offers a contrast between his state of diminished strength and the brightness of the moon, which is a traditional symbol of love.

The effect of the loss of love is also explored by Hardy in his poem *The Going.* In Hardy's poem the final separation is created by death, but it has been preceded by the estrangement of the couple. The feeling of desolation is presented through a first-person perspective, just as in the Browning and Byron poems. Hardy refers, however, to *The yawning blankness* (line 20) of bereavement, an anguished image of loss that differs from the tone of Browning's and Byron's speakers.

The sibilant sound patterning created in the second stanza of Byron's poem, as the speaker asserts *the sword outwears its sheath*, suggests a fragile emotional state while also alluding to physical exhaustion. The *sword* may be read as a phallic symbol suggesting the diminishing of sexual desires or powers, despite *the night* still being *made for loving* (line 9). In *La Belle Dame sans Merci*, Keats also describes the fate of a man who, as a result of the loss of love, is in a state of physical and emotional inertia, *Alone and palely loitering* (line 2). He seems drained of life and is described as being in a *withered* landscape that mirrors his state of mind and body. The knight-at-arms, like Browning's speaker, remains *in thrall* (line 40) to the *Belle Dame*, who has abandoned him *On the cold hill's side* (line 44). The speaker in Browning's poem yearns for his lost love, but unlike Keats's knight-at-arms, he is contemplating the experience of meeting his loved one again, not as lovers but as *Mere friends* (line 11). A sense of resignation to this fate characterizes the latter part of Browning's poem, although in the penultimate stanza the speaker insists that he will keep *in my soul for ever* his lover's *glance* and the sound of her *voice*. The conflicting emotions of these lines suggest an attempt at a pitiful compromise in which the speaker tries to accept the offer of friendship while being excluded as a lover.

In a similar way Byron's poem acknowledges that love is a powerful and irresistible force but not an eternal one, and *the heart must pause to breathe* (line 7). Unlike the speaker in Browning's poem, who clings on to what remains of a past relationship, Byron's speaker acknowledges that he does not have the strength to continue. Matthew Arnold, in his poem *To Marguerite*, similarly laments the fading of passion as he asks *Who order'd that their longing's fire / Should be, as soon as kindled, cool'd?* (lines 19–20). The image of fire counterbalanced by cooling echoes the conclusion of Byron's poem, where the refrain *we'll go no more a-roving* is made more poignant in the romantic *light of the moon*.

Love triangles

From the earliest texts examined here (Chaucer's *Knight's Tale*, for example) the issue of love triangles has been present. Relationships are rarely simple, and partnerships that have begun for romantic reasons (as in *A Room with a View*) or as a business transaction (consider the negotiations described in the Paston letters) or both (as in Jack Absolute's relationship with Lydia in *The Rivals*) can break down if one of the parties is attracted to another person. This is the situation in the extract from A.S. Byatt's novel *Possession*. Dorothy Wordsworth's Journal, however, presents a more unusual love triangle: her beloved brother William Wordsworth is marrying Mary Hutchinson. Dorothy's response to this wedding is far from simple joy at her brother finding romantic happiness. In fact, she appears jealous and depressed about the new relationship. When she accompanies the newlyweds on their honeymoon it suggests the formation of an uncomfortable love triangle.

Activity

Compare the ways Wordsworth and Byatt present love triangles in the extracts from their works. In your answer you should explore links through form, structure and language as well as themes and ideas, and attempt to make wider reading links with prose texts.

Discussion

While Byatt's novel is a work of modern fiction, it is partially set in the Victorian era, which forms the contextual backdrop to the piece. The behaviour and dialogue of the couple in this extract are therefore appropriate to this setting. Dorothy Wordsworth's Journal, however, is not fiction, although it describes a situation that seems somewhat unusual. It is interesting to consider the fact that Wordsworth always intended to share the contents of her Journal with friends and family; it was not merely a private record of her thoughts. Wordsworth is constrained by the social codes of the day and by the fact that marriage relationships are privileged over sibling ones, so that it is expected she should be subordinate to William's new bride in her claims on his love. Her restrained portrayal of her grief on the day of his marriage is all the more touching because of the impossibility of her situation.

The structure of Wordsworth's account moves from her isolation as the wedding ceremony is taking place, through the beginning of the honeymoon as one of a party of three, to her joyous walk with William alone at the end of the extract. When at the very end the pair leave *Mary sitting by the kitchen fire* to go out together, Wordsworth is clearly at her most successful in having *prevailed upon William*.

In the extract from Byatt's novel, the couple are pictured together on a train and begin in strained formality, before discussing in fervent tones how they are to proceed in their relationship. The extract ends with speculation from the perspective of Ash, considering their situation.

The novel makes much use of the couple's dialogue, both to reveal character and to illustrate the tension between them as they attempt to work through the difficulty of their forbidden relationship. The hesitation and fragmentation in Ash's speech as he broaches the delicate subject of whether they are to present themselves as a married couple illustrates his nervousness: *We decided – you decided – to come* (lines 53–54). In Dorothy Wordsworth's Journal there is only one instance of direct speech, when Sara informs her of the imminent arrival of the newlyweds with the brief declarative sentence *They are coming*. This statement has a dramatic effect on her: *This forced me from the bed where I lay, and I moved, I knew not how*[...] *and fell upon his bosom* (lines 11–15).

The extracts differ in their presentation of the wife in the marriage relationship. While Mary is a constant presence in Wordsworth's Journal, neither Ash nor LaMotte refer to Ash's wife, left at home, unaware of the couple's adulterous liaison. Her mere existence is, nevertheless, a critical factor in the couple's behaviour and conversation as they skirt around the difficult question of whether LaMotte wishes to *travel as* Ash's *wife* or be lodged *separately* and respectably elsewhere (lines 55–58). In the extract from Wordsworth's Journal, however, Mary figures from the start. While she is physically approaching as a newly married bride, Wordsworth exclaims *I could stand it no longer, and threw myself on the bed* (lines 9–10), which is a surprising revelation of emotion in what has been to that point a fairly calm, factual account. We should not make too much of the fact that she chooses to absent herself from her brother's marriage ceremony, since wedding customs differed greatly from our own (the actual ceremony was a matter for religious devotion, not family celebration), but we can believe that it would be unendurable for her to watch William marry.

The representation of the outside world in the two texts is interesting. Wordsworth finds consolation in it, especially the natural world. In contrast to the couple in *Possession*, she distracts herself (and fulfils the purpose of her Journal) with details about *sunshine and showers, pleasant talk, love and chearfulness* (lines 21–22). She describes the places they see on their journey and the people they encounter, and her account consequently has a far more expansive atmosphere than the train journey of the lovers in *Possession*.

In Byatt's novel, the reader feels involved in the relationship of the couple within the enclosed space of the train carriage. Once there are *no other passengers* in their carriage, the couple begin to talk (line 32). From this point onwards, there is no mention by the narrator of anything external to the two lovers. The deserted wife is a ghostly presence in the background of their conversation. In the final section of the extract, from line 112, Ash's dream of the woman compared with the reality of her is the only other presence in the carriage.

This idealization of the unattainable woman recalls F. Scott Fitzgerald's novel *The Great Gatsby* (1925), where the young, penniless officer Jay Gatsby falls in love with the rich, beautiful Daisy Fay. Although they seem to agree to marry after the war, when Gatsby does not return with a fortune in order to claim his young bride she marries another rich young man, Tom Buchanan. Gatsby is left with only his 'incorruptible dream' of Daisy for consolation. He dreams of her as 'high in a white palace the king's daughter, the golden girl'. The idealistic language is clearly reminiscent of Ash's fantasies about LaMotte; Byatt even uses the same type of image of a woman on a pedestal: LaMotte is like *a princess in a tower* (lines 115–116). The men in both of these novels are somewhat startled by the reality of these women when they finally engage with them. The reader sees Ash at the end of the extract *observing the ways in which she resembled, or differed from, the woman he dreamed, or reached for in sleep, or would fight for.* In *The Great Gatsby*, when Gatsby finally lures the now-married Daisy to his house, the narrator speculates in a similar vein: 'There must have been moments[…] when Daisy tumbled short of his dreams'.

In her Journal, Wordsworth indulges in no such idealization and there is no dream to be challenged by reality; she describes William as *beloved* (line 14) and his new wife is *my dear Mary* (lines 16–17) or *Poor Mary* (line 18), but there is no room for fanciful description or dreams in this account. Wordsworth allows herself one moment of emotional release, saying *I could stand it no longer, and threw myself on the bed, where I lay in stillness, neither hearing or seeing anything* (lines 9–11). Further than this she does not go.

In the Wordsworths' love triangle, the third party can be escaped from, if only for a time, as shown in the last lines of the extract: *I prevailed upon William to go up with me to the ruins. We left Mary sitting by the kitchen fire.* In *Possession*, the wife is left behind entirely while the couple enjoy their adulterous trip. In Daphne du Maurier's novel *Rebecca* (1938), the unlikely heroine finds it almost impossible to escape the third party in her marriage: the memory of her new husband's dead first wife, after whom the book is named. When the young bride is brought to her husband's family home, she finds the haunting presence of this third party almost as unendurable as Wordsworth seems to find the wedding of her brother. She feels that it is she, the new mistress of the house, who is 'a guest' in the house, and more than this 'an uninvited guest' who cannot measure up to any of the standards set by her predecessor. The novel charts the young bride's gradual unravelling of the mystery of Rebecca's death in order to free herself and her husband from her all-pervasive influence.

In *Rebecca*, at least, the third party is finally banished. In *The Great Gatsby*, it is Gatsby himself (again the 'intruder' in a marriage) who is removed at the end of the text. In *Possession*, Ash returns to his wife but finds that LaMotte is pregnant with his child, so that their love triangle lives on in the person of this illegitimate daughter. The non-fictional love triangle of the Wordsworths was also not easily resolved: Dorothy Wordsworth never married and continued to live with William and Mary. The presentation of all of these different love triangles may be taken as a further illustration that literature will always be interested in the complications and conflicts of love.

Transformative love

The transformative nature of love is an enduring theme of literature. It is explored in a complex manner in both *La Belle Dame sans Merci* and *A Pink Wool Knitted Dress*. In the latter poem Ted Hughes, writing in the late twentieth century, presents a very personal exploration of a kaleidoscope of emotions experienced by the bridegroom during a wedding ceremony, and contemplates the gamble such a commitment involves. In contrast John Keats, writing in the early nineteenth century, looks at the transformative nature of love in terms of its danger and destructiveness; the woman in this poem is seen as a siren who tempts men and then destroys them.

Activity

Compare the ways Keats and Hughes explore the presentation of transformative love in these two poems. In your answer you should explore links through form, structure and language as well as themes and ideas, and attempt to make at least three wider reading links with other poems you have read.

Discussion

Keats opens his poem with an image of a knight-at-arms who is *Alone and palely loitering*, the description suggesting his ghostly pallor and his isolation. He seems to have been almost robbed of life, and he wanders through a desolate wasteland. This sense of a formerly vigorous man who is transformed by the loss of love is also seen in Hardy's poem *The Going*, in which the speaker explores the effect of the death of his estranged wife; like Keats's knight-at-arms, he feels that *All's past amend* (line 36), seeing himself as *but a dead man held on end / To sink down soon* (lines 38–39). Hardy writes in the first person, but the description of the knight-at-arms at the beginning of Keats's poem is offered by an unknown speaker addressing him in the second person. From stanza 4 the knight-at-arms speaks in the first person, telling his story, and by the end echoing the descriptive terms used of him at the beginning of the poem.

In *The Going*, the speaker seems fully conscious of his suffering and the *yawning blankness* he faces (line 20). *The Going* begins with a demand to know why the speaker has been left alone, and its opening tone is one of complaint, but the imagery in *La Belle Dame sans Merci* creates a haunting and ominous effect. The anonymous speaker highlights the signs of anxiety in the knight-at-arms' demeanour and the landscape seems to reflect his emotional state: *The sedge has withered from the lake,/ And no birds sing* (lines 3–4). Similarly the landscape of Elizabeth Jennings's poem *In a Garden* is transformed in the eyes of a woman who describes herself as *lost* now that *the gardener has gone*. The narrator sees her familiar world transformed into something that suggests a kind of menace: *Even the beech tree from next door which shares / Its shadow with me, seemed a kind of threat* (lines 9–10). As in the case of Keats's knight-at-arms, the external landscape reflects the protagonist's mindscape, as the woman feels *Mocked by the smell of a mown lawn* (line 13).

In *La Belle Dame sans Merci*, not until the fourth stanza does the explanation begin as to what may have caused the knight-at-arms' transformation to this ghostly spectre. The reader embarks on a journey along with the questioner to learn about the lady the knight encountered. In contrast, Ted Hughes focuses immediately upon his bride at the beginning of *A Pink Wool Knitted Dress*; her unconventional dress as she stands *at the altar* and the reference to James Joyce in the word *Bloomsday* (line 3) both suggest a transformative blossoming. However, as in Keats's poem there is a shadow looming from second line of the poem, as Hughes comments that this moment of hope and possibility occurred *Before anything had smudged anything*. There is also a similar use of the pathetic fallacy in Hughes's poem, as he opens the second stanza with the simple word *Rain*, which is separated from the rest of the line by a dash and creates a similar effect to that created by Keats's fourth line *And no birds sing*.

John Keats, in a portrait by his friend Joseph Severn, 1819

The transformation of the knight-at-arms is revealed in stanza 4 to have resulted from his meeting *a lady in the meads*, who from the outset is associated with the supernatural, being *a faery's child* who has *wild* eyes. She speaks *in language strange* (line 27). The exotic foods she offers to the knight cast her in the role of temptress, and this is compounded by the use of the word *lullèd* to describe her effect on the knight's state of consciousness (line 33). She draws him into a dreamlike state and he is no longer in control but is transformed into man in *thrall* (line 40).

The haunting, ominous effect is aided by Keats's use of the formal features of traditional ballads. The effect of frequent reiteration is created not simply by repeating words but also by alliteration and assonance, as in *Her hair was long, her foot was light* (line 15) and *made sweet moan* (line 20). Keats slightly alters the traditional ballad form, which has eight syllables with four stresses in the first and third lines, and six syllables with three stresses in the second and fourth lines of each stanza. Keats shortens the last line of each of his stanzas to two stresses and usually four syllables, creating the effect of the stanza being abruptly ended, or of something being absent, or information being withheld. Thus the knight-at-arms' story seems to open up more questions than it answers. It is of course a one-sided account, as we never directly hear the voice of the *Belle Dame*.

Similarly, Hughes's poem offers us only a male voice and one perspective on the occasion of his marriage. Interestingly however, and in contrast to Keats's poem, the mood and tone change at the end of the poem. In the early lines the poem focuses on the speaker and the complexity of the emotions he experiences leading up to the moment of commitment. However, the images of his shabby clothing, of marriage being a *gamble* (line 26) and a state into which he is *squeezed* (line 24) are replaced by an altered perception in the declaration *You were transfigured* (line 39). The description of the bride as *So slender and new and naked* (line 40) suggests her vulnerability.

This sense of vulnerability to pain in love is echoed in the poem *Song* by Aphra Behn, which offers a female voice. The speaker laments the *tyrannic power* (line 4) of love when it is unrequited. She asserts that love, which in this poem is personified as Cupid, has filled her with *desires / Enough to undo the amorous world* (lines 7–8). Thus, like the bride in Hughes's poem she is vulnerable and full of *sighs and tears* (line 9).

The future of the couple in Hughes's poem hangs in the balance between pain and fulfilment, in the game of *dice* which, the last line suggests, their marriage really is. After the transformative moment signalled by the caesura in line 39, the language in Hughes's poem explodes with emotion and there is a sense of the glory of the *spellbound future* that she offers to him (line 47). Like the knight-at-arms, the speaker describes himself as *subjected* (line 46) to this vision of love's fulfilment, but rather than seeing before him an empty and cold landscape, Hughes's speaker sees his new wife *Brimming with God* (line 43); complex sensations are described with visionary splendour. The intensity of this transformation is compounded by the image of his wife *Wrestling to contain* her *flames*. Her *eye-pupils* are *truly like big jewels / Shaken in a dice-cup and held up to me* (lines 50–54). Passion is conjured up through the image of the *flames* but the image of gambling is prominent, and there is still an overwhelming sense of her vulnerability as the bride's eyes are full of *tear-flames* (line 53).

Passionate love

Passionate love has long been a favourite topic for writing in all genres. The extracts from *Far From the Madding Crowd* and *A Room with a View* demonstrate the novel's long-standing interest in the subject. Thomas Hardy's late-Victorian text illustrates the ways in which writers can use natural settings, symbols and allusions to suggest sexual passions that their society does not discuss openly. E.M. Forster is writing in the Edwardian period and addressing the social tensions of his day, using the character of the chaperone Charlotte Bartlett to represent the restrictions placed upon young love by society, as well as drawing on the natural world and symbolic associations.

Activity

Compare the ways Hardy and Forster explore the presentation of passionate love in these extracts from their novels. In your answer you should explore links through form, structure and language as well as themes and ideas, and attempt to make wider reading links with other prose texts.

Discussion

Both extracts are from novels that explore the writers' ideas about love. The scope of the novel form enables writers to create detailed stories and complex portrayals of relationships. Unlike drama, the novel also allows for authorial commentary and vivid descriptions in a narrator's voice.

The settings of the extracts invite comparison. In *Far From the Madding Crowd*, Hardy's scene of flirtatious sword-play is in a chapter called 'The Hollow Amid the Ferns', and the setting suggests that nature itself is creating a perfect romantic setting for love. The shape suggested by the hollow sounds accommodating and inviting, as though nature is providing a secluded, pastoral idyll for the meeting of Bathsheba and Troy. Similarly, in *A Room with a View* Forster's beautiful Italian setting with its fertile *rivulets* of violets, which are said to be *irrigating the hillside* (lines 64–65), is the perfect background for a romantic first kiss. In his novel *Jude the Obscure*, Hardy also uses a natural setting that seems conducive to romance when he places Jude and Arabella 'in absolute solitude[...] Nobody could be nearer than a mile to them without their seeing him'. In all three texts, the writers depict natural environments that lend themselves to romance and the expression of emotion. Each has the apparently magical combination of natural beauty and privacy.

Natural settings are also used in symbolic ways. In *A Room with a View*, the symbolic associations of water are used to suggest fertility. Although no water is present, the violets are described as forming *rivulets and streams and cataracts*. In *Far From the Madding Crowd*, Hardy invokes beautiful natural phenomena involving lights in the sky when he describes Troy's display of swordsmanship as creating an *aurora militaris* (line 53) in Bathsheba's eyes, *resembling a sky-full of meteors close at hand* (lines 40–41). Interestingly, the references to water in this extract come in the form of a *liquid stream* of tears (line 135) as Bathsheba is overcome with emotion and guilt at the touch of Troy's lips; here, water is linked to a biblical story of Moses and suggests repentance rather than fertility.

Both writers also use symbols to represent the vivacity and passion of their characters. Troy's sword is described as a living thing, *quick as electricity, darting* and *emerging*[...] *having apparently passed through her body* (lines 9–16). Troy's swordsmanship allows him, metaphorically, to give Bathsheba dangerous caresses, as the sword becomes an extension of his own body. Hardy also uses the image of a caterpillar, which has *chosen the front of her bodice as his resting place* (lines 78–79) to suggest a serpent-like threat within the idyllic setting of the hollow. The caterpillar is soon *spitted* upon the point of Troy's sword, possibly suggesting his violent dispatch of any male who might offer competition to his passionate pursuit of Bathsheba. Interestingly, Hardy also uses a caterpillar in the description of Jude and Arabella on a hillside in *Jude the Obscure*, as Arabella tantalizes Jude by claiming to see a caterpillar 'of the most loveliest green and yellow you ever came across!' in an attempt to coax him closer to her.

In the extracts from both Hardy's and Forster's texts, however, the kiss is narrated in straightforward terms. Forster states simply that George *stepped quickly forward and kissed her* (lines 78–79). In Hardy's text, the statement is even briefer, and in a past perfect tense that indicates the fleeting moment has passed before it can even be perceived: *He had kissed her* (line 138). The simplicity of these statements works through juxtaposition with the vivid imagery of setting and events that has preceded them, creating a stylistic counterpoint.

The structure of Hardy's prose is interesting here as he creates mystery through narrating events in reverse order: the reader learns of *the blood beating into her face* (lines 130–131) and Bathsheba's tears before the cause of her discomfort is revealed, allowing the chapter to end on the revelation that *He had kissed her*. The extract from *A Room with a View* also uses an interesting structure for the moment of the kiss. Forster has narrated in detail the means by which Lucy is led to George by the apparently mistaken driver, and has vividly described the beauty of the scene, then writes a single, brief sentence to describe the kiss itself; but instead of choosing to end the chapter here, as Hardy does, Forster brings in the image of the chaperone, *Miss Bartlett, who stood brown against the view*. In this way, Forster reminds the reader of the social restrictions upon Lucy and the forbidden nature of the kiss. Although Bathsheba is mistress of her own fate in *Far From the Madding Crowd*, the fact that Hardy chooses to end the chapter with her in tears suggests that she too is aware that her behaviour is bound by the rules of a society that would disapprove of her being alone with the young soldier, let alone allowing him to kiss her. The tears could also represent her distress at her own loss of control.

Unsurprisingly, in both texts it is the male who is portrayed as the active party in approaching the young women. George sees the suddenly arriving Lucy *as one who had fallen out of heaven* (lines 75–76) and is powerless to resist her beauty. Bathsheba is apparently unaware of Troy's intentions until it is too late to prevent the kiss from taking place. Both women are distressed by the kisses. Conversely, in the incident from *Jude the Obscure* quoted earlier, it is Arabella who is presented as attempting to initiate the kiss, pulling Jude 'down beside her', apparently to see a caterpillar, but really to initiate a romantic moment of her own.

All three of the couples under discussion here marry – Bathsheba and Troy, Lucy and George, and Arabella and Jude – but it is only Lucy and George who manage to create a happy and lasting marriage. Jane Austen also appears to warn of the dangers of following the impulses of passion and marrying in haste in her description of the ill-fated romance of Lydia and Wickham in *Pride and Prejudice* (1813). Lydia, carried away by passion and frivolous ideas of romance, elopes with the untrustworthy Wickham, to the detriment of her family's reputation and her sisters' chances of marriage. Hardy could also be seen as warning of the dangers of passionate love here, in the painful relationship that Bathsheba and Troy have unwittingly embarked upon; Forster, however, shows the value of passion when set against the sterility of social restrictions symbolized by Miss Bartlett, *brown against the view*.

Love and the human condition

As times have changed, the ways in which love is represented in literature have moved on. What is interesting about the poems *To Marguerite* by Matthew Arnold and *In a Garden* by Elizabeth Jennings is the way that both represent the changing worlds the poets inhabit. They both reflect upon the human condition and what it means to love in an uncertain world. Arnold wrote in Victorian times, an era of arguably unparalleled changes to the British landscape and customs; the way of life we experience in Britain today was emerging. Jennings wrote at the end of the twentieth century, yet the images she invokes seem to refer back to earlier eras, even biblical times, in a nostalgic and melancholy fashion. Arnold's use of the natural world is more challenging, stark and uncompromising. Both poets use the landscape, both literal and metaphorical, to reflect on the nature of love and the human condition.

Activity

Compare the ways *To Marguerite* and *In a Garden* present love and explore the human condition. In your answer you should discuss links through form, structure and language as well as themes and ideas, and attempt to make wider reading links with other poems.

Discussion

Jennings adopts a classical sonnet form, often used to explore the subject of love. Arnold's poem explores its ideas over four sestets (stanzas of six lines each). *To Marguerite* is part of a longer work entitled *Isolation*. Interestingly, both poets choose regular verse forms and rhyme schemes, which could be said to constrain and restrict, in order to explore their ideas about love and loneliness. Both poets present a series of ideas that seem to reflect the very constraints of the forms chosen.

Jennings sets her poem, as the title indicates, *In a Garden*. The use of the indefinite article suggests that this could be any garden, especially a symbolic pastoral landscape such as the Garden of Eden. Indeed, Jennings foregrounds this idea in line 3, where the garden is described as *a metaphor of Eden*. The *gardener* can be read in this interpretation as either God or a lover, with the image of the garden suggesting that love is something that must be tended gently, not fiercely controlled. Love goes wrong, the poem seems to suggest, when *Everything* is *too neat* and *someone cares / In the wrong way* (lines 11–12). The enjambment across stanzas here allows the phrase *someone cares* to sound momentarily hopeful, but with the closure of the sentence in the following stanza, the reader is left in no doubt as to the symbolic significance of the *mown lawn* that *Mocked* the poet: it seems to represent the gardener's regulation of their love, and his lack of respect for the more free-spirited wishes of his partner.

Arnold uses a similarly symbolic setting, beginning with the metaphor of the *sea of life*, and uses images of *islands* in this sea to evoke the essential isolation of modern life. Pastoral images in the second stanza, with its *glens* and *nightingales*, momentarily suggest a more hopeful mood in their nostalgic hints of a past life of rural harmony. Such images are quickly superseded, however, in the third stanza, as the reader is reminded that all this is just a sad echo of a time when human beings were *Parts of a single continent* as opposed to the modern *enisled* condition described in line 1. In today's world, *We mortal millions live alone* (line 4).

The mode of address in the poems forms an interesting point of comparison. Jennings adopts a first-person viewpoint to discuss feelings of loss and confusion: *I still felt lost and wonder why* (line 8). This personal and intimate approach leads the reader to wonder what was *the bad/ Choice* that the speaker made or avoided (lines 7–8), and who, exactly, *the gardener* is. Arnold begins his poem with a positive-sounding *Yes*, which leads the reader to expect a personal discussion, as does the collective pronoun *We* in line 4. However, as the poem progresses it adopts a more detached philosophical tone as the speaker explores human loneliness and speculates on the actions of a cruel God.

One might contrast this with the beautifully direct and personal effect produced by Browning in *The Lost Mistress*, where he asks direct questions of the addressee: *Tomorrow we meet the same then, dearest?/ May I take your hand in mine?* (lines 9–10). Browning was known for creating vivid narrative personas, writing in the voices of a wide cast of characters, including murderous lovers in dramatic monologues such as *My Last Duchess* and *Porphyria's Lover*.

Both Arnold and Jennings consider the role of God, or faith. Jennings describes her gardener as *Quietly godlike*, adding intriguingly that *he had / Not made me promise anything* (lines 5–6), presumably unlike God in the Garden of Eden (see Notes page 165). The lack of a promise or commitment in love is reflected in the fact that as the poem begins, *the gardener has gone*. Lack of commitment and faith in love, as in religion, seems to be punished in this reading. The poet's *Sickness for Eden* in the final line can be read as a desire for the return of her lover.

Arnold's God is very different. The speaker of *To Marguerite* holds his God responsible for the isolated condition in which he argues that the *mortal millions* are trapped: *A God, a God their severance ruled!* (line 22). The emphatic repetition sounds embittered and angry, very different from Jennings's quiet melancholy. The last words of Arnold's poem protest that an *estranging sea* surrounds every human being and has been deliberately placed there by God. The rage behind his protest is reminiscent of the anger of the poet William Blake. Writing over 50 years earlier, Blake protests at the role of the Church in placing limitations upon love, in his poem *The Garden of Love*. Here Blake describes the intrusion of organized religion into natural love: 'A chapel was built in the midst,/ Where I used to play on the green'. Blake is angry about the role of the Church in inhibiting love, quoting 'Thou shalt not' as the distorting message the Church gives in the name of God, 'And priests in black gowns were walking their rounds,/ And binding with briars my joys and desires'.

It is interesting that these presentations of God and his role in human love are so very different: Arnold, like Blake, appears to feel only the harm caused by restrictive beliefs and practices, whereas Jennings seems to characterize religious commitment (represented by the *promise*) as a positive force. As always, the context of these pieces should be taken into account when considering the differences: the more secular society inhabited by Jennings allows its inhabitants to choose whether to adhere to the *promises* of religion (and love) or not. In Arnold's Victorian society, religious faith was becoming less all-encompassing, but such freedom of choice was not always possible. In the increasingly urban, industrial society, the *longing like despair* that Arnold articulates in stanza 3 sounds hopeless. It is interesting that Jennings, too, ends on a note of longing, in her case for a past that cannot be regained: *Sickness for Eden was so strong*.

Writing about the literature of love

This section has worked through 16 pairings of texts. It would be a useful exercise for you to decide which texts are suitable for comparison with the remaining poem, *The Sun Rising* by John Donne.

Activity

Look back at the Notes on *The Sun Rising* (pages 108–111) and remind yourself of this poem. How does Donne present love here? You should consider the methods and techniques used to present love in the poem, as well as the type of love it portrays.

Discussion

You might describe the love in this poem as passionate love, or transformative love. You might have thought of some of the following features of Donne's presentation:
- personification of the sun
- an involved first-person narrator
- a direct, conversational style

- a setting in a personal, enclosed space contrasting with the geographical scope of the poem
- use of rhetorical questions
- use of imperatives
- the contraction of space at the end of the poem
- use of an apparently logical argument.

Activity

Now consider which of the other texts you have read in this book might usefully be compared with *The Sun Rising*. List these, along with their possible connections to the poem.

Discussion

You might have thought of some of the following:
- *The Knight's Tale* (passionate love)
- *The Wife of Bath's Tale* (sexual love)
- *The Fair Singer* (Metaphysical conceits about love)
- *La Belle Dame sans Merci* (transformative love)
- Shelley's poem *To...* (re-defining love)
- *Far From the Madding Crowd* (passionate love)
- *A Room with a View* (passionate love)
- *The Going* (the linking of conversational style to depth of feeling)

Finally, choose which of these texts you would like to write about in connection with *The Sun Rising* and create your own question based on the models in this book. Write your answer, remembering to use a comparative structure. The following advice may help you.
- Re-read the texts carefully, and plan your answer before beginning to write.
- Try to compare and contrast in each paragraph.
- Use only relevant wider reading material, and offer quotations. Make it clear where the quotations come from.
- Offer alternative readings and consider different possible interpretations.

- Carefully link your theme to the passages you are considering.
- Make sure all of your comments are relevant to your question.
- Check your work carefully.

Form and structure

When writing about extracts you need to comment on form and structure as well as language (see page 235), and to have an awareness of how styles have changed through the ages. You will therefore need to be clear about the literary techniques connected with form and structure that are used in the particular genre you are discussing, and to consider their effect on the way ideas are presented.

Prose forms

The novel is the most common form of modern extended prose fiction. The novel's history is a fairly short one: in the form that we now recognize, novels began to appear in the eighteenth century. **Epistolary** novels take the form of letters sent between characters. Early novels such as *Pamela* by Samuel Richardson were composed in this form. **Picaresque** novels depict the colourful life and times of a rake or rogue and his (or occasionally her) misadventures. **Bildungsroman** is a German term for a novel that describes a coming-of-age story, the formative years of a person growing up and learning about life. **Magical realism** is a modern genre of the novel where elements of the supernatural are blended with the realistic to create surprising effects.

A **novella** is a piece of prose fiction shorter than a novel, but longer than a **short story**. John Steinbeck's *Of Mice and Men* is a famous example of a novella. Some critics argue that this has more ancient roots than the full novel, in the form of serialized works such as Boccaccio's *Decameron* (1353).

Forms of non-fiction prose include letters, essays and journalism. **Autobiography** and **biography** are also prose non-fiction. These texts describe the life of a person; if written by the person who is the subject, they are called autobiography; if written by someone else, they are biography. An autobiography is sometimes referred to as a **memoir**. Novels, of course, may be in the form of fictionalized autobiographies and biographies.

Prose structure

Some elements to consider when writing about the structure of prose are as follows.

- **Use of time**. Consider how the prose is sequenced and whether it has a chronological narrative line or whether time is fragmented. Are events narrated in a linear or a cyclical way?
- **Foreshadowing**. Does the writer include hints of future events at any point in the text?
- **Ellipsis**. Consider whether the text leaves out anything, as small as sentences or as large as whole events, in order to create tension or mystery.
- **Denouement**. Consider where in the text the conclusion of the story takes place. The denouement refers to the way in which the events of the text are concluded.
- **Pivotal moment or turning point**. What is the crucial or significant event in a text around which the events may be said to revolve? Consider where it is positioned in the text and its effect.
- **Repetition / patterning**. Notice the positioning of repeated patterns, events or motifs in texts and the interesting effects that can be created.
- **Contrast / antithesis**. These can be used to build patterns and emphasize themes.
- **Juxtaposition / paralleling**. Placing events or characters close to one another in an unexpected way can produce particular effects.

Activity

Consider the ways in which Margery Brews structures the first Paston letter on page 20.

Discussion

This is one of a series of letters exchanged between Brews and John Paston. Brews opens her letter with the formalities expected at the time. Her particularly rhetorical style in the opening paragraph can also be attributed to the nature of the letter as a Valentine greeting. The second paragraph begins to introduce her concerns and the purpose of the letter as she tells Paston that she will not be well until she hears from him. The inclusion of two sections of her own verse (if that is what they are – see Notes page 91) breaks up the text and, of course, draws attention to the strength of her feelings. The content of these lines creates the climactic moments of the letter. The piece ends with the writer imploring the recipient to maintain secrecy, and Brews signs off in a traditional yet personalized style.

Dramatic form

Some of the basic forms that drama has traditionally taken are discussed below.

Morality plays developed in the late fourteenth century, out of the **mystery plays** of the Middle Ages, which had dramatized Bible stories. Morality plays flourished to the end of the sixteenth century. The characters were personifications of good and evil qualities, and were usually involved in a struggle for the protagonist's soul. The best-known English morality play is *Everyman*. One of the most famous of plays that are contemporary with Shakespeare has many elements of a morality play: Christopher Marlowe's *Dr Faustus*.

Tragedy is a form of drama that has a specific tradition with its roots in ancient Greek theatre. It has been adapted through the ages to explore the anguish and struggle of humankind. It depicts individual and collective human suffering of many kinds, and creates pathos and possibly catharsis (a purging of the emotions) for the audience. Tragedy can take many forms, for example revenge tragedy or domestic tragedy.

Like tragedy, **comedy** also has its roots in ancient Greek drama, and can be defined as a dramatic work that is light and humorous or satirical in tone, and usually has a happy resolution.

Melodrama exaggerates the plot and characters in order to arouse a variety of emotions in the audience. It originated in dramas of the eighteenth and nineteenth centuries in which orchestral music and song were often used to accompany the action.

There was a general movement in the nineteenth century towards reflecting 'real life' more accurately, and this is known as **realistic** or **naturalistic drama**. It portrays characters in realistic settings, using language that approaches everyday speech.

Postmodern drama developed in the twentieth century as a reaction against the claims of naturalistic drama to present 'the truth'. It raises questions rather than providing answers, and audiences are encouraged to reach their own individual conclusions.

It is important to remember that playwrights will often use the features of a variety of forms within one text; for example, Shakespeare's tragedies usually include comic scenes.

Dramatic structure

A comedy will usually begin with an issue, dilemma or problem to be solved; this often involves lovers facing difficulties in pursuing their relationship. The events of the play will usually complicate that initial problem, and the ending will resolve all the complexities in a satisfying way. Comedies often end with a marriage.

Tragedy will generally begin with the hero (or anti-hero) in a position of prosperity or strength. He will be shown making a tragic mistake or revealing a tragic flaw in his character, which causes him to come to ruin. The structure of the play will depict the gradual destruction of not just the hero but those around him who are affected by his mistake. The play will often end with the death of the hero, and others closely connected with him.

Certain techniques are commonly used to allow dramatic characters to express their thoughts and feelings to the audience.

A **monologue** is a substantial speech by a single character, most often to express thoughts aloud, to another character or the audience. From Renaissance theatre onwards, monologues have generally focused on characters revealing aspects of their personality using extended speech. Postmodern theatre often uses the monologue to challenge the boundaries of character portrayal. **Narrative monologues** simply involve a character telling a story or relating facts, and are usually in the past tense.

Soliloquies are similar to monologues, but whereas a monologue is addressed to other people, in a soliloquy the speaker is always talking to himself or herself, as if we are able to hear the character's private thoughts.

Playwrights may also use particular devices linked to the structure of their drama, such as **foreshadowing**, when there are hints as to how events are to develop over the course of the play. In comedy, in particular, **anti-climax** may be used, where there is a build-up to a particular event only for its importance to be downplayed or for it to be unexpectedly deflated, often in a humorous fashion.

Authors often use structural devices to heighten the impact of their main character, for example by beginning the play with other characters discussing the protagonist before the audience has seen him or her. Sometimes the juxtaposition of characters whose personalities or interests directly oppose one another can give structure to a play.

In classical tragedy, ironic reversal (or **peripeteia**) is often used as part of the structure; a character of high status is humbled in a striking way, as happens to Lear and Edgar in *King Lear*, and other characters gain power.

Another component of classical tragedy is **anagnorisis**, or recognition, when a character realizes the enormity or gravity of his or her actions, or finally sees a truth to which he or she has been blind. Othello, for example, does not realize that he has been duped by Iago until Emilia reveals that it was she who stole the handkerchief upon which such a burden of proof had been placed.

See also the features discussed under 'Prose structure' on page 229, as many of these may be relevant to drama.

Poetic form

A poem's form includes its rhythm, its rhyme scheme and stanza structure (if any). When discussing rhyme schemes, it is important to consider the effect they have. For example, rhyming words may gain emphasis, or may link ideas together in an unexpected way. Similarly, the poet uses stanzas of particular lengths for a purpose; they may be regular or irregular, creating particular effects, and the breaks between them may be significant.

Poetry is an ancient art form, and over the centuries particular forms have acquired traditional names and associations. They include the following.

- **Elegy**: a mournful poem, traditionally written in couplets, that commemorates a person who has died.
- **Ballad**: a narrative poem (one that tells a story), often written in quatrains (four-line stanzas).
- **Sonnet**: traditionally a 14-line poem with a regular rhythm and rhyme scheme. It often, but not always, has love as its subject matter.
- **Epic**: a lengthy narrative poem, often relating heroic deeds.
- **Ode**: a poem expressing personal feelings in praise of, or in dedication to, a person or idea.

Activity

How does Elizabeth Jennings use form in her poem *In a Garden*?

Discussion

Jennings uses a regular sonnet form (two quatrains and two triplets), which could suggest that her poem may be about love, although the word does not appear in the text. The first quatrain introduces the setting and the main 'characters' of the poem – *the gardener* and the narrator. A neat coupling is suggested by the poem's regular rhyme scheme in the quatrains, where each line rhymes alternately.

This rhyme scheme continues in the triplets, where it tends to place an emphasis on the final word of each line, with its strong masculine rhyme (a masculine rhyme is one with a single or stressed syllable – here, for example, *long* and *strong*).

The poem uses enjambment across the first and second quatrains, perhaps suggesting a sense of uncertainty. The second quatrain is end-stopped as the poet changes tone and focus with the beginning of the triplets. Enjambment is used to particularly striking effect in the division between the triplets. At the end of the first triplet is the statement *and someone cares*, but this is modified by the completion of the phrase in the final stanza: *In the wrong way*. Thus the hopeful tone of the first triplet is dashed by the second. The symbolic references to the gardener, Eden and God build to create a pattern, gathering significance as the poem progresses. The sonnet form binds these symbolic references together to suggest that the overall topic of the poem is the love of humans and of God.

The poet Elizabeth Jennings, who died in 2001

Poetic structure

The techniques discussed under 'Prose structure' on page 229 are also relevant to poetry. Other features to look at when considering structure in poetry include a **key image**; the positioning of a particular image may emphasize its significance in the poem. **Setting** is often used symbolically in poetry to create particular moods or atmospheres.

The structure of the poem may be **linear** (working logically or chronologically towards an ending) or **cyclical** (returning to where it began, perhaps by repetition of phrases or lines) or even a combination of the two.

A poem may sometimes have a noticeable turning point or **volte** where it changes its direction or focus. In a sonnet, this often occurs after the octave (first eight lines).

Language

When studying and comparing extracts such as those in this book, you need to consider the writers' specific choices of language and how these help to communicate the ideas and feelings that concern the writer.

The language of prose

Some literary techniques and issues to consider when discussing the language of prose are listed below.

- **Metaphorical language**: the use of similes and metaphors in order to create comparisons and vivid descriptions.
- **Personification**: giving human qualities to ideas or inanimate objects.
- **Pathetic fallacy**: description of particular types of weather or natural phenomena to represent particular moods.
- **Dialogue**: the use of direct (quoted) or indirect (reported) speech, or free indirect speech (where the writer adopts the

perspective of a particular character to render his or her ideas, while remaining in third-person narrative mode).

- **Symbolism**: the choice of motifs; or the use of certain ideas, objects or actions as symbols to represent something else of special significance (for example, the association of water with fertility in the extract from *A Room with a View*).
- **Tone**: the mood or atmosphere of the piece.
- **Sentence type**: the variety of sentence types and structures.
- **Repetition / patterning**: repeating particular words, phrases or ideas to create patterns of significance.
- **Narrator**: choice of a narrator who is involved or detached, uses the first person or the third person, who is omniscient (all-knowing) or not, reliable or unreliable. For example, the narrator in *A Room with a View* is an omniscient, third-person narrator who consistently presents events from Lucy's perspective.
- **Puns / wordplay / innuendo**: playing on words to create humour or other effects.
- **Tense**: use of past or present tense.

Poetic language

Many of the techniques described above are relevant to poetic language. The following terms may also be useful when considering the language of a poem.

- **Conceit**: a far-fetched idea or comparison, commonly used in Metaphysical poetry (for example, Marvell's comparison of *The Fair Singer*'s curls to *trammels* or shackles, see Notes page 114).
- **Assonance**: the repetition of vowel sounds to create internal rhymes.
- **Consonance**: the repetition of consonant sounds (called **alliteration** if it occurs at the beginnings of words), which may have particular effects. For examples the plosive sounds 'p' and 'b' often create an angry or agitated effect.

- **Onomatopoeia**: the creation of sound effects by using words that make the sound they describe.
- **Synaesthesia**: the description of one kind of sensation or experience in terms normally associated with another of the senses.
- **Hyperbole**: literary overstatement or exaggeration.
- **Oxymoron**: the positioning of two words with opposite connotations close to each other (for example, *so sweet an enemy* in Marvell's *The Fair Singer*).

Dramatic language

The language of drama varies from the most grave and formal blank verse of tragedy to the songs and bawdy jokes of comedy. While the speech of many of the characters in drama is in prose, the earliest tragedies were written in poetic form and Shakespeare and his contemporaries used blank verse to heighten their dramatic effects. Blank verse is unrhymed poetry of approximately ten syllables per line, with five beats per line. This verse is not only given to noble or heroic characters, but is also often spoken by lower-status characters (such as Caliban, the monster in *The Tempest*) and can convey the complexity of characters and the themes of the play.

Songs have also formed an important part of the language of drama from earliest times. Shakespeare makes extensive use of songs in plays such as *Twelfth Night*, where they form an integral part of the narrative and comment on the choices of the characters.

The language of drama does not solely comprise the words spoken by the characters, however: stage directions are also important, particularly in modern drama. Although the language of stage directions is not spoken onstage, it communicates to the director and audience and can have a transforming effect on the way in which the drama is received. Modern tragedies especially, such as the ones by the American playwrights Tennessee Williams and Arthur Miller, make use of lengthy stage directions to ensure that directors create the mood, atmosphere and actions they intend for their plays.

Activity

Consider the variety of language used by Shakespeare in the extract from *The Tempest* on page 30.

Discussion

The speeches in the extract are in blank verse, as appears fitting for an episode of high drama where two noble characters (Ferdinand and Miranda) meet and fall in love. Their language is full of exclamations of wonder and surprise. Another interesting feature of their language is the way they complete each other's lines of blank verse, suggesting a closeness and affinity that makes them well-matched partners.

When Prospero speaks to Ferdinand it is in a stern and challenging manner, and the cadence of the verse gives weight to his speech. Shakespeare also makes much use of asides here, to create dramatic irony as the audience becomes aware of Prospero's manipulations but the young couple do not.

Before the meeting, Ariel sings an eerily beautiful song about the supposed drowning of Ferdinand's father. The song contributes to the sense of the mystery and wonder of Prospero's island.

Reading the literature of love

Having studied the extracts in this book by considering a variety of interpretations and applying comparative methods, you should now have some detailed ideas about the literature of love and an awareness of how representations of love have altered through time. Clearly from Chaucer to the present day questions about love, passion, marriage and relationships have inspired the greatest writers to explore this fundamental human quality – a quality that is perhaps the hardest to define or to control. The poems and extracts in this book are designed to offer you a taste of the literature of love, and it is hoped that this collection will act as a catalyst to your own reading as you explore writing about love and all its complications throughout the ages.

Essay Questions

1   Focusing on the extracts from *The Wife of Bath's Tale* and *As You Like It*, write a comparison of the ways the writers present women in love. You should consider:
    - the ways in which the writers' choices of form, structure and language shape these extracts
    - how your wider reading in the literature of love has contributed to your understanding and interpretation of the extracts.

2   Look again at the Paston letters and Oscar Wilde's letter to Lord Alfred Douglas. Basing your answer on the letters and, where appropriate, your wider reading on love, compare the ways in which the two writers have used form, structure and language to express their thoughts and ideas.

3   Focusing on *So, We'll Go No More A-Roving* and the extract from *King Lear*, write a comparison of the ways the writers present the end of relationships. You should consider:
    - the ways in which the writers' choices of form, structure and language shape these extracts
    - how your wider reading in the literature of love has contributed to your understanding and interpretation of the extracts.

4   Focusing on *La Belle Dame sans Merci* and the extract from *The Tempest*, write a comparison of the ways the writers present the first meetings of lovers. You should consider:
    - the ways in which the writers' choices of form, structure and language shape these extracts
    - how your wider reading in the literature of love has contributed to your understanding and interpretation of the extracts.

5   Focusing on *The Sun Rising* and the extract from *A Room with a View*, write a comparison of the ways the writers present passionate love. You should consider:

- the ways in which the writers' choices of form, structure and language shape these extracts
- how your wider reading in the literature of love has contributed to your understanding and interpretation of the extracts.

6   Focusing on *The Going* and *In a Garden*, write a comparison of the ways the writers present the death of love. You should consider:
- the ways in which the writers' choices of form, structure and language shape these poems
- how your wider reading in the literature of love has contributed to your understanding and interpretation of the poems.

7   Focusing on the extracts from *The Country Wife* and *The Rover*, write a comparison of the ways the writers present comedic aspects of love. You should consider:
- the ways in which the writers' choices of form, structure and language shape these extracts
- how your wider reading in the literature of love has contributed to your understanding and interpretation of the extracts.

8   Look again at *Death and Love* and *Leda and the Swan*. Basing your answer on the poems and, where appropriate, your wider reading in the poetry of love, compare the ways in which the two poets have used poetic form, structure and language to express their thoughts and ideas.

9   Focusing on the extracts from *Pamela* and *The Art of Coquetry*, write a comparison of the ways the writers present manipulation in love. You should consider:
- the ways in which the writers' choices of form, structure and language shape these extracts
- how your wider reading in the literature of love has contributed to your understanding and interpretation of the extracts.

10 Look again at *A Pink Wool Knitted Dress* and *To Marguerite*. Basing your answer on the poems and, where appropriate, your wider reading in the poetry of love, compare the ways in which the two poets have used poetic form, structure and language to express their thoughts and ideas.

11 Focusing on the extracts from *The Rivals* and *Possession*, write a comparison of the ways the writers present negotiations in love. You should consider:
   • the ways in which the writers' choices of form, structure and language shape these extracts
   • how your wider reading in the literature of love has contributed to your understanding and interpretation of the extracts.

12 Focusing on *The Lost Mistress* and the extract from Dorothy Wordsworth's Journal, write a comparison of the ways the writers present thwarted love. You should consider:
   • the ways in which the writers' choices of form, structure and language shape these extracts
   • how your wider reading in the literature of love has contributed to your understanding and interpretation of the extracts.

13 Focusing on *The Fair Singer* and the extract from *Far From the Madding Crowd*, write a comparison of the ways the writers present love as a conquering power. You should consider:
   • the ways in which the writers' choices of form, structure and language shape these extracts
   • how your wider reading in the literature of love has contributed to your understanding and interpretation of the extracts.

14 Focusing on Farquhar's letter to Anne Oldfield and the extract from *Othello*, write a comparison of the ways the writers present the effects of love. You should consider:

- the ways in which the writers' choices of form, structure and language shape these extracts
- how your wider reading in the literature of love has contributed to your understanding and interpretation of the extracts.

15 Look again at Shelley's *To…* and Aphra Behn's *Song*. Basing your answer on the poems and, where appropriate, your wider reading in the poetry of love, compare the ways in which the two poets have used poetic form, structure and language to express their thoughts and ideas.

16 Look again at the extracts from *The Knight's Tale* and *The Duchess of Malfi*. Basing your answer on the extracts and, where appropriate, your wider reading on love, compare the ways in which the writers have used form, structure and language to express their thoughts and ideas.

17 Focusing on the extracts from *Paradise Lost* and *The Tempest*, write a comparison of the ways the writers present the power of physical attraction. You should consider:
- the ways in which the writers' choices of form, structure and language shape these extracts
- how your wider reading in the literature of love has contributed to your understanding and interpretation of the extracts.

Chronology

The following are some of the most well-known writers who have written about love through the ages.

c. 1343–1400	Geoffrey Chaucer	*The Canterbury Tales, Troilus and Criseyde*
c. 1405–1471	Sir Thomas Malory	*Le Morte d'Arthur*
c. 1552–1599	Edmund Spenser	*The Faerie Queene*
1554–1586	Sir Philip Sidney	*Astrophel and Stella*
1558–1594	Thomas Kyd	*The Spanish Tragedy*
1564–1616	William Shakespeare	*Plays, Sonnets, Venus and Adonis, A Lover's Complaint*
1564–1593	Christopher Marlowe	*Dr Faustus, Edward II, Tamburlaine the Great*
1572–1637	Ben Jonson	*Epicoene, Volpone, Epigrams, The Forest*
1572–1631	John Donne	*Songs and Sonnets, Elegies, Holy Sonnets*
c. 1578–1634	John Webster	*The White Devil, The Duchess of Malfi*
1586–1640	John Ford	*'Tis Pity She's a Whore*
1608–1674	John Milton	*Paradise Lost, Paradise Regained*
1640–1689	Aphra Behn	*The Rover, The Forced Marriage, Love Letters between a Nobleman and his Sister*
c. 1640–1715	William Wycherley	*The Country Wife*
c. 1660–1731	Daniel Defoe	*Moll Flanders*
1670–1729	William Congreve	*The Way of the World*

1689–1761	Samuel Richardson	*Pamela, Clarissa*
1707–1754	Henry Fielding	*The History of Tom Jones, a Foundling*
1730–1774	Oliver Goldsmith	*She Stoops to Conquer*
1751–1816	Richard Brinsley Sheridan	*The Rivals, The School for Scandal*
1757–1827	William Blake	*Songs of Innocence and of Experience*
1759–1796	Robert Burns	*Tam O'Shanter*
1775–1817	Jane Austen	*Northanger Abbey, Sense and Sensibility, Pride and Prejudice, Mansfield Park, Emma, Persuasion*
1788–1824	Lord Byron	*Don Juan*
1795–1821	John Keats	*Lamia, The Eve of St Agnes, Odes, La Belle Dame sans Merci*
1806–1861	Elizabeth Barrett Browning	*Sonnets from the Portuguese*
1812–1870	Charles Dickens	*The Old Curiosity Shop, Dombey and Son, David Copperfield, Bleak House, Hard Times, A Tale of Two Cities, Great Expectations*
1816–1855	Charlotte Brontë	*Jane Eyre, Shirley, Villette, The Professor, Poems*
1818–1848	Emily Brontë	*Wuthering Heights, Poems*
1819–1880	George Eliot	*The Mill on the Floss, Silas Marner, Middlemarch, Daniel Deronda*

1840–1928	Thomas Hardy	*Under the Greenwood Tree, Far From the Madding Crowd, The Mayor of Casterbridge, Tess of the d'Urbervilles, Jude the Obscure, Poems*
1854–1900	Oscar Wilde	*The Picture of Dorian Gray, A Woman of No Importance, An Ideal Husband, The Importance of Being Earnest*
1879–1970	E.M. Forster	*A Room with a View, Howard's End, Maurice, A Passage to India*
1885–1930	D.H. Lawrence	*Sons and Lovers, The Rainbow, Women in Love, Lady Chatterley's Lover*
1890–1979	Jean Rhys	*Wide Sargasso Sea*
1899–1973	Noel Coward	*Private Lives*
1903–1966	Evelyn Waugh	*Brideshead Revisited*
1904–1991	Graham Greene	*Brighton Rock, The End of the Affair, The Human Factor*
1911–1983	Tennessee Williams	*The Glass Menagerie, A Streetcar Named Desire, Cat on a Hot Tin Roof*
1919–1999	Iris Murdoch	*The Bell*
1922–1985	Philip Larkin	*The Whitsun Weddings*
1924–1995	Robert Bolt	*A Man for All Seasons*
1926–2005	John Fowles	*The Collector, The French Lieutenant's Woman*
1930–1998	Ted Hughes	*Birthday Letters*

1931–	Toni Morrison	*Beloved*
1932–1963	Sylvia Plath	*Ariel*
1936–	A.S. Byatt	*Possession*
1940–1992	Angela Carter	*The Magic Toyshop, Wise Children*
1941–	Anne Tyler	*The Amateur Marriage*
1942–	Susan Hill	*Strange Meeting, The Woman in Black*
1943–	Michael Ondaatje	*The English Patient*
1944–	Alice Walker	*The Color Purple*
1954–	Kazuo Ishiguro	*The Remains of the Day*
1955–	Carol Ann Duffy	*Mean Time, The World's Wife*
1956–	Andrea Levy	*Small Island*
1959–	Jeanette Winterson	*Oranges Are Not the Only Fruit, The Passion, Written on the Body, Gut Symmetries*
1963–	Audrey Niffenegger	*The Time Traveler's Wife*
1965–	Khaled Hosseini	*The Kite Runner, A Thousand Splendid Suns*
1966–	Sarah Waters	*Tipping the Velvet, Fingersmith*
1967–	Monica Ali	*Brick Lane*
1975–	Zadie Smith	*On Beauty*